Family Tree Magazine
LIBRARY

FINDING
YOUR
ROOTS
ONLINE

NANCY HENDRICKSON

BETTERWAY BOOKS
CINCINNATI, OHIO

www.familytreemagazine.com

Other fine Betterway books are available from your local bookstore or on our Web site at www.familytreemagazine.com.

07 06 05 04 03   5 4 3 2 1

Library of Congress Cataloging-in-Publication Data

Hendrickson, Nancy
    Finding your roots online / by Nancy Hendrickson.
       p.   cm.
    ISBN 1-55870-635-6 (alk. paper)
      1. Genealogy—Computer network resources—Handbooks, manuals, etc. 2. Internet research—Handbooks, manuals, etc. I. Title.
    CS21 .H46 2003
    025.06929'1'072—dc21

2003005057
CIP

Editor: Sharon DeBartolo Carmack, CG
Production editor: Eric Schwartzberg
Production coordinator: Michelle Ruberg
Designed by: Sandy Conopeotis Kent
Cover designer: Stephanie Strang

DEDICATION
To those who cherish the invisible bond between the present and the past.
and . . .
"Gypsy trails will never fail,
nor gypsy hearts forget."

About the Author

Nancy Hendrickson has authored countless articles on Internet genealogy for *Family Tree Magazine* and writes a regular column for the magazine's weekly e-mail newsletter. She is also the co-author of two books for amateur astronomers. She also is the Webmaster of her AncestorNews.com, a site for beginning Internet genealogists, and a member of the San Diego Genealogical Society. Send her an e-mail at stjoemo@pobox.com to receive a free inscribed bookplate.

Acknowledgments

Who can write a book without pausing a moment to reflect on all the people who helped make it happen? Certainly not I.

In truth, my most heartfelt acknowledgment goes to two women who are no longer living: my grandmothers, Bessie Faulkenberry and Nora Dearing. Many were the hours I spent with both, asking them over and over again about our family. Their colorful tales of Indians, pioneers and covered wagons gave me a lifelong love of history and genealogy. For that I am forever grateful.

Other family members deserve a mention, too. After all, isn't family what genealogy is all about? So a special thanks to my mother, Marjorie Dunn, my sister, Vicki Fite, my brothers, Mark and Herschel Hendrickson, and my aunt, Helen Hendrickson Hjetland. One more hats-off goes to my aunt, Luella Hendrickson Maxwell, who passed away just as I was completing this book. Remembering her love of life and family will always keep me in good stead.

I'd also like to send a big hug and thanks to the wonderful people who have always supported my dreams; in particular, Charlene Crilley.

Writers rely on editors to make them look good, and I'm no exception. So thanks to David Fryxell, editor of *Family Tree Magazine*, and Sharon DeBartolo Carmack, my book editor. Their encouragement, kind words and gentle, helpful prods kept me on track and on schedule.

Lastly, a huge thanks to all of those Webmasters who have posted genealogy data on the Internet. Without you and your Web sites, this book would never have been written.

Nancy Hendrickson
San Diego, California
September 2002

Icons Used in This Book

 Case Study — Examples of this book's advice at work

 Citing Sources — Reminders and methods for documenting information

 Definitions — \di'fin\ *vb* Terminology and jargon explained

 For More Info — Where to turn for more in-depth coverage

 Hidden Treasures — Family papers and home sources

 Idea Generator — Techniques and prods for further thinking

 Important — Information and tips you can't overlook

 Internet Source — Where on the Web to find what you need

 Library/Archive Source — Repositories that might have the information you need

 Microfilm Source — Information available on microfilm

 Money Saver — Getting the most out of research dollars

 Notes — Thoughts, ideas, and related insights

 Oral History — Techniques for getting family stories

 Printed Source — Directories, books, pamphlets, and other paper archives

 Reminder — "Don't-Forget" items to keep in mind

 Research Tip — Ways to make research more efficient

 See Also — Where in this book to find related information

 Step By Step — Walkthroughs of important procedures

 Timesaver — Shaving minutes and hours off the clock

 Tip — Ways to make research more efficient

 Warning — Stop before you make a mistake

Table of Contents At a Glance

Table of Contents

Introduction

My Internet roots run deep—in fact back to 1986 when I first logged onto a DOS-based service called CompuServe. Although I can't remember how many free hours came with the account—I think five—I do remember using them all the first night I logged on. From that day on, I knew cyberspace was my home away from home.

Back then, accessing online genealogy information was next to impossible. What little was available wasn't all that helpful. Truth is, I could find information far more quickly by schlepping to the library. As the Internet grew, popular services like AOL enticed millions of non-computer folks to dip their feet into the water. And once the flood began, there was no stopping the flow of information.

The past few years have been extraordinary in terms of the sheer volume of genealogy data that's been posted online—not only by individuals but by governmental agencies. Today, it's possible to do something I could never have done back in 1986: serious online research.

Being a successful "Internet genealogist" is more than just learning how to "do" genealogy, but you do need to know how to correctly link the ancestors that you find—otherwise, you won't be successful. To find genealogical information online, you have to learn how to find things. For example, if you wanted to know the value of a 1958 Ernie Banks baseball card, you'd head for eBay.com and search Completed Auctions. But where would you go to find ancestors? This book tells all.

Using four techniques—lineage-linked databases, networking, search engines, and online databases—you'll learn how to tease your ancestors out of their Internet hiding spaces. And, once you've found those ancestors, you'll learn how to assess your findings and then structure more online or offline research. Along the way, you'll become an exceptional detective.

Internet genealogy is a blessing, particularly to those who don't live near a major library or whose access to reference books is slim. It allows family members—no matter how distant—to share information and even divide research tasks. The Internet has made our wonderful hobby instantly available to people who otherwise might never have opened a reference book or scrolled through a census microfilm.

True, the accuracy of everything on the World Wide Web is in question; few Webmasters have cited their sources. Always remember that the Internet is just one tool in your search. For many of us, however, finding a few unverified clues can often open the gates to previously unknown research possibilities. And that counts for a lot.

Since going online in 1986, I've met dozens of "Internet cousins," unearthed generations of ancestors, and found more clues than I'll ever have time to research. I wish you the same success.

PART ONE

First Steps in Climbing Your Family Tree

A few years ago *TIME* magazine did a cover story on Americans' passion for tracing their family trees. "Genealogy is America's latest obsession," the article proclaimed. "And thanks to the computer, it's as easy as one, two . . . tree!"

Well, *Time* may have overstated the "easy" part, but it was right about one thing: Americans have embraced Internet genealogy wholeheartedly. In fact, according to a 2000 Maritz Poll, more than thirty-five million Americans use the Internet to trace their family tree. It's no wonder that the Church of Jesus Christ of Latter-day Saints' FamilySearch site was swamped with more than a half-million visitors on its opening day. Or that in its first year of operation, the Ellis Island database tallied more than 2.5 billion hits.

The Internet and computer technology have made genealogy one of the most popular hobbies ever. As more and more records are posted on the Internet, family trees are growing at record rates. Are these Internet genealogy trees as accurate as the ones constructed from original records and library research? Probably not. However, they do provide millions of Americans with the clues needed to track down even the most elusive ancestors.

Does Internet genealogy work? Yes! In the years that I've been online, I've found clues that helped add countless generations to my family tree, met "Internet cousins" who will be lifelong friends, climbed brick walls, and more importantly, discovered the part my own family played in shaping America's history.

If you're new to Internet genealogy, you're in for the ride of your life. In a few hours online, you'll have the opportunity to uncover clues to generations of family and meet cousins you never knew existed. You'll be thrilled at the connections you make and proud of the family you find.

I know you're ready to jump into the search with both feet, but before getting started, let's cover a few of the basics—just to make sure your online research is as successful as possible. Here's what's coming up first:

Chapter One: Family Tree Basics
- Where to start?
- Pedigree charts and family group sheets
- Family interviews
- Types of evidence
- Citing sources
- Online classes
- Learning to be a detective

Chapter Two: Exploring the Net
- Browser-speak
- Why do you need to know this?
- E-mail basics
- Viruses/hoaxes, and firewalls
- What's online, what's not
- USGenWeb

- Military records
- Cemetery records
- Land records
- Census records
- Maps
- Books
- The history in family history
- Migration routes
- Commercial databases

Chapter Three: The Organized Computer Genealogist
- The filing cabinet
- Windows Explorer
- Files: Finding, moving, copying, deleting, saving, renaming
- Organizing your computer's filing system
- Organizing online records
- E-mail: folders and filters
- Free genealogy e-mail addresses
- Free research software
- Compressed or zipped files

ONE

Family Tree Basics

enealogy is about tracing relationships. Whether you think you're descended from European kings or American presidents, your task is the same: prove the relationship. How? By working from the known to the unknown. That means if you've heard family stories about a distant *Mayflower* ancestor, you start with yourself and work backward, proving relationships between each generation—not the other way around.

The Internet is a temptress when it comes to making assumptions. One of these days—and I guarantee it will come—you'll find an online file that promises paradise. It will contain what looks like a multigenerational report on *your* family, traced all the way back to Robert the Bruce or Mary, Queen of Scots. Is it true? Maybe. Without taking your research back one generation at a time, however, and proving those relationships, you have no way of knowing how far off-base the information may be—or whether the people in the file even belong to your family.

Imagine a tree without roots, and you'll have a clear picture of a genealogy based on inaccuracies and assumptions—the first strong wind will send it toppling. Thankfully, though, genealogists pack a powerful toolkit full of forms, records, and methodologies—all for good reason. These devices are the structure around which we grow a deep-rooted family tree. That's why we're starting with the basics.

Warning

WHERE TO START?

Before logging onto the Internet, you'll need to figure out what you know and what you don't. The easiest way to do this is to fill out a pedigree chart based on your own personal knowledge. A pedigree chart shows direct relationships between generations. It identifies a primary person (you), parents, grandparents, and continues until the chart runs off the edge of the page. (Pedigree charts usually have four or five generations per page.) The

Pedigree Chart

No. 1 on this chart is the same as no. 1 on chart no. 1

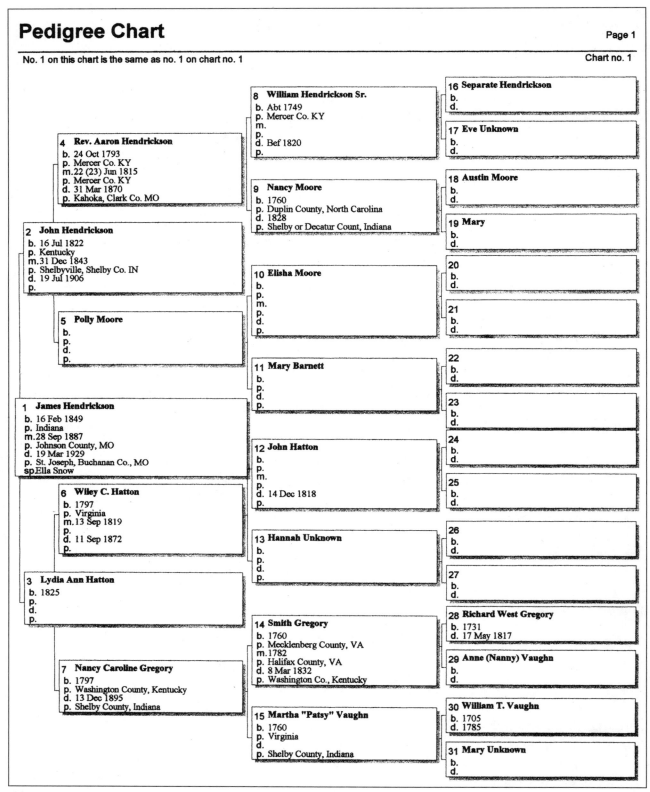

8 William Hendrickson Sr.
b. Abt 1749
p. Mercer Co. KY
m.
p.
d. Bef 1820
p.

16 Separate Hendrickson
b.
d.

17 Eve Unknown
b.
d.

4 Rev. Aaron Hendrickson
b. 24 Oct 1793
p. Mercer Co. KY
m.22 (23) Jun 1815
p. Mercer Co. KY
d. 31 Mar 1870
p. Kahoka, Clark Co. MO

9 Nancy Moore
b. 1760
p. Duplin County, North Carolina
d. 1828
p. Shelby or Decatur Count, Indiana

18 Austin Moore
b.
d.

19 Mary
b.
d.

2 John Hendrickson
b. 16 Jul 1822
p. Kentucky
m.31 Dec 1843
p. Shelbyville, Shelby Co. IN
d. 19 Jul 1906
p.

10 Elisha Moore
b.
p.
m.
p.
d.
p.

20
b.
d.

21
b.
d.

5 Polly Moore
b.
p.
d.
p.

11 Mary Barnett
b.
p.
d.
p.

22
b.
d.

23
b.
d.

1 James Hendrickson
b. 16 Feb 1849
p. Indiana
m.28 Sep 1887
p. Johnson County, MO
d. 19 Mar 1929
p. St. Joseph, Buchanan Co., MO
sp.Ella Snow

12 John Hatton
b.
p.
m.
p.
d. 14 Dec 1818
p.

24
b.
d.

25
b.
d.

6 Wiley C. Hatton
b. 1797
p. Virginia
m.13 Sep 1819
p.
d. 11 Sep 1872
p.

13 Hannah Unknown
b.
p.
d.
p.

26
b.
d.

27
b.
d.

3 Lydia Ann Hatton
b. 1825
p.
d.
p.

14 Smith Gregory
b. 1760
p. Mecklenberg County, VA
m.1782
p. Halifax County, VA
d. 8 Mar 1832
p. Washington Co., Kentucky

28 Richard West Gregory
b. 1731
d. 17 May 1817

29 Anne (Nanny) Vaughn
b.
d.

7 Nancy Caroline Gregory
b. 1797
p. Washington County, Kentucky
d. 13 Dec 1895
p. Shelby County, Indiana

15 Martha "Patsy" Vaughn
b. 1760
p. Virginia
d.
p. Shelby County, Indiana

30 William T. Vaughn
b. 1705
d. 1785

31 Mary Unknown
b.
d.

Figure 1-1

One glance at a pedigree chart, and you'll know which family tree branches need research from the blanks.

HOW TO NUMBER A PEDIGREE CHART

Most genealogy software automatically numbers pedigree charts, but if you're filling out a chart by hand, here's how:

Charts are numbered with the primary person receiving #1. In most cases, #1 will be you.

The number for an individual's father is double the individual's number, the mother is double the individual's number plus one. For example, person #1's father is #2 (double #1) and the mother is #3 (double #1 plus one). Person #2's father is #4, the mother is #5.

What happens when you fill up the four or five generations on one pedigree chart? You start others. If you look at Figure 1-1, you'll see that persons #16 on Chart 1 will become person #1 on their own charts.

birth, marriage, and death data are included for each person, if known. (See figure 1-1 on page 6.)

A second type of form commonly used is the family group sheet. Unlike pedigree charts, family group sheets show all of the vital information about a single family unit. This includes the father, mother, their children, and their children's spouses. As you prepare your searches, you'll fill out a family group sheet for each family you work with. (See figure 1-2 on page 8.)

If you look at figure 1-1, the sample pedigree chart, the most obvious gaps are in the families of Polly Moore and the paternal line of Lydia Hatton.

Figure 1-2, the family group sheet of another branch of the family, shows that there is almost no information on Francis's parents or the spouses of his children. Note, too, that there are only four sources cited for this family: one is from a phone conversation, two from a cemetery book, and another from a family history. There are no birth, death, marriage, or census records to support anything on this page.

As you can see, the blanks in the charts and the scant source material point the way to much-needed future research.

NOW IT'S YOUR TURN

Using the blank forms in the Appendix or your genealogy software (or downloaded from the sites listed on page 9), fill out a pedigree chart, starting with yourself as #1. Fill in as much information as you can from memory, going back as many generations as possible. **When you fill in your chart, take care to**

1. use a woman's maiden name
2. use *about*, *c.*, or *ca.* (abbreviation of the Latin *circa*, or about) if you're estimating dates
3. leave blanks for what you don't know

Tip

FAMILY GROUP SHEET

Husband	Francis Albert Faulkenberry	
Born	25 Sep 1862	
Christened		
Died	20 Sep 1911	
Buried		
Father	Thomas Faulkenberry (–1876)	Mother Martha Wright (–)
Married		
Wife	**Sarah Josephine Dimmitt**	
Born	24 Feb 1868	
Christened		
Died	5 Jul 1935 Lone Jack, Jackson Co., MO	
Buried		
Father	Calvin Manlieus Dimmitt (1841–1917)	Mother Nancy Louisa Markham (1840–1930)
Children		
1	**F**	**Belle Faulkenberry**
Born	14 Jul 1887 Lone Jack, Jackson Co., MO	
Christened		
Died	29 Dec 1918	
Buried		
Spouse		
2	**F**	**Edith Maye Faulkenberry**
Born	13 Apr 1889 Lone Jack, Jackson Co., MO	
Christened		
Died	28 Nov 1942	
Buried		
Spouse		
3	**F**	**Bessie Frances Faulkenberry**[1]
Born	8 Nov 1890 Lone Jack, Jackson Co., MO	
Christened		
Died	30 Dec 1959 Horton, Brown County, KS	
Buried		
Spouse	Herschel Byron Hendrickson (1888–1949)	20 Apr 1913 – Jackson County, MO
4	**F**	**Ina Faulkenberry**
Born	31 Aug 1892 Lone Jack, Jackson Co., MO	
Christened		
Died	17 Mar 1895	
Buried		
Spouse		
5	**M**	**Elmer Albert Faulkenberry**
Born	18 Nov 1894 Lone Jack, Jackson Co., MO	
Christened		
Died	16 Oct 1941	
Buried		
Spouse		

Source Citations

1. Helen Hendrickson Hjetland, Phone conversation, 4/30/2000.
2. Russell Helmig, *Lone Jack Cemetery*, (Russell Helmig, 37102 E. 50 Hwy., Lone Jack, MO), p47.
3. Wilma Faulkenberry Mallicoat, *A Faulkenberry Family Tree*, (compiled by Wilma Faulkenberry Mallicoat, 102 E. 9th, Lee's Summit, MO 64063 1986), p371.
4. Russell Helmig, *Lone Jack Cemetery*, (Russell Helmig, 37102 E. 50 Hwy., Lone Jack, MO), p48.

Figure 1-2
Use a family group sheet to detail all known information about a single family unit.

WHERE TO FIND CHARTS

If you have a genealogy software program such as Family Tree Maker or Personal Ancestral File, you will be able to easily plug your family information into computerized chart templates. Many charts are also available for free on the Web (as well as in the back of this book). Visit these sites to download free pedigree charts and family group sheets:

Free Downloadable Forms—*Family Tree Magazine*
<www.familytreemagazine.com/forms/download.html>
A host of forms and charts, including pedigree charts and family group sheets, available for download as PDFs or text files.

Ancestors—Charts & Records
<www.pbs.org/kbyu/ancestors/charts>
Downloadable charts and records in PDF format from the PBS *Ancestors* series' Web companion.

Ancestry.com—Ancestral Chart
<www.ancestry.com/save/charts/ancchart.htm>
Five-generation ancestral chart (PDF) and other forms.

LESSER THAN/GREATER THAN SYMBOLS

Throughout this book and others, you may see Web addresses surrounded by lesser than or greater than symbols: < >. We use these to ensure other punctuation marks aren't mistakenly thought part of the URL.

4. include the person's middle name, if known
5. include all pieces of evidence, even if they are conflicting
6. put question marks around guesses, e.g., born 10 Jan ?1853? or born 10 Jan [1853?]

Did you notice as you filled in your pedigree chart that the number of your ancestors doubles with each generation, i.e. two parents, four grandparents, eight great-grandparents, sixteen great-great-grandparents? In fact, in the book *Unpuzzling Your Past* (Cincinnati: Betterway Books, 2000), author Emily Anne Croom estimates that if you traced each of your lines back to 1650, you could have had as many as four thousand ancestors living at that time!

Next, fill out a family group sheet for your parents' family and as many nuclear families as you desire. At the least, these will include yourself, your parents, grandparents, and probably great-grandparents. Although it seems time-consuming now, take the time to do family group sheets for the siblings of your parents, grandparents, etc. Later on in your research, there will be times when the only open door to solving a mystery is the back door through a sibling's family.

While filling in your charts, keep a couple of questions in mind:
1. Can I prove this fact? If so, how?
2. If not, what information do I need to prove it?

The answers to these questions will help form your research goals. For example, you may think that your great-grandfather was born in Cincinnati. However, if you can't prove it, what documentation will you need? A birth certificate? Cemetery record? Obituary? What do you think? Make that determination and you've just created a research goal.

TALKING IT OUT

You'd be surprised at the number of family stories remembered by your older relatives. Oftentimes, they are the only members of your family who have personal knowledge of the people who died before you were born. In fact, they can remember events that you will never find mentioned in any record or database. For that reason alone, it's important to interview them as soon as possible. Sadly, there isn't a genealogist alive who hasn't said, "I wish I had asked my _____ [fill in the blank] these questions before he or she died."

Oral History

When interviewing, don't confine yourself to date questions (e.g., When were you born?) or ones that can be answered with a simple yes or no. Instead, ask questions such as

- How did your parents meet?
- What family stories have been handed down to you?
- What did your grandparents look like?
- What sticks out in your mind about your parents or grandparents?
- Where did you grow up?
- What was your school like?

Not only will the stories flesh out your family's genealogy, they will probably be loaded with clues. I recently found my great-great-grandfather thanks to something my grandmother told me nearly forty years ago. You just never know when the mention of a single name or place will lead to your big break—so tuck them away in a safe place.

SORTING OUT THE STORIES

Once you start interviewing the family, I promise you'll get conflicting data. While Uncle Jim may remember that Grandpa's first wife was from Kentucky, Aunt Caroline is certain it was Alabama. In addition, you'll get differing dates, names, spouses, religions, hometowns, and churches.

But no matter how farfetched or illogical it may seem, write down the story and who told you what. In truth, it's probable that each piece of information may contain a tiny grain of fact. For example, Uncle Jim and Aunt Caroline may both be right—maybe Grandpa's first wife was born in Kentucky, but moved early on to Alabama.

Also take note of name variations, both given and surnames. Everyone in your family may have called your great-granny Lizzie, but it's possible her real name was Margaret Elizabeth. Our ancestors weren't a tenth as concerned about spelling as we are, so it's common to see a surname spelled with

Tip

several variations, such as Hendrickson, Hendricksen, Hendrixson, and Hendriksen.

Make sure you keep ongoing notes, either in your genealogy notebook or software, about what you learn during these oral interviews.

Over time you'll find that every time you talk to a family member, it becomes an interview of sorts, because you'll develop the habit of listening for family information, even during an informal phone call. Whenever I learn any tidbit about the family during a phone call with my aunts, I make a note of it in my genealogy software. (See figure 1-3 below).

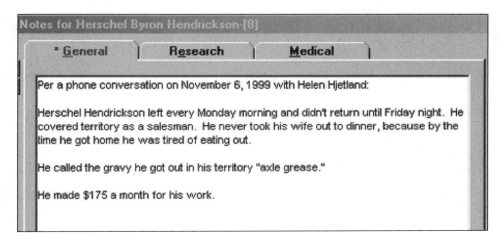

Figure 1-3
Even a telephone conversation can include interesting facts about a family member.

TYPES OF EVIDENCE

Once you've gathered basic facts about yourself and other living relatives, start looking for other evidence to help prove family relationships or serve as confirmation of family stories. There are two types of evidence: primary and secondary. Primary evidence is an eyewitness account or a record created at the time of an event by someone with knowledge of the event. Secondary evidence is information that's passed through an intermediary. A story a relative tells you about a Revolutionary War ancestor, for example, would be secondary evidence, or hearsay.

ORAL HISTORY

The basis for Alex Haley's wildly popular (and fictional) *Roots* was an oral tradition handed down through the generations. For most genealogists, those oral traditions are just as valuable today as they were for Haley.

Every family has stories of past events and more current ones. In my family, a favorite is how I rescued my brother, Mark, from a sewer he had fallen into—and how Mom hosed him off before letting him come in the house! One of Mark's favorite stories is how my cousin and I scared him when we told him that a lion had escaped from the San Diego Zoo and had been seen in the vicinity.

Although future generations won't be able to trace a lot of family information from those stories, they will learn a bit about our childhoods—and our humor.

Other family stories help paint a historic picture of the times. For example, in a 1969 interview with Great-Aunt Dolly, she said

> Somewhere near the first day of August in 1862, they [Civil War raiders] came by to burn my grandfather's home. Grandmother was expecting a baby at the time. She begged them to let her keep the chest of drawers that had the baby clothes in it, and the feather bed. They did, but burned the home.

> They were going to take Grandpa with them but Aunt Mary told them they couldn't take her father. She followed them down the road and they finally said, "Turn the old devil loose, he won't be any good to us anyway." That night my father was born on the feather bed in the potato patch. A few days later the Battle of Lone Jack was fought. Aunt Mary, the one who saved her father, came up and helped take care of the wounded on both sides.

Aunt Dolly had a great story, even though the facts were somewhat skewed, partly because she wasn't there. She's repeating a family legend. The battle of Lone Jack took place in August, and Aunt Dolly's father was born in September. As with most oral traditions or family stories, however, there is usually a grain of truth.

Interviewing family members in person is by far the best approach. When you're sitting across the table from someone, it's far easier to ask a follow-up question or to clarify something on the spot.

If you do have the opportunity to conduct in-person interviews, take along a camcorder or tape recorder. I taped Aunt Dolly's story, then later transcribed it. I wish camcorders had been around then, however; I'd love to pop the tape in the VCR and re-live that afternoon.

Oral History

INTERVIEW TOOLS

If you're doing an in-person interview, make sure you have fresh batteries for your tape recorder, or a freshly souped up camcorder or digital camera battery. Also, be sure to prepare your interview questions in advance; there's no point in conducting an interview if you don't know the questions you want to ask!

If you're interviewing by mail or e-mail, be sure to let your relative know what you're doing and how much you'd appreciate their help. Always include a self-addressed, stamped envelope (SASE). Make this process as easy as possible: Type out your questions and then leave big enough blanks for their responses. Also, encourage them to write on the back of the page if they need more space.

Lastly, if you've asked a lot of questions, let your relative know that it's okay for them to return the paper without every question answered. Some

INTERVIEW RESOURCES

Emily Anne Croom, in *Unpuzzling Your Past*, 4th ed. (Cincinnati: Betterway Books, 2001), says, "No amount of library research can duplicate or replace what these people [family members] can tell." In fact, she thinks interviews are so important in genealogy research that she wrote an entire chapter on how they can help solve family puzzles.

Her book details how to prepare for an interview, the vital questions to ask, how to handle touchy subjects, doing interviews by mail, how to tape an interview, and mistakes to avoid.

Other resources

Bringing Your Family History to Life Through Social History by Katherine Sturdevant (Cincinnati: Betterway Books, 2000)

50 Family History Interview Questions
<www.scrapbookscrapbook.com/FamilyTree/familytreequestions.html>

How to Conduct Oral History Interviews
<www.audiotapes.com/product.asp?ProductCode='UGAC9820'>

Oral History Interviews
<www.dvjc.org/history/guide/contents.shtml>

relatives may hesitate to return an incomplete form, so it's better to get something than nothing.

WRITTEN DOCUMENTS

This is the paper trail that records some part of your ancestor's life. They may be an official document, such as a will, land grant, birth certificate, insurance policy, or military discharge paper. They can also be a program from a funeral, an invitation to a wedding, a newspaper article, or a membership card. If you are descended from a family of pack rats, you're especially lucky!

While going through scraps of paper, be on the lookout for anything that helps prove a relationship, verifies an assumption, or offers more clues. Look for written documents in places such as

Hidden Treasures

- baby books
- calendars
- diaries
- diplomas
- family Bibles
- letters
- newspaper clippings
- photo albums
- yearbooks

Think of your own life and the paper it has generated. For example, many of these records probably exist for you:

- birth certificate
- car registration
- census reports
- church membership
- credit card applications
- diplomas
- enlistment/discharge papers
- house deed
- insurance policy
- invitation to your wedding
- marriage license
- newspaper announcement of your engagement
- report cards
- school enrollment
- Social Security card
- will

Figure 1-4
Cherished family mementoes, like this grade school diploma, can be scanned into your genealogy software.

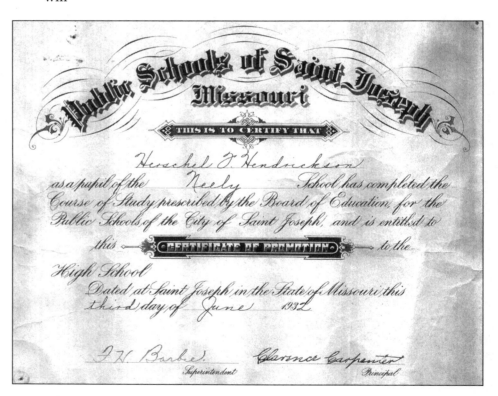

Your ancestors created records, too—perhaps not as many as you, but certainly as important. In fact, the further you go back in time, the more detailed some records become, while others may be less detailed. Some land records, for example, contained far more genealogically-relevant information than any you'll see today. Modern mortgage papers may be lengthy but only because they're filled with legalese. The land records of your ances-

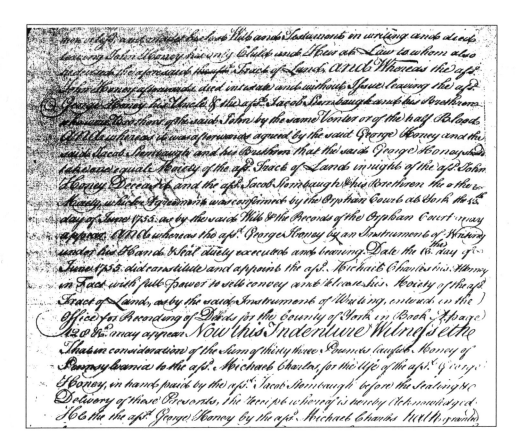

Figure 1-5
Even though old documents can be difficult to read, they often contain gems of family information. *Phyllis Boozell Quarg*

tors were more detailed to prove the chain of title, which sometimes included relatives.

Figure 1-5 above is a page from a microfilmed 1756 York County, Pennsylvania, deed. (Only part of the deed is reproduced here.) The deed reveals the following relationships:

> George Honey is the brother of the deceased Nicholas Honey, whose only child John inherited the land. John is also deceased and did not leave a will, nor did he have children. Nicholas did leave a will. Jacob Stombaugh and his brothers are described as "Brethern of the said John by the same Venter" [Latin, meaning "of the same womb or mother"] or of the half blood.

This shows that Nicholas Honey was the second husband of the Stombaugh brother's mother and that she and Nicholas had a son John. Further research proved this to be a fact. The deed says that John is the only son of Nicholas Honey, so if John is the only son of Nicholas Honey, and he has a half-brother Jacob Stombaugh, then Nicholas' wife (John's mother) was married previously to a man named _____ Stombaugh.

Wills, too, can often contain clues about family relationships, particularly if you're looking for female ancestors. Your ancestor's will might contain a statement similar to this: "I leave three cows to my daughter Mary, wife of Jonathan Maysfield."

Wills also can contain clues about possible family conflict. The will of

John Snow evenly divided the proceeds of his estate between all of his children, both male and female. He specified that his daughter Mary's proceeds be administered by her brothers, however. Did this reflect John's concern that his daughter's husband might spend all her money, or that he felt she was incompetent to manage her inheritance? Or, was she merely under legal age?

Benjamin Franklin's will left no doubt about his feelings toward his son, William (a pro-British sympathizer). "The part he acted against me in the late war, which is of public notoriety, will account for my leaving him no more of an estate [than] he endeavoured to deprive me of."

What other types of records did your ancestors leave?

Idea Generator

- church records
  membership, attendance, behavior (like swearing or dancing), baptisms, marriages, burials
- civil or criminal records
- court
  probate
  adoption
  divorce disputes
- federal/state
  census, taxes
- immigration
  ship passenger lists, naturalization papers, passports
- land records
  purchase, sales, bounty land warrants, land grants
- military records
  enlistment/discharge papers, pensions, commendations
- vital records
  birth, marriage, death records

Remember, no matter what type of records you're searching, the goal is to find the ones that help prove relationships and put flesh on the bones.

CITING SOURCES

It happens to every genealogist: the nightmare of finding a critical piece of data and six months later not remembering the book, Web site, or microfilm where it originated. You can avoid this trap by remembering to cite all of your sources as you go. This simply means keeping track of where you found things and noting them in a standardized form (see sidebar on page 17).

Citing Sources

Citing the source of the information you find serves a couple of purposes. One, it allows other researchers to easily relocate the same piece of data. If you found a birth date in a letter, the source of the date would be the letter itself, and the citation would look something like this:

Letter from Jason M. Grover to Minnie Grover, 10 January 1915; held in 2002 by Sally Jameson (111 Main Street, My Town, CA 92111).

CITING YOUR SOURCES: DOS AND DON'TS

Books

Do: Sharon DeBartolo Carmack, *Your Guide to Cemetery Research* (Cincinnati: Betterway Books, 2001).

Don't: That book on cemeteries I found at the library.

Web Sites

Do: State Library of Massachusetts—Genealogical Resources <www.state.ma.us/lib/genealogy/genelett.htm>, printed information on obtaining vital records, 12 October 2002.

Don't: Obtain vital records info, Mass State Library

E-Mail

Do: "Texas Land Records," e-mail message from John Smith <jsmith@xyz.com> to author, 18 December 2002.

Don't: E-mail from Jack on Texas land.

For complete information on citation formats, see *Evidence! Citation & Analysis for the Family Historian* by Elizabeth Shown Mills (Baltimore: Genealogical Publishing Company, 1997)

The Sleuth Book for Genealogists by Emily Anne Croom (Cincinnati: Betterway Books, 2000)

If someone wanted to see the letter, clearly that person would need to contact Sally Jameson.

A second purpose of citing sources is to give other people a (somewhat subjective) means of analyzing the quality of the data. If you found a birth date on a personal Web site, you have no way of knowing the accuracy of that date—unless, of course, the Webmaster cited his sources so you could verify the data. If this citation is to another Web site, that's not saying much for its accuracy.

If you're unsure of how to format source citations, pick up a copy of Emily Anne Croom's *The Sleuth Book for Genealogists* (Betterway Books, 2000). Croom's book contains an easy-to-follow documentation guide.

Online citation guides include:

Citation Style Guides for Internet and Electronic Sources
     <www.library.ualberta.ca/guides/citation/index.cfm>

A Cite for Sore Eyes—Quality Citations for Electronic Genealogy Sources
     <www.oz.net/~markhow/writing/cite.htm>

"Citing Your Sources" by the Board for Certification of Genealogists
     <www.bcgcertification.org/skillbuilders/skbld959.html>

"How to Cite Sources" by John Wylie
     <www.genealogy.com/genealogy/19_wylie.html>

Internet Source

ONLINE CLASSES

If terms like "probate" or "bounty land warrants" send you scurrying for your genealogy dictionary, take heart. There isn't a genealogist on earth who hasn't had to fess up to something she didn't know. In my case, it was GEDCOM and Soundex (see Glossary). Yours may be something else.

Fortunately, **there are several Web sites that offer free genealogy classes.** Most of them are self-directed; all you have to do is go to the site and read the material. You may even want to download and print the lesson for a genealogy learning notebook. Other classes involve posts to a message board by both students and teacher.

The class subjects range from simple to complex, and include things such as how to send for Civil War records and where to look for cemetery records. Even if you're not new to genealogy, it's possible there's a subject you haven't studied before or need to brush up on.

Online Classes at Genealogy.com
<www.genealogy.com/university.html>

Self-led classes on Internet genealogy, tracing immigrant origins, genealogy basics, and beginning genealogy. For those pesky genealogy terms, follow the link to Glossary.

Mother Hubbard's Cupboard Online Classes
<www.rootsweb.com/~genclass>

Free classes for beginning researchers. Several courses on researching ethnic ancestors, including Irish, German, Scottish, English, African American, Australian, and Hispanic.

RootsWeb Guide to Tracing Family Trees
<http://rwguide.rootsweb.com>

Thirty-one lessons written by genealogists Julia M. Case, Myra Vanderpool Gormley, and Rhonda McClure. Wide variety of subjects explored, including church records, newspapers, taxes, and city directories. Major source of information on ethnic research.

Family History
<www.generations.on.ca/family-history.htm>

Step-by-step introduction to tracing your family tree. Sections include information on interviewing, charting, taking photos, and documenting your family history.

In addition to free offerings, you can also sign up for these fee-based classes, which offer more coverage and in-depth study:

Brigham Young University Independent Study
<http://ce.byu.edu/is/site/catalog/pe.dhtm>

Choose from a large array of online courses in family history, categorized as introductory, record types, and regional/ethnic. A few of the introductory courses are free; the rest are available for twenty dollars each. Many BYU online classes can be taken for personal enrichment or for college credits.

Genealogy Online Training Courses through Ancestry.com
<www.myfamily.com/isapi.dll?c=home&htx=gentraining>

For $29.95, students receive four weeks of eight lessons from a genealogy expert, plus thirty days of access to Ancestry databases. Current offerings are Irish Research, Scottish Research, Beginning Genealogy Computer Class, and Writing a Family History.

National Genealogical Society Online Learning Center
<www.ngsgenealogy.org/Courses/Course.cfm>

The National Genealogical Society currently offers an introduction to genealogy as well as a course on using the federal census in your research. Courses are thirty-five dollars for NGS members, fifty dollars for nonmembers. After completing the course you will receive a twenty-five dollar discount toward the NGS sixteen-lesson home study course.

National Institute for Genealogical Studies
<www.genealogicalstudies.com>

In conjunction with the University of Toronto, the National Institute for Genealogical Studies presents a series of courses (basic, intermediate, advanced, and elective) for amateur family historians and aspiring professional genealogists. These Web-based courses are designed to lead to Certificates in Genealogical Studies with specialization in various countries.

DEDUCTIVE SKILLS

Before we jump off into ancestor hunting, let's talk about what it takes to be a successful genealogist—whether online or off.

Building a family tree requires you to ask logical questions and then analyze the problem from many angles. A genealogist is like a detective—always working from the known to the unknown, searching out clues that will break open a case. Before long, you'll find you have honed your deductive skills to such a fine edge that you'll be able to guess "whodunit" before the end of every mystery.

When you climb your family tree, you'll be looking at facts that may not seem to connect. However, as you analyze what you know, then apply some deductive reasoning, possible scenarios will emerge. From there, you'll establish a game plan to prove your theory.

For example, if you know that a branch of your family lived in Virginia in 1743 and didn't reappear until 1840 in Missouri, what might you deduce? Obviously the family moved, but when, why, and along which route? This is the moment in the search where your inner detective steps in and begins asking questions:

- Did the family move to get free land?

Notes

COMBINING OFFLINE AND ONLINE RESEARCH

As you become more skilled at online research, you'll find that some of your greatest successes will come with blending sources from the Internet with those offline.

One of my online searches targeted finding a connection between the Missouri and Texas branches of my Faulkenberry family. I found an amazing amount of information on the family, thanks to online histories, census, and pension reports. I didn't discover the fate of David, the Texas patriarch, or his son, Evan, however, until buying the book *The Border Wars of Texas*, by James DeShields (Austin, Texas: State House Press, 1993).

The book relates how the pair's hunting party was attacked by about thirty "dastardly redskins." David was wounded, managed to swim across the river, but was found dead the next day. According to an Indian tale, Evan "fought like a demon" before being killed. At the time of that search, the information about David and Evan's death was not available online—or if it was, I couldn't find it.

If you can learn to move effortlessly between the library and your computer, your success is guaranteed.

- Did neighbors move with them?
- What were the major migration routes from Virginia to Missouri?
- Was there a war or disaster in their part of Virginia in 1743?
- How would they have traveled: by river or overland?
- Is it possible the family stopped for a generation or so in North Carolina or another state along the way?

From these questions, you'll begin to formulate a research plan. Your steps will probably include searching indexes for the federal census beginning in 1790 and then the actual census, reading a Virginia state or county history, pouring over period maps, or researching migration routes. Before long, you'll have created a research checklist to take with you online or to the library.

Chapter One Checklist
- Fill out pedigree charts and family group sheets.
- Interview relatives.
- Search for records at home.
- Cite your sources.
- Begin thinking like a detective. For practice, what clues can you find in your own birth certificate?

Printed Source

Recommended Reading

America's Best Genealogy Resource Centers, by William Dollarhide and Ronald Bremer (Bountiful, Utah: Heritage Quest, 1998)

Bringing Your Family History to Life Through Social History, by Katherine Scott Sturdevant (Cincinnati: Betterway Books, 2000)

First Steps in Genealogy, by Desmond Walls Allen (Cincinnati: Betterway Books, 1998)

The Handy Book for Genealogists, edited by George B. Everton, 10th edition (Draper, Utah: Everton Publishers, 2002)

Map Guide to American Migration Routes, 1735–1815, by William Dollarhide (Bountiful, Utah: Heritage Quest, 1997)

Organizing Your Family History Search, by Sharon DeBartolo Carmack (Cincinnati: Betterway Books, 1999)

Unpuzzling Your Past, by Emily Anne Croom, 4th edition (Cincinnati: Betterway Books, 2001)

Your Guide to Cemetery Research, by Sharon DeBartolo Carmack (Cincinnati: Betterway Books, 2002)

Your Guide to the Family History Library, by Paula Stuart Warren and James Warren (Cincinnati: Betterway Books, 2001)

Your Guide to the Federal Census, by Kathleen W. Hinckley (Cincinnati: Betterway Books, 2002)

WHAT'S NEXT?

Why the Internet is like the biggest variety store on earth . . .

TWO

Exploring the Net

I f you believe all the media hype, finding your ancestors on the Internet is as easy as logging on and clicking a button. I wish it were so—and perhaps one day it will be. True, there are tens of thousands of genealogy-related items online, but compared to the data contained in books, microfilm, and original records, it's a drop in the bucket. The good news is, it's a large drop.

GENEALOGIST, MEET THE INTERNET

The Internet started life in 1969 as a network named ARPANET. The network was funded mainly by U.S. military sources and consisted of several individual computers connected by leased lines.

In the 1980s, ARPANET was replaced by a separate new military network and a network of scientific and academic computers funded by the National Science Foundation. The Internet as we know it is a relatively new member of the family, with its commercial roots only extending back to about 1992.

Today's Internet is a massive grouping of millions of computers, all linked together on a network. All of the computers can communicate with one another through the network. Briefly, here's how it works.

Your home computer communicates with the computer owned by your Internet Service Provider (ISP). Your ISP then talks to other ISPs around the world via fiber-optic lines, undersea cables, or satellite links. When you want to view a specific Web page, your server sends a request, which makes a series of hops between the user's server and the server hosting the page on the Internet, asking that it be sent to you.

BROWSER-SPEAK

To view Web pages, you'll need a software program called a browser. New computers come with at least one browser preinstalled, either Netscape Navigator or Microsoft Internet Explorer (IE). There are many other browsers available, such as Opera and NeoPlanet, but Netscape and IE are the two most popular.

If you are using America Online (AOL), you can still use Netscape or IE. They are more robust (fully-featured) than the AOL browser. Just launch either browser (by double-clicking on the icon on your desktop) once you've logged onto AOL.

Although the toolbar (the icons running across the top of the page) on IE and Navigator vary, they contain the same basic tools. These include a backward and forward navigation button (these allow you to go back or forward to a Web page you were just on), a home page, print, refresh (or reload), and favorites (or bookmarks). Both programs also offer a history feature, which automatically saves the sites you've visited recently, and a search button, which is essentially the browser's own search engine. (See figure 2-1 below.)

Figure 2-1
Internet Explorer toolbar.

Browser Bookmarks

Have you ever found a great Web page, but couldn't remember where it was or how to get back to it? We all have.

Using a feature on your browser called Bookmarks or Favorites, you can keep track of all of those important pages where you found a possible family connection or discovered a county history. You'll definitely want to bookmark the site and return from time to time to see if any new information has been added.

Tip

Bookmarking a page is simple. Using Netscape, just click Bookmarks, then Add. A bookmark will automatically be added for whatever page is currently displayed.

On IE: While on the page you want to bookmark, click Favorites, then Add.

Caveat: If you bookmark all the pages you want to remember, at some time in the future, you'll have hundreds of bookmarks, and it can be an unorganized mess. Although you can search Netscape for a bookmark containing a specific keyword, it's not always easy to remember what sites you marked or how they were named. To search your bookmarks, click Booksmarks/Manage Bookmarks/Edit/Find Bookmarks.

Besides adding new bookmarks, you can also rename them, file them into folders, and delete them. Creating new folders and moving bookmarks (or favorites into them) is a great way to keep your genealogy sites organized. For example, you'll probably want to create a new folder named Genealogy, and then create sub-folders for specific areas, such as states or surnames.

When you use the Bookmarks window to organize your bookmarks, Netscape Navigator updates the Bookmarks menu automatically. Click the Bookmarks button to pop open the Bookmarks menu, and select Edit (or Manage in newer versions of Netscape) Bookmarks or press Ctrl+B.

If you're using IE, just click Favorites, then Organize. Follow the directions to add new folders, delete or rename favorites, or move them to a new folder.

For more information, see

Organizing Bookmarks in Netscape
<www.stanford.edu/group/itss-customer/docs/329.bookmark2.html>
Using and Organizing Favorites
<www.iup.edu/helpdesk/service/pc/software/ie50/ie50.shtm>

WEB PAGE ADDRESSES

Definitions

Each Web page has a unique "address." If you want to get to a specific Web page, you need to tell the browser its address. **In Internet lingo, this is known as a Uniform Resource Locator (URL).**

A URL looks like this <www.familytreemagazine.com/store/>

Without boring you with the technical details, a URL tells the network which Web page you want to view on your browser. In this instance, you're telling the network that you want to go to the Web site of *Family Tree Magazine* <www.familytreemagazine.com> and view the page that contains the bookstore (store).

This page <www.familytreemagazine.com/articles/feb02/livinghistory.html> tells the computer you want to read one of the online articles (articles) from the February 2002 (feb02) issue on Living History (livinghistory.html).

As you can tell, URLs are organized a lot like the directories on your own computer. For example, your computer contains a main directory called Windows, and several subdirectories, among them "icons," "system," and "start menu." In the example above, familytreemagazine.com is the main directory, articles a subdirectory and feb02 a sub-subdirectory!

WHY DO YOU NEED TO KNOW THIS?

Web site addresses do change, but if you understand the basic structure of a URL, you can often find a page even when it has a different address. For example, if you click on a link to <www.someaddress.com/pedigrees/jerryjones.htm> and you get a message saying the page cannot be found, just delete the jerryjones.htm part of the address. Then, hit Enter on your computer and see what comes up. Oftentimes you'll be able to find the page from a new or corrected link.

HOW TO SET YOUR HOME PAGE

When you first log onto the Internet, the first page you'll see in your browser is your "home page." Although the home page is usually set by default to one chosen by your computer manufacturer, you can select any page you want as your home page.

For example, you may want *Family Tree Magazine* to be your home page because it contains up-to-date information on what's happening in the genealogy world. In addition, its Site of the Day will point you to valuable resources.

To set your home page:

Netscape Navigator:
- Open Netscape Navigator.

- Click Edit on the top toolbar, then Preferences.

- In the center of the menu box where it says Location, type in <www.familytreemagazine.com>

- Click OK at the bottom of the box.

- That's all there is to it! Now, whenever you go online, the home page of *Family Tree Magazine* will be the first page displayed on your browser.

Microsoft Internet Explorer:
- Open IE, click Tools, then Internet Options.

- On the box that pops up, click the General tab, then in the Home Page address box.

- Type www.familytreemagazine.com

- You're set!

E-MAIL BASICS

E-mail is a great tool for keeping families connected. You can use e-mail to send a family newsletter (see chapter ten), let everyone know about your latest findings, or just send a photo of the reunion. In addition, once you get online and start leaving queries, e-mail will be your link to other researchers. Here are a few e-mail basics.

Create a Signature File

Have you received e-mails from someone and at the bottom it says something like "Researching the Harris family of Santa Barbara County, California"? **That is part of what is called a signature file.** It's a file created by a user that is automatically inserted at the bottom of every message sent. The value is keeping your researched surnames in front of the public eye. Who knows

\di'fin\ *vb*

Definitions

FUN BROWSER TOOLBARS

Want a browser toolbar with a little something extra? Download *The New York Times* add-on for Internet Explorer and every ten minutes you'll get an updated newscast. Or, add the Alexa toolbar to get information on every site you visit, including site statistics and contact information. <www.microsoft.com/windows/ie/previous/webaccess/default.asp>

If your IE toolbar is still looking a little boring, download toolbar wallpaper. After running the download, just close IE, start it up again, and choose Toolbar Wallpaper from the Tools menu and pick your wallpaper! (I'm partial to Tubular.)

Don't worry Netscape users! You can easily change browser themes by going to this Web page <http://home.netscape.com/themes/6_2/index.html> and clicking on the Import Theme button. In addition to the pre-installed Modern and Classic themes, check out my favorite, Toy Factory. Once the theme is downloaded, click View/Apply Theme. The next time your browser is opened the new theme will be displayed.

---

when an e-mail recipient may be researching your family or may know someone else who is.

To create a signature file, refer to the Help menu of whatever mail software you are using. For Outlook Express users, click Tools/Options/Signatures. In the box titled Edit Signature, type in whatever you want to appear in your signature file. Next, check or uncheck the option of whether you want the signature added to all outgoing mail.

E-mail Etiquette

Use capital letters judiciously. This means DON'T MAKE ALL OF YOUR WORDS LOOK LIKE THIS BECAUSE IT COMES ACROSS LIKE SCREAMING! You CAN use capitals, however, to emphasize an occasional word.

If you're new to e-mail, you'll probably be mystified by strange groupings of letters that occasionally appear in your messages, such as BTW or LOL. These are actually acronyms, or the cyber version of shorthand! A few favorites are

- BTW—by the way
- LOL—laughing out loud
- IMHO—in my humble opinion
- TTFN—ta ta for now

While acronyms are important, it's surnames that genealogists try to put in all caps, e.g., "Searching for John SMITH family, circa 1850, Cincinnati, Ohio." This makes skimming bulletin boards, e-mails, and mailing lists easier.

VIRUSES

Viruses are nasty little pieces of computer programming code that make your computer do things you didn't want and didn't authorize. The wide body of unwanted critters is called malware, or malicious software. Malware comes in different varieties, including true viruses and programs called Trojan horses.

Viruses are pieces of code that are replicating. They attach themselves to a file and every time the file is opened, the virus is opened and activated. Viruses can also reside in computer memory, and every time your computer opens or modifies a program, the virus is activated. Over time, left unchecked, the virus will replicate itself onto many programs.

A Trojan is technically not a virus because it doesn't replicate itself and spread to other programs. A Trojan is a program that appears to be one thing but it's actually something else. For example, you could download a program that you believe to be a new game. Once launched, however, the program is really a "stealer"—a program designed to steal your user name and passwords.

Guarding against viruses, Trojans, and other malware is as easy as buying and installing anti-virus software. The most popular manufacturers are McAfee (VirusScan) and Symantec (Norton AntiVirus software). With more than five hundred viruses discovered on a weekly basis, these companies keep close tabs on the latest malware.

Important

When you buy and install an anti-virus program, you can configure it to automatically scan your incoming and outgoing mail, any e-mail attachments, and any downloads. This ensures that you can open an e-mail attachment without worrying that it's carrying a known virus that will infect your system.

Note: The text portion of e-mail messages cannot contain a virus. The only way to get a virus from an e-mail is to open an infected attachment. The virus rides along in the attachment, not the e-mail message itself. Be cautious about opening attachments, even when they appear to come from someone you know. The current crop of viruses and worms can "borrow" a recognizable e-mail address, so the attachment may look like it comes from someone you trust, but didn't really. Having anti-virus software is not a guarantee that your computer won't get infected.

Anti-virus software can also be configured to launch itself at a predetermined day and time (e.g., every Friday afternoon at two o'clock), and download the latest virus definitions to your system. By doing this, you'll have the most up-to-date protection. However, if you install anti-virus software and don't keep definitions current, a new bug could hit the computer world and your software won't detect it because it's not on the list of definitions. Follow the instructions in your software Help file to set up your download.

My system is set to download virus definitions once a week, and my entire system is scanned weekly for viruses. To set up your anti-virus protection, follow the instructions that came with your software package. Options include protecting on start-up (recommended), automatically repairing or quarantining an infected file, and setting a specific time for scanning your system. Norton's AntiVirus software, for example, also has an option called LiveUpdate; this allows your computer to automatically go online and download the latest virus definitions.

Virus Hoaxes

Every so often you'll receive an e-mail from a well-meaning friend that warns you of a new virus and encourages you to send the message along to all your friends. These messages are usually hoaxes. How they get started and how they spread is a mystery. If you receive such a message and want to verify its authenticity, just go to the McAfee Web site page on virus hoaxes: <http://vil.mcafee.com/hoax.asp?of McAfee http://mcafee.com/>.

Below is a sample of the Friends virus hoax, which is sent via e-mail:

> ATTENTION VIRUS NASTYFRIEND99
> There is a new virus, which will be infecting computers on May 15. This virus will take all your e-mail contacts and ICQ contacts and send to those contacts. Please forward this e-mail to everyone you know and do not open any email with the subject "HI MY FRIEND!!!"

Another possible hoax e-mail suggests that you delete critical computer files by making you think those files are infected.

Warning

FIREWALLS

If you are using a cable modem or another type of "always-on" connection to the Internet, you are particularly at risk for someone trying to hack into your system through an open port. Many service providers provide firewalls, meaning that outside hackers can't get into your system, even though you have an always-on connection.

If your ISP doesn't provide a firewall, pick up a copy of a personal firewall program such as Norton's Personal Firewall or BlackICE <www.networkice .com>. These programs will intercept any incoming attempts to access your system.

Although some major ISP providers like Earthlink provide firewall security, you need to contact your own provider for information on firewall coverage. If you are using the Windows XP operating system, you can use the built-in Internet Connection Firewall (ICF) by following configuration directions at <http://support.microsoft.com/default.aspx?scid = kb;en-us;q2 83673>.

WHAT'S ONLINE, WHAT'S NOT

When you visit one of the major genealogy information Web sites, you will likely need to search its database to look for facts about your family. A database is a large collection of information organized for quick searches and retrieval. Genealogy databases typically contain transcribed records or compiled family histories. For example, a marriage database might include the name of the bride and groom, the date, the town in which the ceremony was performed, and the county.

What you often won't find are the "extras" that appear on an actual record. These may include the names of the witnesses, minister or justice of the peace, and peripheral notes such as "performed at the home of the bride's brother, Jonathan Sutton."

Database-friendly information contains basic "name-date-place" data, such as

- cemetery records (date and place, but not art carvings)
- immigration records
- land records
- marriage data
- military rosters

What types of records aren't database-friendly? Those that contain text that doesn't easily fit into a name, date, or place field. These include things such as

- medical records (type and length of illness, attending physician)
- military enlistment papers (soldier's physical description, any notes by recruiting officer)
- pension files (may contain description of military service, including specific battles and health of the ancestor)
- probate files (itemized property list, debts)
- wills (detailed account of individual's last wishes)

This doesn't mean you won't find an online pension file, because it's possible that someone transcribed and uploaded it to a Web page. In fact, volunteers work daily to transcribe tombstone inscriptions, probate files, wills, and even Bible records. However, it's more likely to be sitting on a volunteer's personal Web page than on a large, database-driven site. There is an exception, though, called the USGenWeb.

USGenWeb
<www.usgenweb.com>

In 1996, a group of Kentucky genealogists began a project that revolutionized Internet genealogy. Their idea was to provide an online home for genealogy data from each Kentucky county. They wanted the information to be organized so researchers visiting the county Web pages could easily access genealogical and historical information. In addition, they wanted access to the information to be free.

Several months later, as the KyGenWeb Project neared completion, other volunteers began creating Web sites for other U.S. states and counties. Thus, USGenWeb was born. **The goal of the USGenWeb was to create genealogical Web pages for every county in the United States.**

The USGenWeb county pages are maintained by volunteers and are freely searchable by anyone with Internet access. Excellent information exists at

Notes

SEARCH FOR TRANSCRIBED RECORDS IN THE USGENWEB ARCHIVES

The USGenWeb Digital Library (Archives) contains transcriptions of public-domain records, such as census records, marriage bonds, wills, and other historical documents. You can search using either the National Archives <http://searches.rootsweb.com/htdig/search.html> or State Archives search engines <www.rootsweb.com/~usgenweb/ussearch.htm>.

While you're at the USGenWeb <www.usgenweb.com>, don't forget to search the county pages themselves. Many counties have an on-site search engine, which will save you from scanning through every document on the site.

For example, if you go to the Lincoln County, Kansas, home page <http://skyways.lib.ks.us/genweb/lincoln/index.html> and enter Hendrickson in the search box, you'll see a display of eighty-four results—including some pretty unbelievable tall tales.

the national and state level, but the heart and soul of the USGenWeb lies at the county level.

The county Web page content and quality will depend on the volunteers who administer the county. However, you will always find links to local research facilities and a query page. Additionally (depending on the volunteer), you may find

- a county history
- a "snail mail" list of county resources
- a list of surnames being researched in this county as well as e-mail addresses of researchers
- look-up volunteers
- a county mailing list
- transcripts of probate files
- wills

Phyllis Miller Fleming is the county coordinator of the Shelby County, Indiana, USGenWeb site <www.ingenweb.org/shelby/index.htm>, and one of the volunteers who helps get those hard-to-find files on the Web. A few years ago, Fleming went into the Shelby County courthouse in search of an old probate file. She was shocked to learn that all of the historic records were in boxes in the courthouse basement—and in no particular order. Fleming dove in and began organizing the records, then posted the names and types of files on the Shelby County USGenWeb pages.

If a visitor to the Shelby County site wants a copy of a file, Fleming will happily copy it and send it along. Her only payment is a request that the person transcribe the file and send her the transcription to be posted to the Web site. (See figure 2-2 on page 31.)

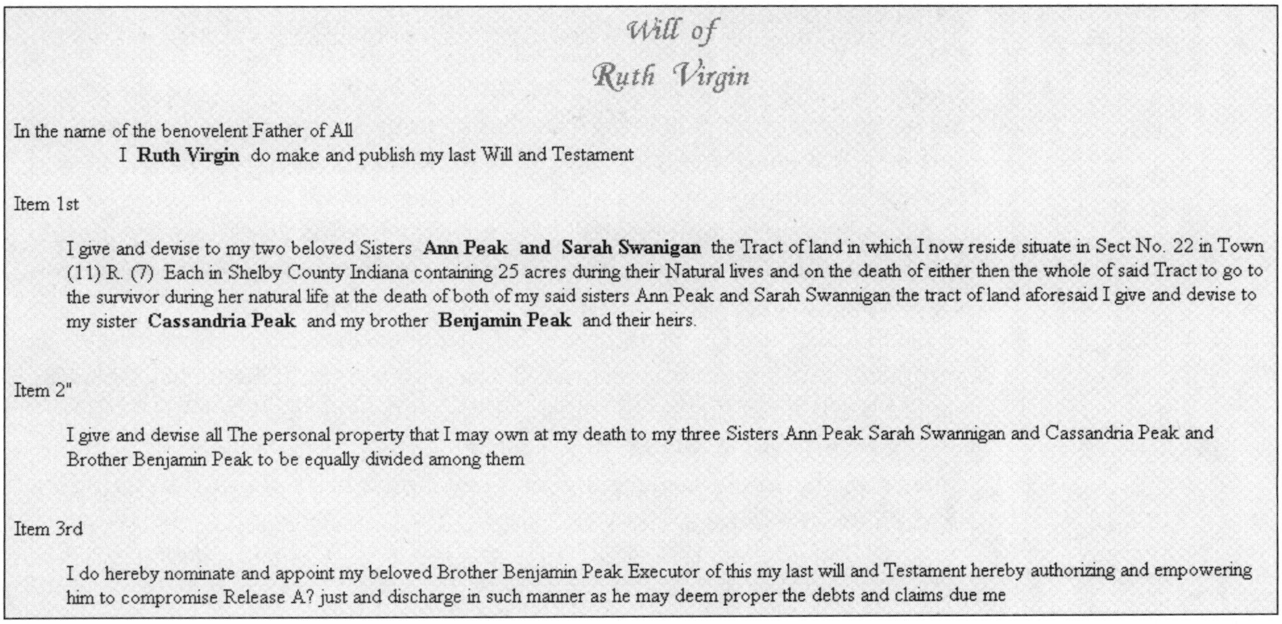

Will of
Ruth Virgin

In the name of the benovelent Father of All
      I **Ruth Virgin** do make and publish my last Will and Testament

Item 1st

    I give and devise to my two beloved Sisters **Ann Peak and Sarah Swanigan** the Tract of land in which I now reside situate in Sect No. 22 in Town (11) R. (7) Each in Shelby County Indiana containing 25 acres during their Natural lives and on the death of either then the whole of said Tract to go to the survivor during her natural life at the death of both of my said sisters Ann Peak and Sarah Swannigan the tract of land aforesaid I give and devise to my sister **Cassandria Peak** and my brother **Benjamin Peak** and their heirs.

Item 2"

    I give and devise all The personal property that I may own at my death to my three Sisters Ann Peak Sarah Swannigan and Cassandria Peak and Brother Benjamin Peak to be equally divided among them

Item 3rd

    I do hereby nominate and appoint my beloved Brother Benjamin Peak Executor of this my last will and Testament hereby authorizing and empowering him to compromise Release A? just and discharge in such manner as he may deem proper the debts and claims due me

Figure 2-2
Volunteer efforts by USGenWeb County Coordinators can result in the posting of probate files, wills and other family documents.
Phyllis Miller Fleming

Other USGenWeb volunteers are busily transcribing different genealogy-related information. For example, the Pension Project, which is in its infancy with only a few posts, has a goal of transcribing all military pension-related materials for all U.S. wars prior to 1900.

If you are researching a U.S. family, a visit to the USGenWeb is a must. This is the place to leave queries and communicate with other researchers who are either tracing your family or one of your family's neighbors. If I had to pick one online resource for American genealogy, it would be USGenWeb.

Other Volunteer Projects

Another exceptional volunteer project is that of the Emigrant Savings Bank <www.genexchange.org/esb/index.cfm>, one of the most important genealogical source materials for New York City. The bank opened in 1850 and was run by Irish immigrants for Irish immigrants. It contains records for immigrants who lived in California, Michigan, Florida, New York, New Jersey, Delaware, Maryland, Alabama, and Missouri. The transcription of thousands of records was done by one volunteer: Monica Bennett.

Civilian Draft Registration Cards

<www.genexchange.org/draftcard.cfm>
About 1.3 million Civilian Draft Registration Cards were transcribed and contributed by Raymond H. Banks. Completed transcribed cards are searchable by surname, first name, or county.

Okay, ready to explore what you can expect to find online?

Military Records

Let's say you've heard stories about Great-great-grandpa Joe's stint in the Union Army during the Civil War. You may even be lucky enough to own his letters or wartime diary. Or perhaps family stories exist about how he survived a wound at Gettysburg and went on to take part in the Grand Review in Washington, DC, at the end of the war.

Although many family stories have grown with time, they usually contain a grain of truth. But wouldn't it be great to find out more about Joe, including the regiment he served in and the battles he witnessed?

A Civil War soldier generated a lot of paperwork, commonly known as compiled military service records. These include the enlistment papers he signed when he volunteered, muster rolls, and payrolls. Compiled military service records don't include much genealogical information, but they sometimes give the soldier's place of birth, age, and a brief physical description. (See figure 2-3 below.)

Figure 2-3
This Civil War enlistment of James Knox gives his place of birth (Highland Co., Illinois) and a brief physical description (blue eyes, light hair, fair complexion, 5 feet, 8½ inches tall).

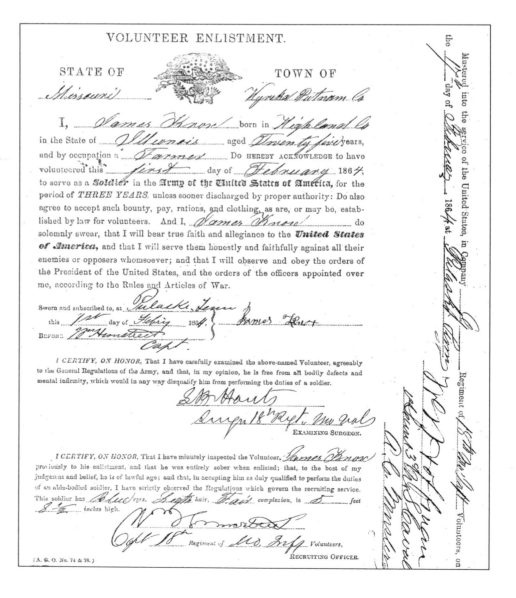

The most useful genealogical information in military records is in pension files. (See figure 2-4 on page 34.) These might include the names and ages of a wife and children, as well as the place of marriage.

Unfortunately, compiled military service records and pension files are not data you will routinely find online; in fact, the only time you will find it is if another researcher transcribed or scanned the papers and uploaded them to the Internet. (See page 36 for information on ordering military records.) What you will find online, though, are

- military rosters
- regimental histories
- descriptions of battles

Military Rosters

Military rosters are simply lists that include the soldier's name, rank, company, and regiment. Although not all military rosters of all soldiers are online, there is a high percentage.

For example, an online search in the Illinois Civil War Veterans Database <www.library.sos.state.il.us/departments/archives/datcivil.html> for my great-great-grandfather, Calvin Dimmitt, returned a list of soldiers with the Dimmitt surname. Calvin was on the list and shown as serving in Company E of the 65th Illinois Infantry.

What the roster did not reveal was that he was captured at Antietam, he was part of a prisoner exchange the following day, deserted, disappeared for a few years, ended up in Tennessee, rejoined the Union Army, and married a local girl. (See figure 2-5 on page 35.)

Another database, Illinois Civil War Rosters from the Adjutant General's Report <www.rootsweb.com/~ilcivilw/regros.htm>, was a bit more revealing. I learned that the 65th Illinois Infantry was known as the Second Scotch Regiment or Cameron's Highlanders, and that its soldiers signed up for three years of service. In addition, it showed the 65th was in service from 1 May 1862, to 26 July 1865 and that the regiment was filled with volunteers from Boone and McDonough counties. Finally it listed, under Company E, Calvin Dimmitt as a deserter.

Regimental Histories

A second type of online military record is a regimental history. This is a detailed account of a regiment's activities beginning from the day it was organized. Unless your ancestor was a commanding officer, it's unlikely you'll find his name in a regimental history. You will learn which battles he was in, however, and the dates of those battles.

An online search for the regimental history of the 65th Illinois included its activities from spring 1862 until 13 July 1865, when the regiment was mustered out. Included in the description was the action where Calvin Dimmitt was captured:

> The Regiment was ordered to Martinsburg, VA, and, on its arrival, was
> brigaded with the Hundred and Twenty-fifth New York and Batter M,

Figure 2-4
James Knox's Civil War pension declaration lists the regiments in which he served as well as his occupation and place of birth.

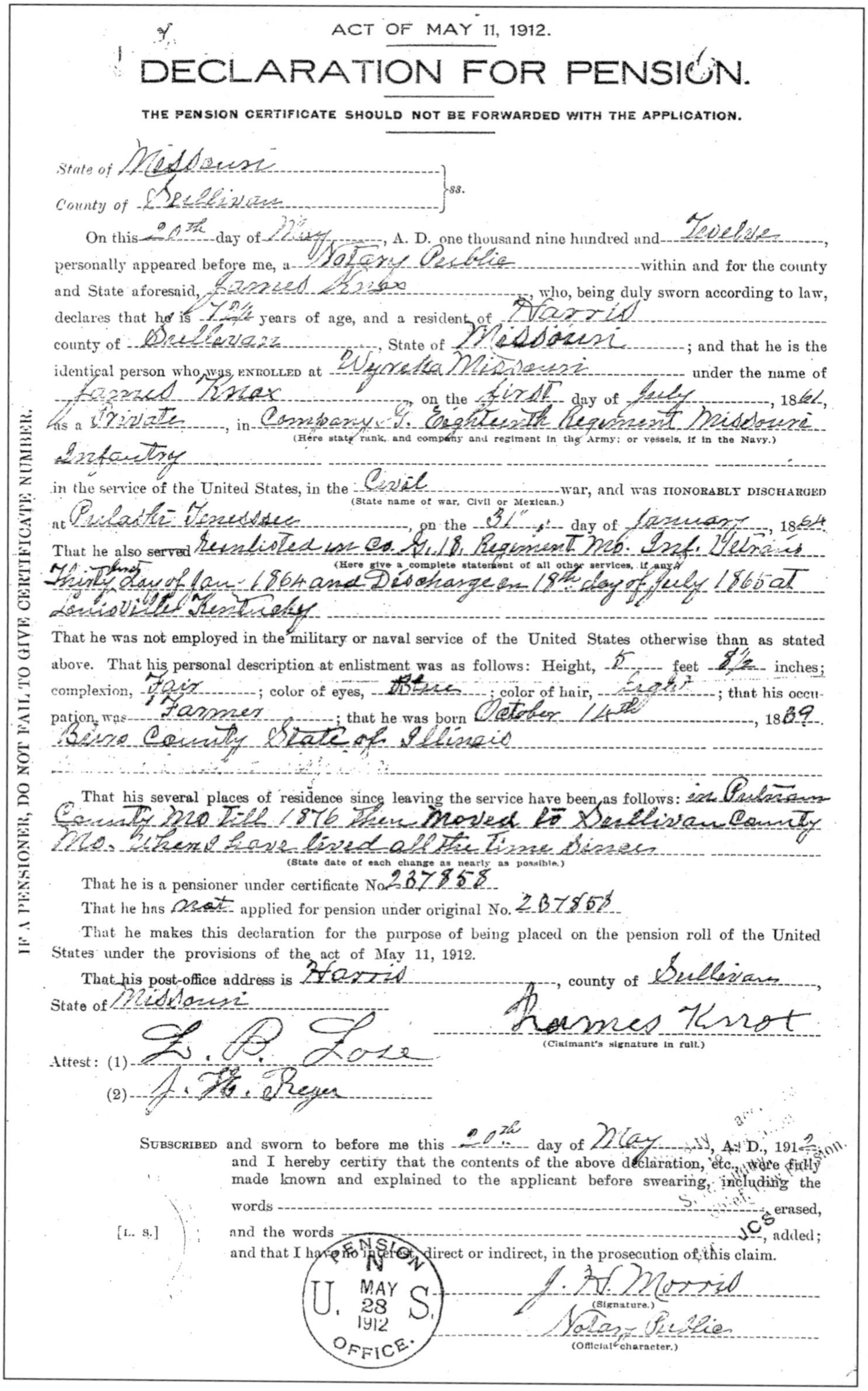

ACT OF MAY 11, 1912.

DECLARATION FOR PENSION.

THE PENSION CERTIFICATE SHOULD NOT BE FORWARDED WITH THE APPLICATION.

State of *Missouri*

County of *Sullivan* } ss.

On this *20th* day of *May*, A. D. one thousand nine hundred and *Twelve*, personally appeared before me, a *Notary Public* within and for the county and State aforesaid, *James Knox*, who, being duly sworn according to law, declares that he is *72* years of age, and a resident of *Harris* county of *Sullivan*, State of *Missouri*; and that he is the identical person who was ENROLLED at *Wyretta Missouri* under the name of *James Knox* on the *First* day of *July*, 1861, as a *Private*, in *Company S. Eighteenth Regiment Missouri Infantry*
(Here state rank, and company and regiment in the Army; or vessels, if in the Navy.)

in the service of the United States, in the *Civil* war, and was HONORABLY DISCHARGED
(State name of war, Civil or Mexican.)

at *Pulaski Tennessee* on the *31* day of *January*, 1864. That he also served *Reenlisted in Co. G. 18 Regiment Mo. Inf. Vetrans*
(Here give a complete statement of all other services, if any)
Thirty first day of Jan. 1864 and Discharge on 19th day of July 1865 at Louisville Kentucky

That he was not employed in the military or naval service of the United States otherwise than as stated above. That his personal description at enlistment was as follows: Height, *5* feet *8½* inches; complexion, *Fair*; color of eyes, *Blue*; color of hair, *Light*; that his occupation was *Farmer*; that he was born *October 14th*, 18*39*, *Bond County State of Illinois*

That his several places of residence since leaving the service have been as follows: *in Putnam County Mo Till 1876 Then Moved to Sullivan County Mo. Where have lived all the time Since*
(State date of each change as nearly as possible.)

That he is a pensioner under certificate No. *237858*

That he has *not* applied for pension under original No. *237858*

That he makes this declaration for the purpose of being placed on the pension roll of the United States under the provisions of the act of May 11, 1912.

That his post-office address is *Harris*, county of *Sullivan*,
State of *Missouri*

James Knox
(Claimant's signature in full.)

Attest: (1) *L. B. Lose*

(2) *J. H. Reger*

SUBSCRIBED and sworn to before me this *20th* day of *May*, A. D., 1912, and I hereby certify that the contents of the above declaration, etc., were fully made known and explained to the applicant before swearing, including the words _____ erased, and the words _____ added; and that I have no interest, direct or indirect, in the prosecution of this claim.

[L. S.]

J. H. Morris
(Signature.)

Notary Public
(Official character.)

U. S. PENSION OFFICE MAY 28 1912

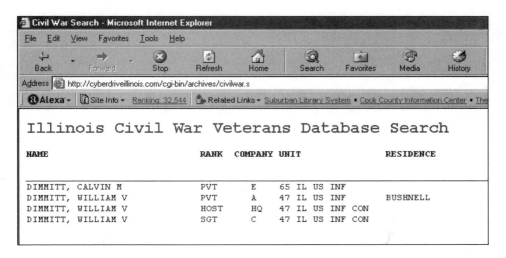

Figure 2-5
Some states, like Illinois, are beginning to post historic records on the Internet. *Illinois State Archives*

Second Illinois Artillery, under command of Colonel Miles. When Colonel Miles surrendered at Harper's Ferry, the Sixty-fifth were made prisoners by the enemy. On the succeeding day, the Regiment was parroled [*sic*] and sent to Chicago, where it remained until April, 1863 . . . <www.rootsweb.com/~ilcivilw/history/065.htm>

Although finding regimental histories online used to be a rarity, today you can find histories for nearly every outfit. Visit the Civil War Resources section of A Barrel of Genealogy Links <www.genealogytoday.com/barrel>, which includes links to most regimental histories on the Net.

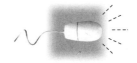

Internet Source

Battle Descriptions

No matter which wars your ancestors served in, there's likely more than a few Web sites that can help you find out more about the conflict and your ancestors' experiences in it—certainly in a general sense, and perhaps even specific instances. *Family Tree Magazine*'s Web site lists a large number of Web sites categorized by each war the U.S. has participated in at <www.familytreemagazine.com/articles/apr02/milsites.html>, along with links to today's military sites. You may find out what your ancestors' lives could have been like during the war, or you may find out a whole lot more.

Finding battle descriptions of major Civil War engagements is easy; locating Revolutionary War ones is a bit more difficult. That said, I found a wonderful description of the 1780 South Carolina Battle of Hanging Rock—an action described by one of my ancestors in his pension records.

One of the most interesting things I learned was that the battle was observed by a thirteen-year-old president-to-be, Andrew Jackson. The battle description said Jackson later modeled his own fighting style after the engagement at Hanging Rock <www.inmyattic.com/lancaster/history/history_hangingrock.htm>.

Cemetery Records

As genealogists, we want to know every little tidbit about our ancestors' lives, including their final resting place. I remember the exhilaration I felt

---

ORDERING MILITARY RECORDS

The National Archives and Records Administration is the official repository for military records. Holdings include

Regular Army: Enlisted personnel, 1789–October 31, 1912; officers, 1789–June 30, 1917

Navy: Enlisted personnel, 1798–1885; officers, 1789–1902

Volunteers: 1775–1902

Marine Corps: Enlisted personnel, 1789–1904; some officers, 1789–1895

Coast Guard: 1791–1919 (includes predecessor agencies)

Confederate States: 1861–1865

Veterans Records: 1775–1916 and bounty land warrant applications, 1775–1855

Detailed information on military records held at NARA can be found at <www.archives.gov/research_room/genealogy/research_topics/military.html>.

To order military service records, 1776–1916, use Form NATF 86; for 1917–present use Standard Form 180. Pension records may be ordered using Form NATF 85. To obtain forms 85 and 86, send an e-mail addressed to inquire@nara.gov. Provide your name and mailing address, the name of the form, and the number of forms you need (limit five). You may also obtain forms by writing to the following address:

National Archives and Records Administration
Attn: NWCTB
700 Pennsylvania Avenue NW
Washington, DC 20408-0001

You may receive Standard Form 180 electronically at <www.archives.gov/facilities/mo/st_louis/military_personnel_records/standard_form_180.html>.

You can also research these records on microfilm at the National Archives in Washington, DC, and at some of its branches. Visit <http://www.archives.gov> to search the NARA catalog and find branch locations. Some records may also be available at the Family History Library and its centers. Search for a Family History Center near you at <www.familysearch.org/Eng/Library/FHC/frameset_fhc.asp>.

---

on the day I finally discovered the burial site of my third-great-grandfather.

Thanks to volunteers, millions of names from cemeteries are being transcribed and uploaded to the Net. Again, you'll find information that's database-friendly, like names, dates of birth and death, the location of the cemetery, and possibly the burial plot number. If your ancestor was buried in a military cemetery, rank and unit are often listed. What you likely won't find in a searchable database are tombstone transcriptions, like "beloved wife of," a quote from a Bible verse, or the artwork, (which is often an important and overlooked clue).

GUIDE TO CEMETERY RESEARCH

Learn how cemeteries can help fill in the holes in your family history with *Your Guide to Cemetery Research* by Sharon DeBartolo Carmack (Cincinnati: Betterway Books, 2002). Using this book, you can determine when and where a person died, how to locate cemeteries, analyze headstones and markers, interpret funerary art, safely make a tombstone rubbing, and conduct a cemetery survey.

This book is a comprehensive, in-depth resource that's perfect for genealogists, researchers, and historians. It goes beyond strict cemetery research to cover cemetery and death-related terminology, clues offered by headstone art, and cemeteries' role in our culture and history.

This guide also examines the funeral customs of various ethnic groups, includes a social history of death that reveals both the usual and unusual ways in which your ancestors coped with and celebrated death, and contains numerous Web sites linking to cemetery transcriptions.

When I went to Cemetery Records Online <www.interment.net> and searched for Hendrickson burials in California, one of the hits was my own father's records, including birth and death dates, the location of the cemetery, and the plot number. Because he is buried in a military cemetery, his rank and unit are also listed.

When doing online cemetery research, remember to bring your inner detective along and be alert for any clues. For instance, a query for the surname Faulkenberry returned an interesting listing for a J.W. Faulkenberry, Company C, 2nd South Carolina, who was buried in the Point Lookout Confederate Cemetery in St. Mary's County, Maryland. I don't know if this person is part of my family, but because I do know some of the Faulkenberry's served in the Confederate Army, it's certainly worth further investigation.

Stop: If J.W. was your ancestor, what would this listing suggest, and what kind of research plan would you develop? List four possible questions this burial might prompt.

_____
_____
_____
_____

What thoughts do you have about researching these questions?
_____
_____
_____

Reminder

For More Info

For more on land records, see *Locating Your Roots: Discover Your Ancestors Using Land Records*, by Patricia Law Hatcher, (Cincinnati: Betterway Books, 2003).

Land Records

If your ancestor lived in a public land state and had a land grant (see Glossary), it's possible you'll find his land patent at the Bureau of Land Management <www.glorecords.blm.gov>. These records contain details of the original transfer of land from the United States government to an individual. Any subsequent resale of the land is not included in this database.

See chapter seven for more on using Bureau of Land Management records.

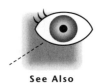

See Also

Census Records

Every ten years since 1790, the federal government has conducted a census of its population. Although the census was originally designed to be a "head count," it has evolved into one of the most valuable tools for American genealogists.

Census records are filled with genealogy clues. They can contain the birthplace of an individual or his parents, as well as ages of everyone in the household. The first census lists only the name of the head of household and the number of people living there. Beginning in 1850, however, the census taker (enumerator) wrote down the name of every free person living in the household.

See chapter seven for more on searching census databases.

UNTANGLING THE FEDERAL CENSUS

Census research is one of the first and most important steps in constructing a family tree. Everyone from genealogists to historians use the federal census for researching family histories. Deciphering census data, however, is not always easy. *Your Guide to the Federal Census,* by Kathleen Hinckley (Cincinnati: Betterway Books, 2002) <www.familytreemagazine> acts as a personal "research assistant." It examines the nuts and bolts of census records and the types of information available. It also reveals where to view the censuses online and off, and how to find most ancestors quickly.

WHAT ELSE IS ONLINE?

If you think of the Internet as a genealogist's version of Wal-Mart, you'll have a good idea of what's online. In other words, there's a little bit of everything.

As much as we love records, we don't live and die by them alone. We are story weavers and our family tapestries include whatever puts flesh and blood on the names in our pedigree files.

For instance, if you are descended from a Revolutionary War veteran, wouldn't it add more interest to your family history book (you are going to write one, aren't you?) to include a first-hand account of the battles he took part in? Or a period map of where he lived? Or what the wife and kids were doing on the home front? How fascinating it would be to read a copy of his local newspaper or a popular book of the time.

Luckily, these types of items can be found online. How to find them will be covered in chapter six (Search Engines), but for now, here's a preview of what's available to you—and most of it is free of charge.

Maps

The Library of Congress <http://memory.loc.gov/ammem/gmdhtml/gmdhome.html> holds more than 4.5 million maps, and a small percentage of them have been digitized and posted online. Typical maps include:

- an 1849 depiction of the California gold fields
- an 1862 pen-and-ink manuscript drawn on tracing cloth, showing "line of Hooker's advance," roads, houses and names of occupants, fences, vegetation, drainage
- an 1859 St. Louis city map
- an 1836 map of lands assigned to Indians west of Arkansas and Missouri
- a map of the 1773 "Potomack and James rivers in North America shewing their several communications with the navigable waters of the new province on the river Ohio."
- an 1893 map showing the proposed route of the Tennessee, Alabama, and Georgia railroad

Other Web sites contain maps of American migration routes (wouldn't these be great in your book if the images are in the public domain!), street maps, exploration trails, railroad routes, Indian territory, historical city maps, county maps, westward expansion, the Oregon Trail, territorial growth, and military expeditions.

Maps can be of great help in pinning down exactly where your ancestor lived. If you've "lost" a generation, migration maps can provide clues for possible places they may have stopped along the way.

Books

In 1995, the University of Michigan and Cornell University began a joint project of digitizing books that documented American social history from the antebellum period through reconstruction.

The collection, called Making of America <http://moa.umdl.umich.edu>, currently contains more than three million book and journal pages that have been scanned and uploaded. **While you may not find a direct reference to your ancestors in any of these volumes, you will discover details about their daily lives.**

I searched the MOA collection for Lone Jack, Missouri, the home of several of my ancestors. The search returned twelve hits. My favorite was a diary excerpt from 9 June 1858, *Beyond the Mississippi: from the great river to the great ocean. Life and adventure on the prairies, mountains, and Pacific coast*, by Albert D. Richardson. It reads

> Beyond the Waukarusa we found one solitary "black-jack" (oak.) In Missouri there is a flourishing town named Lone Jack from a tree of this species whose pleasant shade and a cool spring at its roots, made it a favorite camping-place for early travelers.

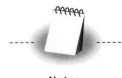

Notes

At night, we sought refuge from a thunder storm in the hospitable log house of Ottawa Jones, a Pottawatomie half-breed, educated and bearing no appearance of Indian extraction. His white wife was a native of Maine. Both had been adopted into the Ottawa tribe, and he was chief of the band. For his Free State sympathies the Border Ruffians had burned his house, whose blackened ruins were standing a few yards from the present dwelling.

First-Person Narratives

During the Depression, the Works Project Administration began interviewing average Americans and writing their life histories. The Library of Congress collection of the Federal Writers' Project includes 2,900 documents representing the work of more than 300 writers <http://memory.loc.gov/ammem/wpaintro/wpahome.html.>

The life histories contain stories of the Alaskan gold rush, life on the Oregon Trail, slave narratives, and accounts of everyday life. You may not find your ancestor's Oregon Trail story, but reading accounts from other travelers will offer insight into the conditions they faced along the two thousand-mile journey. This collection is searchable by keyword.

The History in Family History

"Doing" genealogy means "doing" history. Our ancestors were eyewitnesses to the events that we read about in history books. They debated slavery, heard about the capture of Geronimo, and shook their heads over the death of a fellow named Custer at the Little Bighorn.

While searching for ancestors online, you'll be surprised at how often you'll move back and forth between genealogy sites and history sites. For example, were any of your ancestors old enough to have fought in the French and Indian War or the Mexican War? It's pretty hard to know unless you know the dates of those wars. Where will you find them? History sites.

Reminder

The more we know about the time in which our ancestors lived, the better detectives we become. When gold was discovered in California, is it any wonder that your Oregon ancestors all poured south? Or, if your ancestor "disappeared" for a generation or two, did it coincide with opening new land to settlers?

Would you like to join the Daughters or Sons of the American Revolution <http://dar.org> <www.sar.org> but can't find a soldier in your history? Membership is based on a link to a patriot, not necessarily a soldier. Patriots included gunsmiths, ferry operators, town treasurers, and ministers who gave patriotic sermons.

The Internet is a rich source for historical documents. For example, the Library of Congress has digitized copies of documents from the Continental Congress and the Constitutional Convention <http://memory.loc.gov/ammem/bdsds/bdsdhome.html>. Read, for example, the 1782 report by Mr. Beresford, Mr. Jefferson, Mr. Chase, Mr. Spaight, and Mr. Read regarding the state of Indian affairs in the Southern Department.

If your ancestor lived in South Carolina or Georgia during this time period, you can read the official government stance about Indians who sided with Great Britain during the Revolutionary War.

Another key online resource for finding historical documents and records is the Archival Research Catalog (ARC) <www.archives.gov/research_r oom/arc>, which is the online catalog of the U.S. National Archives and Records Administration's nationwide holdings in the Washington, DC, area, Regional Archives and Presidential Libraries. You can perform a keyword, digitized image, and location search, or do more advanced searches by organization, person, or topic. Microfilm publications may be searched via the Microfilm Publications Catalog <www.archives.gov/research_room/alic/res earch_tools/search_microfilm_catalog.html>.

The Library of Virginia has a digital library program <www.lva.lib.va.us/ dlp>, that includes an Index to Wills and Administrations, a War of 1812 searchable database, a marriage index, and land records index.

OTHER HISTORICAL DOCUMENTS ONLINE

A 1607 List of Jamestown Settlers
<http://englishamerica.home.att.net/places/va607001.htm>

An 1862 Letter From General McClellan to President Lincoln
<http://americancivilwar.com/documents/mcclellan_lincoln.html>

Hessian Army Life, 1776–1777
<www.hillsdale.edu/dept/History/Documents/War/EMAmRev.htm>

Major-General Sir John Burgoyne's Report of Bunker Hill Major
<www.hillsdale.edu/dept/History/Documents/War/EMAmRev.htm>

The *Mayflower Compact*
<http://members.aol.com/calebj/compact.html>

Rare Maps of Colonial America
<www.libs.uga.edu/darchive/hargrett/maps/colamer.html>

Migration Routes

In a conversation with a member of the San Diego Genealogical Society, I mentioned that I was trying to track down a branch of the family who lived in Kentucky. She said, "You know that a lot of early Kentucky settlers came by way of Ohio, don't you?" Well, I didn't know that, but it got me started looking at migration patterns.

Our ancestors traveled pretty much the same way we do today—over the path of least resistance. Why climb a mountain if someone has already hacked a road through the wilderness?

Early American settlers colonized the East Coast. At that point, the only roads were a few along coastal areas or waterways such as the Hudson River. As settlements spread inland from the coast, more and more roads

---

BRING YOUR FAMILY HISTORY TO LIFE

Katherine Scott Sturdevant's book, *Bringing Your Family History to Life Through Social History* (Cincinnati: Betterway Books, 2000) shows you how to use social history—the study of ordinary people's everyday lives—to add depth, detail, and drama to your family's saga.

She'll provide you with the instruction you need to accurately investigate your family's unique history, including their

- daily lives—use the Elements of Social History as the background context of your family history

- family photographs—learn how to find, acquire, care for, analyze, copy, and display them

- oral histories—record your family's oral traditions and folklore and learn the best methods for formulating questions that draw out the social history you're looking for

- home sources and material folk culture—collect the artifacts and materials already within your family, such as heirlooms, memorabilia, and photographs

In addition, you'll learn how to build and sharpen your research skills, including

- writing letters to collect historical information from hard-to-reach sources such as distant family, state institutions, or local towns

- easing yourself into college and university library research with confidence

- creating an accurate cultural context in which to understand the actions and influences of your ancestors, as well as produce a written account of historical and social value

---

were built and traveled. These are most likely the routes taken by your ancestors. Get out a map and pinpoint where they started and where they ended. It's likely that today's highways run on top of those old roads—the path of least resistance.

For a detailed look at old roads and migration patterns, pick up a copy of William Dollarhide's book *Map Guide to American Migration Routes* (Bountiful, Utah: Heritage Quest, 1997). Priced at less than ten dollars, it's an indispensable addition to your genealogy library.

Cyndi's List: A Mega-Genealogy Portal

If you've been doing online genealogy for more than a week, you've undoubtedly heard about a Web site called Cyndi's List <www.cyndislist.com>. This portal (meaning it's a gateway to other sites) was created by Cyndi Howells in 1996, as an outgrowth of her personal set of genealogy bookmarks.

Today, Cyndi's List welcomes fifteen thousand visitors daily, includes close to 166,000 genealogy links, with fifteen hundred links added monthly. Sites are organized alphabetically within one of 150 categories. Although you won't find actual family data on Cyndi's List, you will find links to any number of topics that will assist your research.

The best way to use Cyndi's List is if you have a general topic of interest. For example, if you know you have a Quaker ancestor, but don't know anything about searching Quaker records (or even where to find them), go to Cyndi's List and click on Quaker. Next, you'll find the Quaker category further organized by

Tip

- general resource sites
- history
- how-to
- libraries, archives, and museums
- locality specific
- mailing lists, newsgroups, and chat
- people and families
- publications, software, and supplies
- queries, message boards, and surname lists
- records: census, cemeteries, land, obituaries, personal, taxes, and vital
- societies and groups

In all, there are 140 Quaker links to explore, depending on the type of information you're seeking. If you're starting from square one, visit the general resource sites for an overview on the Quaker faith; if you've already used William Wade Hinshaw's *Encyclopedia of American Quaker Genealogy* (Ann Arbor, Michigan: Edwards Brothers, 1930–1950), follow the How To link for more information on Hinshaw's system of abbreviations. Are you keen on networking with other Quaker researchers? Then follow the Mailing List links.

Another excellent way to use Cyndi's List is to track down state-specific resource sites. If your family settled in South Carolina, for instance, go to the United States/South Carolina category and explore through more than thirteen hundred South Carolina related links. There, you'll find links to sites with South Carolina maps, military rosters, records, religion, and culture. If you need to hire a professional researcher who is skilled in a specific area, you'll find links to researchers in the state categories.

For anyone who has discovered "over the sea" ancestors, Cyndi's List is a good jumping off place for getting your feet wet. For example, if you've just discovered you have Swedish ancestors, click on the Sweden link, and you'll find dozens of useful reference sites, like a Swedish Research Outline or tips on the language, locating churches, and Swedish naming customs.

Whenever you start a new area of research, be sure to visit Cyndi's List for links to obtaining vital background information.

PAY AS YOU GO: SUBSCRIBING TO COMMERCIAL DATABASES

As much as everyone loves "free genealogy" (more in chapter four), the day will probably come when you subscribe to a commercial database service.

Internet Source

These sites contain thousands of genealogy-specific databases or other hard-to-come-by family files. Currently, the two largest players are Ancestry.com <www.ancestry.com> and Genealogy.com <www.genealogy.com>. Both offer an assortment of subscription plans, including monthly, quarterly, and annual (most economical) billing options.

Ancestry.com

Ancestry allows you to choose a subscription plan that includes access to all databases, or pick only the major databases you need, e.g., census images, historical newspapers, and United Kingdom/Ireland, for example.

One of the latest collections is the United Kingdom/Ireland database, which contains parish and probate records, lists of Irish immigrants, and the Pallot Marriage and Baptism Index. The parish and probate database (the largest of the U.K. databases) contains fifteen million birth, death, and marriage records from historical registers dating from 1538 to 1837. You'll even find some older, non-parish records from as early as the twelfth century.

The Irish immigrants database contains an index of 600,000 immigrants into New York City, 1846–1851. Information can include destination, gender, residence, and nationality. The Pallot Marriage and Baptism Index contains four million names of marriages and baptisms in the London area. Marriage records date from 1780 to 1837.

Ancestry.com's databases are the genealogical version of a Sunday smorgasbord—the table is laden with every type of goody imaginable. Bite into Massachusetts town vital records; Aiken County, South Carolina, cemetery inscriptions; or Texas land title abstracts. Munch your way through the Leavenworth, Kansas, death index, or feast on Virginia marriages before 1824. I'd be surprised if you didn't find an ancestor or two in an Ancestry.com database.

If you have only a three-month period (the shortest available subscription) and can devote several hours to searching, it's probably worth the thirty dollars to search every applicable database and store the information you find until you're working on that particular branch of the family. I've subscribed to Ancestry off and on for several years—and have discovered several "break-through" records, opening dead ends in my search.

Genealogy.com

Genealogy.com's roots go back to the mid-1990s, when Brøderbund Software created FamilyTreeMaker.com, a companion site for the company's popular software. At first, the majority of the site's content was dedicated to FTM users and purchasers of the extensive line of genealogy-related CD-ROMs.

Over time, the site became Genealogy.com, a major stopover for anyone in search of ancestors—not just FTM users. Today, in addition to subscription databases, you'll find a powerful search engine along with a whole bag full of free resources, including lessons, how-to articles and genealogy message boards on the Net. It also offers almost one hundred celebrity family trees, which are free and cover a variety of lineages.

The Genealogy.com subscription plans range from monthly to annual access. You can get a package deal that includes a copy of the popular Family Tree Maker software, along with access to the Genealogy Library, World Family Tree, and International and Passenger Records. Genealogy.com recently partnered with Heritage Quest to make digitized images of all census records available and, like Ancestry, they are actively indexing these records. Of particular interest to genealogists is the World Family Tree collection, which includes hundreds of thousands of actual family trees which can be viewed online or downloaded into the desktop.

Warning

Keep in mind that the family trees included in the World Family Tree collection have not been verified for accuracy. It's a good bet however, that they contain leads and clues to further research. In addition, if you find a family tree that contains information on your family, you can contact the submitter and begin networking.

A plus for users of the Family Tree Maker software is you can go online directly from within the FTM program (as long as you have Internet access) and request a Genealogy.com search for any individuals in your family tree.

As a service to the genealogy community, this commercial site offers the ability to search all of its sources, including personal Web sites, message boards, family home pages and the Social Security Death Index (all free). The search will also contain hits in commercial databases like World Family Tree and historical records.

Other Commercial Databases

Origins.net
<www.origins.net>
Pay-as-you-go database with English and Scottish records.
MyTrees
<www.mytrees.com>
Formerly Kindred Konnections, over one billion names in lineage-linked database.

Chapter Two Checklist

- Check your own computer to see if it has anti-virus software. If so, configure the software to automatically check your system and download definitions.
- Explore the USGenWeb site <www.usgenweb.com>.
- Search for a cemetery record <www.interment.net>.
- Search for a map at the Library of Congress <http://memory.loc.gov/ammem/gmdhtml/gmdhome.html>.
- Fill out the Military Actions sheet for as many of your ancestors as possible (see form in Appendix).

WHAT'S NEXT?

Everything you ever wanted to know about your computer . . . and more.

THREE

The Organized Computer Genealogist

By nature, I'm not the world's most organized person. In fact, I have a habit of tucking things away in such safe places I can never find them again. But getting organized—and staying organized—is a way of life for anyone who wants to climb the family tree.

Although it's not in the realm of this book to guide you through organizing your at-home genealogy filing system, I am going to give you a few tips to make sure the computer end of your research stays organized. If you follow these simple suggestions, you'll never have to worry about finding your way back to an important Web site or losing a valuable e-mail message.

For those of you who feel you need help from the ground up, pick up a copy of Sharon DeBartolo Carmack's *Organizing Your Family History Search*. (Cincinnati: Betterway Books, 1999).

YOUR COMPUTER'S WINDOWS FILE STRUCTURE

When Windows was first introduced, it replaced an operating system named DOS. Compared to DOS, Windows was easy to navigate, user-friendly, and didn't require users to remember strings of commands like:

```
c:\
cd \utilities
c:\utilities
c:\utilities\makebackup.exe
```

Unlike the text-based DOS, Windows is graphical—almost everything you'd want to do can be done by clicking on an icon, which is a graphic symbol on the computer's display screen that suggests the purpose of an available function. However, your computer still has a basic file structure just as it did in DOS; it's just hidden behind Windows' pretty face.

It's possible to get through most of your computer life not knowing a thing about the computer's file structure. **As an Internet genealogist, however, there will be times when you'll need to know how to perform simple tasks such as**

Important

GET ORGANIZED!

At last, a book to help you organize your genealogical research! *Organizing Your Family History Search* by Sharon DeBartolo Carmack (Cincinnati: Betterway Books, 1999), is a friendly and practical guide that shows you how to reduce the ever-mounting piles of papers, books, and other materials, so you can spend more time researching and less time hunting for information lost somewhere on your desk or computer.

As experienced genealogist Carmack can testify, few hobbies generate more paperwork than genealogy. In this guide, she successfully tackles the arduous process of organizing family research, from filing piles of paper to streamlining the process as a whole. She reveals how to create a flexible filing system that can expand with new data; how to take notes according to this filing system; how to set up an efficient work space, and how to store photos, CD-ROMs, archival correspondence, and more.

Additionally, genealogists will receive long-term guidance, learning how to create logs, charts, and plans in a special research notebook designed to track progress and keep information straight on research trips. Carmack even offers techniques for preserving precious family histories for future generations through wills and archives. Easy-to-copy charts, forms, and checklists take you through every step:

- Create filing systems that not only keep your research straight, but also grow with your needs.

- Get a handle on correspondence, so you can eliminate duplicate requests and locate your findings quickly and easily.

- Plan productive research trips using special journals that help you record essential information while you're on site.

- Define your research goals and establish projects around those goals.

- Develop a storage system for CD-ROMs, disks, books conference materials, microforms, and other miscellaneous research necessities.

- Prepare a "bag of essentials" for special trips to gravesites, interviews, repositories, and more.

- Protect delicate family artifacts, including documents, photos, diaries, and other materials.

- Organize and preserve your research for future generations by publishing your genealogy, making provisions in your will, or donating your work to an archive.

finding, copying, and moving files. Don't worry. It's really easy. First, let me show you a different way to think of your computer.

THE FILING CABINET

Because computers can run such a wide variety of software, it's easy to forget they are basically electronic filing cabinets. The Windows Operating System is structured in a way that most users see only a graphical interface, not the "filing cabinet" structure that underlies all of your family pictures, GEDCOM files, and Web browsers. Let's take a look at how computer files are structured and how you can use the structure to keep your genealogy work more organized.

Computers generally have three or more drives. They are

- hard drive
- floppy drive
- CD-ROM drive

If you have a device like a Zip drive or a SanDisk (it downloads photos from digital cameras), the system sees them as drives too. For now, the only drive we really care about is your hard drive, most commonly assigned the letter C. Think of your hard drive as a *filing cabinet*. Within every filing cabinet are file *folders*. The folders on your computer are called directories. Folders are used as organizational tools. The ones in your home filing cabinet may be called

- bills
- taxes
- medical
- car repair

The directories on your computer have names like

- My Documents
- GEDCOM
- Family Photos
- Johnson Surname

Within each folder are pieces of paper, or *documents*. The documents are the equivalent of your computer's files. A file is nothing more than a document of some kind, maybe a family story written on your word processor or a Family Tree Maker surname file. (See figures 3-1, 3-2 and 3-3 on page 49.)

There's an easy way to see the file structure in action. It's called Windows Explorer.

WINDOWS EXPLORER

Think of Windows Explorer as your own personal file manager. It knows the whereabouts of all of your files. To access Windows Explorer, click Start,

Figure 3-1
Your Computer.

Figure 3-2
Your Directories.

Figure 3-3
Your Files.

Programs, Windows Explorer. **If you want to use the shortcut, the Windows key plus E will open it, too.**

Note: To access Windows Explorer if you are running the Windows XP operating system, click Start, then point at All Programs, then Accessories. You'll find Windows Explorer tucked away in the Accessories category.

On the left side of the Explorer window you can see a list of every folder (directory) in your file cabinet (hard drive). As you can see, each directory can have as many subdirectories as you wish. For example, my Surnames directory currently has nine subdirectories. (See figure 3-4 below.)

Tip

Figure 3-4
Faulkenberry is a subdirectory in the directory Surnames.

On the right side of the window is a list of the subdirectories and files within the highlighted directory. In Figure 3-4, I highlighted Faulkenberry (a subdirectory in the directory Surnames). In the right window, you can see that there are two text files in that directory, Faulkenberry and Fortenberry, as well as a sub-subdirectory called Photos.

Does this seem confusing? If so, just think about the filing cabinet. It can have as many folders as you need. For instance, what if you have a folder titled The Kids. Within The Kids folder, you can have subfolders titled Johnny, Martha, Karen, and Tim. Within each of those folders are documents for each child: immunization records, school achievement awards, team awards, and report cards. If you want to get really organized, you could make sub-subfolders, such as The Kids/Johnny/Awards! Okay, now that you know the basic structure, let's see how you can use it to organize your genealogy files and online research.

FINDING FILES

A year or so ago, a fellow online genealogist named Mike Gregory sent me a text file containing information on several generations of my Gregory line. The file began with my tenth-great-grandfather, Robert Gregory, who was born about 1549, in Stockwith, Lincolnshire, England.

The file traced the family as it moved to Virginia and later to Kentucky. Mike kindly included a transcription of an important will and detailed research notes. And, if that wasn't treasure enough, all his records included sources. I immediately printed his notes, then promptly forgot where on my computer I had saved the original file. Doesn't seem like a problem, does it? It wasn't, until another Gregory researcher asked me for a copy of the file. Thankfully, finding it was a breeze. Here's one of the ways to do it.

Windows lets you locate a file based on the file's name (or part of the name), date and/or the text included in the file. To search, open Windows Explorer, then click on Tools, then Find/Files or Folders. In Windows XP, you can use the Search button on the toolbar. If you know the file name, just type it in the named box. In my case, I knew the file contained the name Gregory, but I couldn't remember if Gregory was the actual file name. I did remember that I had saved it as a Microsoft Word file. **When I searched, I used the asterisk as a wildcard.** That means I could type in an asterisk for whatever part of the file name I don't know.

Tip

I typed *gregory*.doc This let the computer know I was searching through my entire hard drive (c:) looking for any Microsoft Word file (has a .doc extension) that contained the word *gregory*. I used the asterisk in front of and behind *gregory* because it's possible I was looking for a file called mygregoryfamily.doc. See figure 3-5 on page 51 for the result.

The file I was searching for was named Descendants of Robert Gregory, and I had two copies of it: one in a directory called Family and another in a Windows/Temp directory.

Oh yes, I almost forgot to mention that Windows likes to make tasks as simple as possible by giving you more than one way to do things. In this case, you can access the Find/Files or Folder search box by clicking Start, then Find. In Windows XP, click Start, then Search.

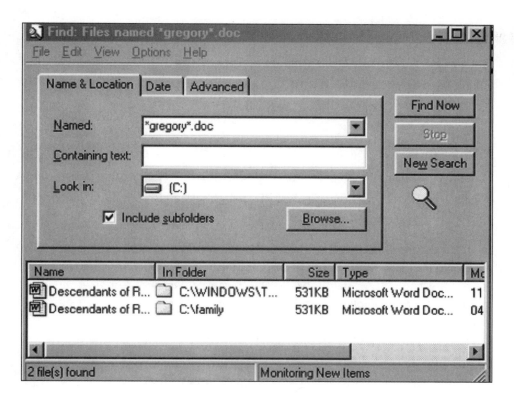

Figure 3-5
Windows will track down
missing files, even if you can't
remember the file's full
name.

MOVING FILES

Now that I found the Gregory file, don't you think it would be a good idea
to move it to my Surname/Gregory subdirectory? This is how to move the file:
With Windows Explorer open, in the left side of the window click on Family
(remember, that's where the Gregory file is located), and in the right side of
the window, right-click on the file Descendants of Robert Gregory. When I
right-click, a box pops up with several choices. Click on Cut.

Next, move the scroll bar in the left side of the window until you can see
the directory you want to move the file to. In this case, I scrolled down to
Surnames and highlighted the subdirectory Gregory (the subdirectory may not
be showing if the main folder hasn't been opened). I can then put my arrow
anywhere in the right side of the window and right-click again. From the menu
box, click Paste and the file will automatically be moved to the new location.

COPYING FILES

What if you have a file that contains information on more than one surname? For example, my Gregory file contains data on the Gregory and
Hatton families. If I file it under the Gregory directory, in a year from now
will I remember it has Hatton information? Unlikely!

Fortunately, copying files is as easy as moving them. In fact, you use the
exact same process, except when you right-click, this time select Copy. Then,
just scroll to the new directory and select Paste.

If your file contains information on five different surnames, you don't have
to Copy and Paste five times. Once the file is copied it is actually sitting on a

"clipboard." The clipboard is a type of non-permanent memory; in other words, if you turn off your computer, whatever's on the clipboard is not saved. Once you've pasted the file into the directory, just move to the second and right-click Paste, and the same with the third, fourth, and fifth. That file remains in the clipboard until you copy another file (or part of one).

DELETING FILES

Would you ever want to delete a file? Sure. Do you remember when I searched for the Gregory file and there were two copies of it? One was in the Family directory and another in a Windows/Temp directory. I don't need both, so I'll delete the copy in the Windows/Temp directory.

Warning

The computer is picky about the Windows directory. That's because it contains all files needed to run your computer and doesn't want you deleting something the system needs. **So if your unwanted file is in a Windows directory or subdirectory, be** *absolutely certain* **it's not a system file.**

In this case, I know that my computer doesn't need Descendants of Robert Gregory to run properly. So I'm going to delete it.

With Windows Explorer open, I scrolled down the left side of the window to the Windows directory. (Windows ME and XP tend to hide the folders in the Windows directory to protect them.) You will see many, many subdirectories. I clicked on Temp. In the right side of the window, I scrolled down until I saw the file Descendants of Robert Gregory.

Next, I right-clicked the file name and on the pop-up box, clicked Delete. Another pop-up box appeared, asking me if I'm sure that I want to send the file to the Recycle Bin. I clicked yes and the file was deleted.

UNDELETING A FILE

Did you know that when a file goes to the Recycle Bin, you can get it back? Here's how: Open Recycle Bin on your desktop, then highlight the name of the file you want to un-delete. In Windows, once the file name is highlighted, just click on Restore. All deleted files will remain in your Recycle Bin until you open Recycle Bin, click File, and click Empty Recycle Bin.

SAVING FILES

When Mike Gregory sent me the original file, I saved it to my system. Back then I wasn't as organized as I am now, which is why I couldn't find the file. But you can save files to any directory or subdirectory you wish. So, why not start out right and start saving genealogy files to the most appropriates directory?

Oftentimes, your computer is set to automatically save files to a directory called My Documents. This system works fine until you get so many files

MORE WINDOWS HELP

Need more help figuring out how to make Microsoft Windows work for you? Professional genealogist and well-known author Rhonda McClure guides you through the popular operating system with a genealogy focus in her ninety-minute instructional video *Windows for Genealogists* (Hurricane, Utah: The Studio). Order your copy online at <www.123genealogy.com>.

that management and organization is difficult. For example, my weekly anti-virus scan is currently checking more than 180,000 files on my computer. I have a pretty good memory, but not that good.

When doing your family research, it makes sense to save files in surname, locale, or general research directories. For instance, at the time I received the Gregory file, if I had placed it in my Gregory directory I wouldn't have had any problems finding it. (See figures 3-6 below, and 3-7 on page 54.)

Most Windows applications have the same basic toolbar running across the top of the screen. From the toolbar, you can choose to save a file in any directory you wish. When you're ready to save the file

- click File
- click Save
- name the document
- click on the pull-down menu on the Save In box and choose a directory where you want to save the file
- click Save

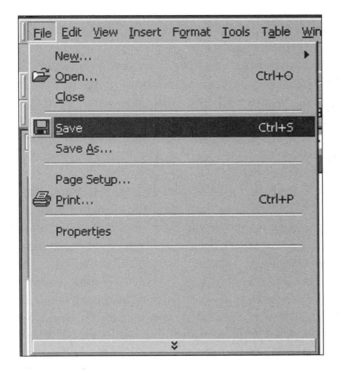

Figure 3-6
Save a file using the File pull-down menu.

Figure 3-7
Where do you want to save a file? Windows lets you pick a directory from a pull-down menu.

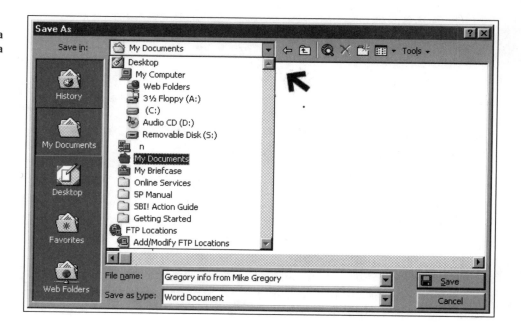

If in a year from now, you don't remember where you saved the file, just use the Find feature described above.

RENAMING FILES

Notes

An Internet cousin sent me a file containing the transcript of an 1850 census microfilm for Shelby County, Indiana. Listed among the residents were family members from one of my main research branches. The file, which had been sent as an e-mail attachment, was named 1850shelby.txt. Is that a file name I'll remember in the future? Probably not.

There are two ways I can rename this file. The first is by using the Save As menu command. Save As differs from the Save command, only in that it gives you the opportunity to save the file using a different name than the original. So when I receive a file, I can rename it using Save As. But when you do this, leave the file extension (.doc or .txt, for example) as is, because these are specific to the program that created the file. Renaming the file extension may render the file unopenable.

A second way to rename a file is by opening Windows Explorer, highlighting the name of the file, right-clicking and choosing the Rename option. When you click on Rename, the computer puts a small rectangle around the current file name. Just type whatever name you want in the rectangle and the file is automatically renamed.

The key to effectively naming files is choosing a name that makes sense to you. The length of the file name isn't as important as whether you can easily find the file a year after it was created. For example, it would be easier for me to find a file named "mikegregory.doc" than one named "jan03_1496.doc" or "mg.doc".

YOUR TURN: ORGANIZING YOUR OWN SYSTEM

Decide how you can best organize the computer directories to optimize your genealogy research. Here are some file structure ideas. Check to see if you need new directories for

- surnames
- locales
- cemeteries
- books
- research tasks
- Internet correspondence

Or maybe you want to structure your directories like this

- surnames
    - Web sites
    - researchers
    - cemetery listings
- locales
    - Missouri
    - Kentucky
    - Indiana
    - Kansas

Or even like this

- surnames
    - Faulkenberry
        - Web sites
        - correspondence
        - other researchers
        - Missouri
        - North Carolina
        - Virginia
    - Gregory
        - Virginia
        - Williamsburg photos
    - Hendrickson
        - Kentucky
        - Indiana
        - Kansas
        - Missouri

The only "right" way to structure your files is the one that works best for you. Take a little time to plan out your structure and don't worry if the structure changes over time. It's very easy to rename, move, or copy.

ORGANIZING ONLINE RECORDS

Now that your files are whipped into shape, it's time to organize your online records. These are all the bits and pieces of information you find on the

Internet and may include
- e-mail messages
- records
- e-mail addresses
- Web site URLs
- queries
- mailing list subscriptions

E-MAIL

There are a couple of different ways to organize e-mail messages. The first is by copying important e-mail messages (Control-C) and pasting (Control-V) them into a word processing program. To do this, you simply highlight the text in the message (by clicking and dragging your mouse over the text) and then pull down the Edit menu and select Copy. Open your word processing program (Microsoft Word or WordPerfect, for example), and select Paste from the Edit menu to place the text into a new document. Then save the file to the appropriate directory. For example, I received an e-mail from my Internet cousin, Gene Bird, who guided me to Lincoln County, Kansas, research on my Hendrickson line. He sent me one of his findings via e-mail.

I cut and pasted that information into a text file, and then saved it in my Hendrickson directory under the name hen_lincolnks.doc. I also cut and pasted the same information into my genealogy software program under my listing for William Hendrickson and Martin Hendrickson. What other way could I have organized my e-mail?

E-mail Folders and Filters

As you know, your e-mail program is organized by folders, with the usual ones being the Inbox, Trash, and Sent. You can create as many folders as you want, however. For detailed help on setting up folders, consult the Help file in your software.

Tip

I have created folders for my most researched surnames. Whenever I get e-mails pertaining to any of these surnames, I move them from my inbox to the appropriate folder. **Note: It's easy to move e-mails into different folders by using the "drag and drop" method.** Simply click on the message, and while you're holding down the left mouse button, drag the message into the new folder.

I also created a Missouri folder for the odd bits and pieces of information that don't really belong in a surname folder. This includes period descriptions of towns, a church history, and cemetery locations. Another folder is called Subscriptions. This folder is where I move any e-mail pertaining to subscriptions of all kinds. These include the welcome messages that are sent when you subscribe to a mailing list. I also move e-mails there that remind me that a commercial database subscription or newsletter subscription is coming due.

Whenever new mail arrives, I move it to the most appropriate folder. For example, when Gene Bird sends me an e-mail, it is almost always in relation to my Hendrickson line, so I move the e-mail to the Hendrickson folder. However, another way of automatically moving Gene's e-mails is by setting up an e-mail filter. An e-mail filter automatically performs an action on incoming messages, based on user-specified criteria. For example, I can create a filter that automatically files any message from Gene into my Hendrickson folder. I can create actions that filter by e-mail address and subject line. Here's how to set up message filters.

Netscape Navigator

To set up a filter, click Edit/Message Filters. Choose the parameters for the filter, e.g., subject line=Missouri, or sender=John Smith, then specify to which folder to move the e-mail.

IE

Click Tools/Message Rules/Mail. Checkmark the appropriate box (in this case, "where the from line contains people" and the "move it to the specified folder").

E-mail filters work differently in each e-mail program. However, most allow you to filter mail by sender's e-mail address, name and/or subject keyword. Outlook Express, for example, allows you to set several different filters by defining "message rules." A rule is set by first defining the condition (i.e., if the subject line contains a specific word), then the action (like moving the message to a specific folder). For information on setting filters in your e-mail software, refer to its Help file.

ONLINE SOURCES

When I first started doing genealogy research, I was terrible at keeping accurate records. In fact, I'm too embarrassed to confess how many times I've searched the same census microfilm, all because I didn't write down everything I should have the first time. Going back over the same census—or visiting the same Web site—multiple times because you didn't take good records is a waste of time. That time could be better spent searching new sources. Of course there will be times when you'll return to a Web site (see below), but at least you'll do it for a good reason, such as seeing if new records have been posted. Here are the types of online sources to record and file.

- Web site URLs where you found data
- Web sites you posted queries on
- Web sites that didn't have what you wanted, but you want to check back at a later date, just in case new information is added
- Web sites with free databases
- Web sites where you didn't find anything useful (to avoid revisiting sites that yielded negative results)

Idea Generator

YOUR GENEALOGY E-MAIL ADDRESS

Another way of organizing your research is to get a free E-mail account that you use only for genealogy correspondence, if you prefer to keep your personal/professional e-mail separate from your family history research e-mail. Set up your free e-mail account through *Family Tree Magazine* at <www.familytreemail.com>. All you have to do is choose your e-mail name, fill out a short form, and you've got mail! Your address will be username@familytreemail.com. You can access your account through the site once you log in with your user name and password. (If you want to write me, mine is genealogywriter@familytreemail.com.)

RESEARCH SOFTWARE

Once you begin using the online techniques from this book, the information about your family will begin to roll in. Do you know what software you'll use to store it? I use a free program called EditPad Lite <www.editpadpro.com/editpadlite.html>. Alternatives to EditPad are Window's Notepad or WordPad (both free), or even your own word processing software, like Microsoft Word or WordPerfect. You can set up files by surname or locale and add information to the file whenever you do online research. If you're comfortable using database software, like Microsoft Access, you can even set up a genealogy database to hold whatever information you've located. I like EditPad because it lets me have an unlimited number of files open at the same time, and it shows the file names in tabs across the top. See figure 3-8 on page 59 for what it looks like.

GENEALOGY SOFTWARE

The easiest way to keep all of your research records and notes is by using genealogy software. These programs, designed especially for family tree research, allow you to enter all of your family names, dates, photographs, scanned images and research notes into a single file. Once data is entered, the software can then produce a variety of reports like a pedigree chart, family group sheet or even pages for your Web site.

Some of the most popular genealogy software programs are:

Family Tree Maker <www.familytreemaker.com>

Legacy Family Tree <www.legacyfamilytree.com> (free)

The Master Genealogist <www.whollygenes.com>

Personal Ancestral File (PAF) <www.familysearch.org/eng/paf/> (free)

Family Origins <www.formalsoft.com>

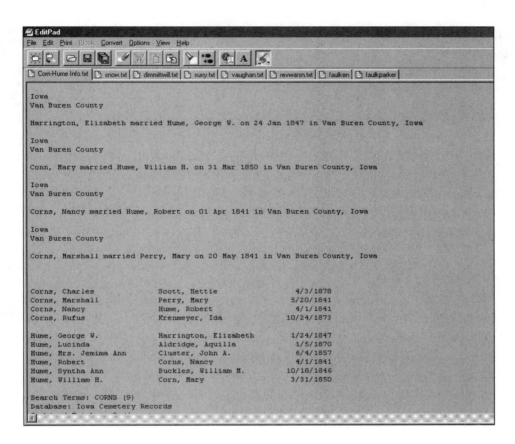

Figure 3-8
Using EditPad Lite, you can open an unlimited number of files at the same time.

As you can see, I use EditPad to save text file copies of wills, census information, Revolutionary War testimony—in other words, everything. Besides tracking online data, you can use EditPad or the software of your choice to keep track of the queries you posted. When leaving a query, just open your query file, note the URL site, add a brief note about the query you posted, and the date. It won't hurt to go back to that site at least once a year and recheck that your original query is still online. I like to post on a yearly basis, so I always have a current query that's easily found by other researchers, as some sites archive queries after a year.

Another use for research software is to keep a list of URLs where you *didn't* find information. Maybe the URL was a total bust, or maybe the Webmaster was in the process of posting information, but as of yet, you haven't found any that pertained to your family. I found an info-packed Web site for the Hume/Home family. Since Hume is one of my surnames, I wondered if it connected to me. At the time, I couldn't find a connection, but I kept a record of the Web site just in case I find new information that indicates I should go back to that site and check it again.

DOWNLOADING FILES

It's certain that one of these days you'll want to download a file or program from the Internet to your computer. Your first thought is probably "no I won't, because I don't want to get a virus." Don't worry. **If you configured**

Reminder

your anti-virus software as suggested in chapter two, it will automatically scan any downloaded files.

What would you download? When I searched the FamilySearch site <www.familysearch.org> for more information on Frances Easley, I found GEDCOM files that traced her family to 1588. Of course, I immediately downloaded the GEDCOMs for further research and examination. *GEnealogical Data Communication* (GEDCOM) is a standard format for exchanging genealogical data. It is used to easily share information between different genealogy software programs. For example, if you use Family Tree Maker, your software can create a GEDCOM file which can be read by someone using Legacy Family Tree or PAF.

To download a file, just click on the file name (in FamilySearch, click the Download link). Your browser will pop up a box asking you if you want to open the file, save it, or cancel the operation. (Browsers vary a bit in how they handle this, but the process is basically the same). Click Save. Another box will pop up, asking you in which directory to save the file. Use the pull-down menu to select your GEDCOM directory, then click Save. (See figure 3-9 below.)

Figure 3-9
You may want to save all of your downloaded GEDCOM files into a GED directory.

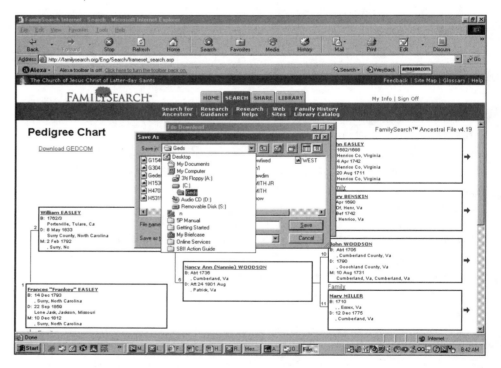

You can also right-click the file name, and in IE pick the menu choice Save Target As, then go ahead as above and pick the directory in which to download your file. Using Netscape Navigator, right-click and choose the menu item Save As.

COMPRESSED OR ZIPPED FILES

Sometimes files or programs are so large that they are compressed to make downloading faster. PC files are compressed into a .ZIP file, and MAC files into a .SIT format. You can tell if a file is compressed because the name of the file will end in either .ZIP or .SIT, e.g., hendrickson.zip.

To run or open a compressed file, you'll need to uncompress it using special software like WinZip <http://winzip.com>.

FOR AOL USERS ONLY

If you are downloading from AOL, select the Download Now or Download Later button at the bottom of the file description window. As a default, the download location is set to America OnlineDownload (also indicating the version of AOL you are using).

- **Select Download Now:** Double click the file name or the e-mail attachment, then click Download Now. The Download window will appear. Click OK and the download will begin. As the download continues, you'll see a progress bar that will tell you approximately how long it will take to download the file (this is also the case in Netscape and IE). Some files are so small, you will barely have time to see the progress bar. Once the download is complete, you can find the file in your default download directory.

- **Select Download Later:** Double click the file name or the e-mail attachment, then click Download Later. The file will be placed in a "queue," awaiting download. Choosing Download Later allows you to pick several files for downloading. For example, if you are on the FamilySearch site and find several GEDCOMs you want to download, you can queue them all before starting the download. When you're ready to begin downloading, click File from the menu bar, then Download Manager, then Start.

Did you know that while your files are downloading, you can use your computer for other tasks?

If your file is compressed, AOL can uncompress it automatically. Turn on this option by clicking Members from the top menu bar, then Preferences, then Download. Make sure "automatically decompress" is selected.

Chapter Three Checklist
- Explore Windows Explorer.
- Find a file.
- Move a file.
- Delete a file (be careful!).
- Copy a file.
- Rename a file.
- Decide if you need new genealogy directories. Then create them.
- Sign-up for a free genealogy e-mail account <www.familytreemail.com>.
- Create new e-mail folders, if needed.

WHAT'S NEXT?

The search begins.

PART TWO

The Search

D o you know how to eat an elephant?" asked a friend. "Not a clue," I responded. "It's easy," he said. "Just do it one bite at a time."

The Internet is a lot like that elephant—especially when it comes to climbing your family tree. With millions upon millions of Web sites, in no particular order, how in the world can you find a single ancestor? One bite at a time. Or in this case, four bites:

1. Lineage-linked databases
2. Networking
3. Search engines
4. Other databases

Chapter Four: Search Strategy #1:
Free Lineage-Linked Databases

Lineage-linked databases are files organized by descendancy. This means they usually show an individual and her line of descent. The largest free lineage-linked databases online are maintained by the Church of Jesus Christ of Latter-day Saints' Family Search <www.familysearch.org> and Ancestry/ RootsWeb WorldConnect <http://worldconnect.rootsweb.com>.

Both of these sites are fully searchable, and in total contain more than one billion names. In chapter four, you'll learn

- how to structure a search goal
- why you need to search using different criteria
- how to go back and forth between FamilySearch and World Connect
- how to interpret search results
- the thought process of a detective
- when to add search criteria, when to delete them
- the basics of interpreting clues

Chapter Five: Search Strategy #2:
Networking

Networking means connecting with other people who are already researching your family tree. If you think the odds of doing that are slim, think again. Remember that the number of your ancestors doubles with each generation, i.e., two parents, four grandparents, eight great-grandparents, sixteen-great-great-grandparents. And by the time you go back twelve generations you have more than four thousand ancestors. According to recent surveys, there are 544.2 million people online worldwide, with 181.2 million in the United States and Canada. If you crunch the numbers, the odds of finding an online cousin are actually very good. You'll see just how easy it is in chapter five. In addition, you'll discover how to

- find mailing lists
- join mailing lists
- post a query that will increase your chances of getting results
- locate surname sites
- find personal Web sites maintained by Internet cousins

- submit your name to one of the biggest surname lists on the Web
- increase your odds of connecting with other researchers

Chapter Six: Search Strategy #3:
Search Engines

You've probably run into genealogy-related search engines. These scour genealogy-only sites for your surname. You can be even more successful—particularly when you're looking for a specific piece of information—by using search engines such as Google <www.google.com> or AltaVista <www.altavista.com>. Most good search engines—by good, I mean the ones that return hits most relevant to your search—allow users to structure complex searches. That means you can create a search with a high probability of pinpointing exactly what you're looking for. After reading chapter six, you'll be structuring searches like a pro. Chapter six will teach you

- how to do "search engine math"
- how to structure complex search terms
- where to find the best search engines
- search techniques to locate oddball pieces of information
- why you need to use multiple search engines
- basics of locating Internet cousins using search engines

Chapter Seven: Online Search Strategy #4:
Databases and Transcripts

These are the searchable collections of a variety of data. They may contain GEDCOMs, births, burials, city directories, pioneers, or ship's passenger lists. Some of the databases are free, others, such as the ones at Ancestry.com and Genealogy.com, are available through a subscription.

Online transcripts are genealogically relevant pieces of information that have been copied (usually by volunteers) and uploaded to the Internet. The most common transcripts you'll find are federal census returns. Other transcripts you might find include wills, probate files, and headstone inscriptions. Chapter seven contains tips and techniques for searching online databases. Databases include these record types

- cemetery
- census
- immigration
- land
- marriage
- military

Chapter Eight: Peripheral Resources

I guarantee you'll be surprised at the wealth of information available from these "peripheral resources," even though many aren't even genealogy sites. Here's the chapter where you'll find out which president your great-grandpa may have voted for, how great-great-granny may have dressed, or what games were popular a century ago. Site topics included are

- books

- history
- maps
- photographs
- state resources

PUT THEM TOGETHER

In reality, most of your searches will entail using all four strategies: free lineage-linked databases, networking, search engines, and online databases and transcripts. For example, if you search a database site and find a reference to your great-grandmother's marriage, what would you do next? You'd obtain a copy of the record, but you also might try to find other people searching for her family. And you'd probably look for information about where she lived, where she might have come from, where her parents were married, and where she's buried.

As you go through this section, you'll find actual case studies of online research, first for each technique, then for all combined. By the time you finish, you'll be prepared to eat even the biggest elephant.

FOUR

Search Strategy #1: Free Lineage-Linked Databases

Step By Step

GET READY . . .

Let's start with the easy stuff.

For our first search, the goal will be simply to "find something" about a specific ancestor. To do that, we'll cast a wide net, which means searching the two free lineage-linked databases that contain more than one billion names. Why not start where we have plenty to search?

Begin by picking an ancestor or two that you'd like to research. However, be sure to choose someone that you know *something* about—a full name and birth date, for example, so you can identify the correct person online. Save your brick walls for later in the book. Because the sites we're going to search first are those with lineage-linked databases, our search will hopefully tell us something about the individual's children, spouse, or parents. If you're searching for someone with a common name, you may get hundreds of search results, so be sure to gather as much identifying information as possible about the individual first—either from your interviews, home sources, or prior research.

For example, what if you go online to locate your great-granddad Joseph Cooper and the search returns five hundred Joseph Coopers? Unless you know something more than his name, it will be impossible for you to determine which (if any) of these men are your ancestor. If you know the name of Joe's wife, parent(s), kids, or the date and place of his birth, it will help narrow the field.

GET SET . . .

Before going online, gather your tools just like you would for a library trip. Have your pedigree chart and any family group sheets that include your target individual. If you want to keep all your notes in electronic format, fire up your copy of EditPad Lite (see chapter three), your favorite word processing program, or your genealogy software program. Next, open a new file and name it whatever surname you're looking for (or open the appropriate file in your genealogy software). Then, as you search, make notes in that file of the date of the search, the Web site or sites you searched, and your results. If you don't find anything with this particular search, note that too.

If you get in the habit of keeping research notes as you move from Web site to Web site, it will help you become a more efficient researcher. It's hard to remember all the sites you visit and your findings; keeping consistent (and current) notes will make it easy to plan future online research.

A note of caution: Just because you find something online doesn't mean it's accurate. Think of your online finds as the clues that lead to original records.

GO!

For this search, our "wide net" will include the two free Internet sites that contain the largest collection of online GEDCOM files: FamilySearch.org and Ancestry/RootsWeb.com.

FamilySearch.org <www.familysearch.org> is the site maintained by the Church of Jesus Christ of Latter-day Saints. **It is the largest single site of free genealogy data on the Internet**—its searchable databases contain more than 900 million names. For now, we'll search its three primary databases: Ancestral File (AF), Pedigree Resource File (PRF), and the International Genealogical Index (IGI). Ancestral File has millions of names and some vital information, organized into pedigrees and family groups. Pedigree Resource File is an index to FamilySearch's PRF CDs. PRF has replaced Ancestral File as the database people submit to. The information at FamilySearch is limited to the individual in question, and there's no way to view a family or pedigree chart. Instead, the researcher is directed to a given CD. The IGI has names of deceased persons worldwide and some vital information.

Internet Source

When you first log onto the FamilySearch site, click the Search tab. To begin your search, the system requires that you fill in at least a surname. Other search options are first name, name of spouse, name of parents, events (birth, marriage, death), a date range, and locale. If you want to specify a U.S. state, you must first select United States in the pull-down country menu.

Although you can specify "use exact spelling," this option is not recommended because a surname can have several different spelling variations. If you force the system to use exact spelling, there's a good chance you'll miss the very record you were looking for.

When the search is completed, results will be displayed by database groups, e.g., the number of hits in IGI-North America or the Pedigree Resource File. Click on results from each of the hits to see more detailed records.

If you find too many names, narrow your search by adding another piece of information, such as a parent or spouse's name. Each time you specify additional search criteria, it will reduce the number of records found. With a surname of Smith, this filtering method is almost compulsory. If your search returns too few names, use only minimal input, such as surname or the surname plus the country. (See figure 4-1 below.)

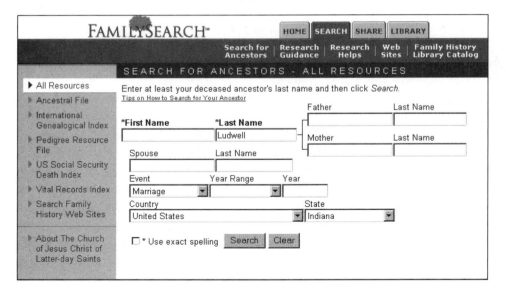

VARIATIONS ON A THEME

As Grandma used to say, "there's more than one way to skin a cat." Same with searches. **Keep in mind that the pedigree files on this site were submitted by thousands of individuals.** It's possible (and likely) that the same individuals will show up in several different files, with slightly different information. For example, one file may list a daughter as "Jenny," another may show her as "Jiny." This means you may need to conduct this search more than once, using different approaches. How can you do this? Try entering the individual's name and the father's name but not the mother's; or enter the mother's but not the father's. Try a spouse's surname and a father's surname or use a surname and country only. Remember, being a genealogist is like being a detective. If one line of questioning doesn't work, switch to another.

Even if you find information with your initial search criteria, search again using different criteria. Here's why: If you know an ancestor had the sur-name of Ludwell and was married in Indiana, you may use Ludwell and Indiana as your search criteria—and you may find that marriage record. What you may *not* find is Ludwell's birth in Tennessee. If you search for Ludwell and Tennessee, you may not find Ludwell's grandmother's birth in Virginia. Play around with adding and subtracting search filters.

Are you ready to walk through a couple of real searches? If you're online, do these along with me.

CASE STUDY: THE HUME SEARCH ON FAMILYSEARCH.ORG

One of my weakest lines is through my maternal grandmother. This is what I know: Her great-grandfather's name was Robert Hume. Robert Hume

Reminder

Case Study

married someone named Nancy Corn or Corns. One of Robert and Nancy's children, Sarah, married James Knox.

I entered Robert Hume in the search box, with spouse surname of Corn. I did not specify exact spelling because I didn't know if her name was Corn or Corns, and I didn't know if Hume was really Humes or maybe even Home (a variant spelling of Hume). The search returned twenty-five hits from the Social Security Death Index (SSDI) and one from the IGI. Since Social Security didn't exist when Robert Hume lived, I knew none of the twenty-five returns could be him. The one IGI result was a marriage record for Robert Hume and Nancy Corns, married on 1 April 1841 in Van Buren County, Iowa. Was this my ancestor? I have no idea. My grandmother's family lived in northern Missouri—close enough to Iowa—but I don't have any further evidence that this Robert Hume and Nancy Corns are mine.

By the way, if you're following along online, did you notice the blank box next to Robert Hume's name, and above it the notation "select record to download"? If you check the box and click the notation, a GEDCOM file will download into your computer. It will contain the information you see on the page, including the Batch Number (see pages 79-81).

Next, I searched for Robert Hume without a spouse in Iowa, Robert Hume in Missouri, and just plain Robert Hume. The Iowa and Missouri results didn't tell me more than I already knew. The "plain" Robert Hume search turned up 155 results, too many to be of help because I didn't know enough about Robert to know if any of them were mine.

I then tried a Nancy Corn search and got 143 results—again, too many to help because I didn't know anything more about her than her name. Next, I typed in Nancy Corn and Iowa. This search yielded only a couple of results, but one of them was the Corn Family Genealogy Web site. I clicked on it and found a post that mentioned the Hume/Corn marriage I found earlier along with a listing of several family members, none of whose names I recognized. What did jump out, however, was the statement that two of Nancy and Robert's children were "living in Putnam County, MO in 1860." Putnam County, Missouri, is where my grandmother's family lived. I still didn't know if these were my ancestors, but I now had more clues to follow.

I went back to the FamilySearch site and clicked the button to download the GEDCOM file—a choice you'll probably want to make too. Just remember, none of this data has been checked for accuracy, so proceed with caution. That means don't make assumptions. At this point I had pretty much exhausted the FamilySearch resources. Next, I'll run this search through Ancestry/RootsWeb.

Ancestry/RootsWeb
<http://worldconnect.rootsweb.com>

The Ancestry/RootsWeb WorldConnect project is one that allows users to upload their family trees to the Internet. Files are submitted to WorldConnect by means of GEDCOM files. Currently, this searchable database contains more than 215 million names.

Definitions

SOUNDEX

The Soundex is an indexing system based on the way names sound, rather than how they are spelled. For more information on the Soundex and how to code names, go to <www.archives.gov/research_room/genealogy/census/soundex.html>.

Important

When you first go to the WorldConnect page, click Search All Databases. This will take you to a global search form. It can be used for simple and advanced searches (the differences will be discussed later in this chapter).

Search Strategies

Search criteria includes surname, first name, names of parents and spouse, birth and death places, and birth and death years. You can also click a box called Fuzzy Search (this will search using Soundex), which will look for names spelled in various ways. You must enter information in at least one of the search fields. Use the same strategies as on FamilySearch: If you get too many results, fill in more fields; if too few results, fill in fewer fields. Also, try variant spellings.

Since these GEDCOMs were submitted by many different individuals, it's possible you'll find names spelled with several variations. I have seen my own surname spelled Hendrickson, Hendrixson, Hendrixsen, Hendricksen, and Hindrixson. So when you search, be as creative with your spelling as your ancestors were.

WorldConnect's global search form can be used for both basic searches and advanced searches. **You must enter search criteria in at least one field**; you decide how many fields you wish to specify. You can search using a trailing wildcard, which is a minimum of three letters followed by an asterisk that traditionally replaces up to five characters. For example, John* will return Johnson, Johnsen, Johnston, etc.

Entering just a surname will return the broadest possible search results. If you want to narrow the hits, you can enter a first name, a first initial, or a first and middle name. If you enter a first and middle name, the system will look for those two names in any order. For instance, if you enter Vicki Noreen the system will return Vicki Noreen and Noreen Vicki. Although you can narrow a search by adding a place name to an individual name search, you can also search for GEDCOMs that contain a specific place name. Why would you do this? When you are searching for ancestors from a small town or village, searching for just the place name will return files of other people who lived there, too. You might turn up an in-law, blood relative, or allied family.

When you add a location to your search criteria, use the same variant spellings as you did with a surname. Since the files were submitted by many people, and none of them are checked for spelling or typographical errors, you may find misspellings. If you're searching for a place in Massachusetts, you may have to enter Masachusetts and other spelling variations.

Search Results

After your search is completed, a page is displayed with the results. At the top of the box you'll see the number of matches found. Each page displays a maximum of twenty-five matches. Follow the links at the bottom of the page if there are more than twenty-five matches.

The left column lists the matches according to your search criteria. If you were searching for a surname, it will be displayed in this column. If the date and place of birth are available in the file, they will be shown, as will the date and place of death. On the right column is the name of the database; this is the file name of a specific family tree. Click on that link to go to the index page of that particular database. On each page, you'll find a link to the e-mail address of the submitter. It's also possible to find links to the submitter's own Web page. (See figure 4-2 below.)

	Results 1-1 of 1					
	Birth/Christening			Death/Burial		
Name	Date	Place		Date	Place	Database
HUME, Robert Marion	18 Apr 1815	New Lexington, Perry Co, OH		Abt 1883	Cowley Co, KS	1905457
🔍 📷 🔴 Father: John HUME Mother: Sarah McCLELLAND Spouses: Nancy CORNS, Josephine A. GHEEN						

Figure 4-2
WorldConnect search results display basic information about the individual—enough for you to decide if this is a potential ancestor. *Copyright © 2002 and under license from MyFamily.com, Inc., all rights reserved*

In the left column, under the name of your match, you may find icons of a magnifying glass, a blue silhouette, and a red pedigree chart. Click on the magnifying glass to conduct the same search at Ancestry.com (more on this commercial site in chapter five). The blue silhouette indicates that the family tree includes descendants of the person in the "name" column. The pedigree chart indicates there are ancestors of the person in the "name" column. Other icons include an open book (listing sources) and a note page (indicating the individual has notes).

ANCESTOR AND DESCENDANT REPORTS

Once you've located an ancestor and clicked on his or her name, you'll notice a menu running across the top of the page. It looks something like this:

> Index | Descendancy | Register | Pedigree | Ahnentafel | Download GED COM | Add Post-em

Clicking on Descendancy, *Register*, Pedigree, or Ahnentafel will generate ancestor and descendant reports.

The Descendancy report displays an outline of the individual's descendants, up to a maximum of ten generations. The *Register* report displays up to six generations.

A *Register* report lists the information about a specific person, in narrative format, then works forward through the person's descendants for a given number of generations. Each person is given an identifying number. It is named for and based on the numbering system used in the *New England Historical and Genealogical Register*. (See figure 4-3 on page 72.) Click on Pedigree to produce either a traditional chart or a text-only format. Lastly, the Ahnentafel (German for "ancestor table") option will show up to six generations of the "selected" individuals' ancestors. (See figure 4-4 on page 72.)

Figure 4-3
Click on the menu at the top of the page to display different report formats like *Register* or pedigree. *Copyright © 2002 and under license from MyFamily.com, Inc., all rights reserved.*

1. **Robert Marion HUME** was born 18 Apr 1815 in New Lexington, Perry Co, OH, and died Abt 1883 in Cowley Co, KS. He was buried in Widener Cemetery, Rock, Cowley Co, KS. He was the son of **2. John HUME** and **3. Sarah MCCLELLAND**. He married Nancy CORNS 1 Apr 1841 in Van Buren Co, IA. She was born 9 May 1824 in PA, and died Abt 1861 in Putnam Co, MO. He married **Josephine A. GHEEN** 29 Aug 1865 in Perry Co, OH. She was born Abt 1844 in OH. She was buried in Widener Cemetery, Rock, Cowley Co, KS.

Children of Robert Marion HUME and Nancy CORNS are:

i. Sarah HUME was born 31 Jul 1842 in Van Buren Co, IA, and died 7 Mar 1905. She married James KNOX 14 Oct 1858 in Putnam Co, MO, son of John Milton KNOX. He was born 14 Oct 1839 in IL, and died 29 May 1920.
ii. Maria HUME was born 1844 in Van Buren Co, IA. She married John Milton KNOX 30 Mar 1864 in Putnam Co, MO, son of John Milton KNOX.
iii. Charles Elmer HUME was born 1846 in Van Buren Co, IA.
iv. William Henry HUME was born 13 Mar 1849 in Van Buren Co, IA, and died 3 Jun 1924 in Powersville, Putnam Co, MO. He married Georgian Ann KIRK 11 Feb 1872 in Putnam Co, MO. She was born 29 Feb 1853 in MO, and died 1933 in Powersville, Putnam Co, MO.
v. Margaret HUME was born Abt 1850 in Van Buren Co, IA. She married Henry CORNS 23 Feb 1868 in Putnam Co, MO. He was born Abt 1845 in IA.
vi. Caroline HUME was born Abt 1853 in Putnam Co, MO. She married James Henry WILSON 24 Jan 1875 in Putnam Co, MO.
vii. Augustus Wallace HUME was born Apr 1859 in Putnam Co, MO. He married Charity HAGER 21 Dec 1882 in Cowley Co, KS. She was born Sep 1865.
viii. Robert Alvin HUME was born Abt 1860 in Putnam Co, MO.

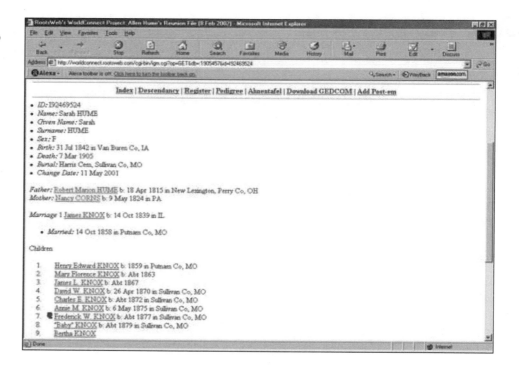

Figure 4-4
Sample Ahnentafel report. *Copyright © 2002 and under license from MyFamily.com, Inc., all rights reserved.*

DOWNLOADING WORLDCONNECT GEDCOM's

You may download GEDCOMs if the submitter of the material chose that option when she uploaded the file. You can tell if you have the option by the Download GEDCOM link on the page. The file will begin with the person shown on the page you're viewing. The maximum number of generations you can download may be determined by the submitter, but it is usually ten generations.

ADDING A POST-EM

The WorldConnect project has a spiffy option to add a Post-Em note, the equivalent to a yellow sticky note. You can add a Post-Em to let other researchers know you are searching this family too (always be on the lookout for a networking opportunity); or you can post a note if you have conflicting data about a specific person or event. You can use the interactive form to add a new Post-Em or edit an existing one. You'll find the Post-Em option on the top menu of the individual record page. (See figure 4-5 below.)

Your Name	Nancy Hendrickson	(required)
Your Email		(required)
If you'd like to link to a page with additional information, enter the page reference before (optional)		
URL		
URL Title		
Note (required)	I am researching the Hume family and would like to connect with other family researchers. My link is through Robert Hume and Nancy Corns.	
Password		(Required)
Preview Post		

Figure 4-5
Notify other researchers of your interest in an individual by adding a Post-Em note. *Copyright © 2002 and under license from MyFamily.com, Inc., all rights reserved.*

Let's get back online and see where we can take the Robert Hume search on WorldConnect.

CASE STUDY:
THE HUME SEARCH ON WORLDCONNECT

From the WorldConnect home page, I clicked Search All Databases and entered Robert Hume, with the option to search using Soundex. Results: 3,115! I changed the Soundex to search using the "exact spelling" option and the number of hits dropped to 290, because only those files with the exact spelling of Hume were included. Although I could start going through the 290 hits at this point, I decided to search for Robert Hume with a spouse of Corns. There were only two hits, but they were dandies.

Case Study

Both files were submitted by the same researcher. The most current file had been recently updated and included source citations (which are helpful if they refer you to the original records, but too often they refer to other GEDCOMs instead). When I clicked on Robert Hume's name (in order to display his individual record/family group sheet), it showed a list of his children. The link from his oldest daughter, Sarah, showed her marriage to James Knox (my second great-grandfather), and their children, including Bertha who was my great-grandmother.

Because the file's submitter included his sources, it will be far easier for me to verify the facts by checking those sources citing the original documents. Without the sources, though, the information would have yielded many valuable clues that would have formed the basis for a research plan.

TACKLING A MORE COMPLEX SEARCH

Another branch of my family settled in a small town in Missouri named Lone Jack. I purchased a booklet called *The Story of Lone Jack*, and it said that in the spring of 1837, "Warham Easley, Galen Cave and John Snow, all three of whom were brothers-in-law" had come indirectly from North Carolina. The book also noted that Galen Cave and John Snow died from cholera within a few hours of each other in 1851.

I knew John Snow was married to a woman named Frances (Frankey) Easley. I didn't know anything about her family or the Caves. Since these three families were all related by marriage, I decided to attack the group of them as one.

The Lone Jack booklet stated that Galen Cave, John Snow and Warham Easley were brothers-in-law, however I had no idea how they were related— did John marry Galen's sister, did Galen marry John's sister, did John marry Warham's sister, was Galen John's wife's brother? I didn't have a clue, so I started untangling the relationships by searching for Galen Cave. I went to <www.familysearch.org>, clicked on Search, then entered the name Galen Cave in the search box. This search returned one Galen in the Ancestral File and three in the IGI. With so few results, I could easily check all of them. If I had gotten more than a couple dozen results, I would've gone back to the search screen and added a filter such as Missouri or North Carolina. The three IGI results were vital records from North Carolina; the Ancestral File showed a birth record from Orange County, Virginia. Two of the IGI records didn't give enough information for me to know if this was the Galen Cave I was looking for. The third was a marriage record of Galen Cave and Susannah Frances Easley from 6 January 1828 in Surry County, North Carolina. Date-wise and spouse-wise, this could be my man.

The real gold came when I clicked on the Ancestral File record, however. It, too, showed Cave's marriage to Easley, but more important, it showed that this Galen Cave died in 1851 in Lone Jack, Missouri. Fortunately, there was even more.

Warning

Ancestral File records show how families are linked (although they don't list sources). You can choose various displays of records, including information on the individual, a family group sheet, or a pedigree chart. On the Ancestral File page for Galen Cave, there were links to both a pedigree chart (the link is Pedigree) and a family group sheet (the link is Family). There was also a link to Susannah Easley's name, and a link on her individual record to Family. (See figure 4-6 on page 75.)

Here's what all this means. If I click on Cave's Family link it will show me a family group sheet of his and Susannah's family. If I click on Pedigree it will show his pedigree chart (which may contain only a few names or many generations). In this case, the pedigree chart didn't include any of his ancestors. When I clicked on Susannah Easley's name, it showed both of her parents (William Easley and Sarah Smith), and when I clicked on the pedigree chart, I ended up with Easley records back to 1588, including previously unknown surnames of Woodson, Benskin, Miller, Ferris, Winston, and Porter.

Boy, was it tempting to dive in, but I still didn't know exactly how Cave, Snow, and Easley were related. A word of caution: Always be leery of pedi-

Figure 4-6
Click on the Family link to see a family group sheet displayed. *Reprinted by permission. Copyright © 1999, 2001 by Intellectual Reserve, Inc.*

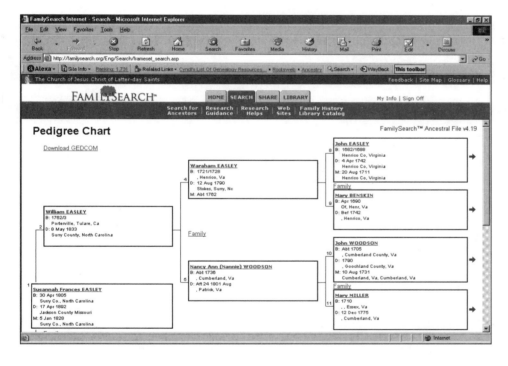

Figure 4-7
Sometimes you can strike it rich by finding a file with generations of ancestors. Remember, each generation needs to be verified in original sources. *Reprinted by permission. Copyright © 1999, 2001 by Intellectual Reserve, Inc.*

grees like this one that take you back to the Middle Ages. They are often inaccurate. (See figure 4-7 above.)

Think It Out

This is the point where many searches go astray. When you luck into finding generations of unknown family in one click, it's tempting to jump back generation after generation, downloading GEDCOMs like mad. **Remember**

Reminder

to verify the connections in original documents; you don't want to end up with the wrong ancestors. Let's save that search for later and focus on our original search goal.

Is it possible that Galen Cave was related to John Snow and Warham Easley through his marriage to Susannah? Let's think it out. The only way for people to be brothers-in-law is by marrying sisters, or through their own sister's marriage. So, Cave and Snow could be married to Easley sisters, or Easley could be married to a Snow or Cave sister, or some combination of the two. The best place to start, then, is to find a list of Susannah's siblings. Her siblings would not be on her pedigree chart, would they? No, because pedigree charts do not include siblings—only information on an individual's lineage. To see Susannah's siblings, we'd need to see the family group sheet for her parents.

SNOW/CAVE/EASLEY: PART II

With Susannah's individual record displayed on the screen, I clicked on her father, William Easley. Now, with his individual record displayed, I clicked on Family so the view would change to that of a family group sheet. What facts stood out?

- William's father's name was Waraham
- William's son's name was Warahm [*sic*] (Was this one of the brothers-in-law?)
- William had a daughter named Frances (Was this Frankey?)

As I scrolled down through the other children, another name popped out: One of Susannah and Frances' brothers was Stephen Isaac Easley. Why did that catch my eye? Because Frankey Easley and John Snow's son (my second-great-grandfather) was named Stephen Isaac. Great clues, but can I prove this Frances is my Frankey? Not from the information I have so far.

SNOW/CAVE/EASLEY: PART III

I decided to try a different tactic by searching for Warham Easley, the second of the brothers-in-law. I went back to the original search screen and entered Warham Easley. The search returned seventy-one matches. That was definitely too many for me to wade through. Next, I entered his name and specified North Carolina as a locale. I thought since Galen Cave had been married in North Carolina, and the three men had come "indirectly from North Carolina," perhaps there would be some Easley record there, too. This second search returned four hits in the Ancestral File:

Warham EASLEY
Gender: M Birth/Christening: 10 Aug 1821, NC
Warham EASLEY
Gender: M Birth/Christening: abt. 1744 Stokes County, NC
Warham EASLEY

Gender: M Birth/Christening: 1759, Stokes, NC
Warham W. EASLEY
Gender: M Marriage: abt. 1824, North Carolina

The first person was possibly too young, the second and third people seemed too old. The 1824 marriage in North Carolina, however, made the fourth person on the list a strong possibility. When I clicked on the fourth name, it went to Warham's individual record, showing his 1796 birth in Surry County, North Carolina, his 1824 marriage, and his 1874 death in Lone Jack, Missouri. Warham's parents were William Easley and Sarah Smith. When I clicked on William and Sarah's Family link (from Warham's individual record page), it showed one of their children was Frances "Frankey" Easley. When I clicked on Frankey's name, it showed her marriage to John Snow. Finally, a connection!

If I had clicked on William's name from Warham's individual record page, however, (which would take me to William's individual record page) and *then* clicked Family, it would show only the reference to Frances, not Frances "Frankey." (See figure 4-8 below.)

Why would one group of records show Frances only, and another show Frances "Frankey" married to John Snow? **The files were submitted by different people.** If you don't find what you are looking for in one family group sheet, try looking on another.

Important

TAKE A BREATHER

What have we learned so far? I know Susannah Easley married Galen Cave and that Frankey Easley married John Snow. Warham Easley was the

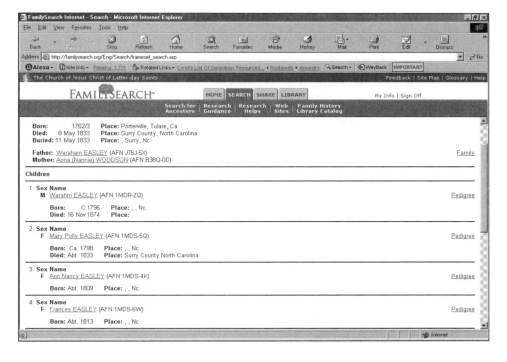

Figure 4-8
Family Group Record for William Easley. *Reprinted by permission. Copyright © 1999, 2001 by Intellectual Reserve, Inc.*

brother of both Susannah and Frankey. Sometimes a picture really is worth *more* than a thousand words. (See figure 4-9 below.)

Figure 4-9
I often draw a rough chart while researching online, just to keep relationships straight in my own mind.

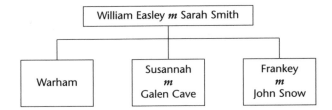

SNOW/CAVE/EASLEY: PART IV

Finally, I plugged the name John Snow, with the spouse surname of Easley, into the search box. Although I already had the connection of the three men, I wanted to see what else I could find. The most amazing discovery was a pedigree chart showing generation after generation of John's grandmother, Elizabeth Ballard. This was another file that went back to the 1500s—one that definitely will need verification in original records. As a nice wrap-up, after poking through generations of pedigree charts and family group sheets, I discovered that John's Aunt Jenny married a man named Bartlett Cave. They had a son, Galen. If this is the same Galen Cave who was Susannah's brother, then John Snow and Galen were not only brothers-in-law, they were cousins! However, to prove these relationships I'll need to track down original records offline.

Tip

Note: If you found family in the Ancestral File or Pedigree Resource File, you can contact the person who submitted the information. Follow the Submitter links for contact details. AF gives the year of submission in the contact's "submission number." This gives you a better idea of whether the person might still be at that address.

ADVANCED FAMILYSEARCH TIPS

Before moving to the next chapter, let's go over a few neat tricks for getting even more from the three FamilySearch databases: Ancestral File, IGI, and Pedigree Resource File. You'll get the most from these tips by getting online and following along with me.

Ancestral File

Ancestral File lists names and vital statistics of millions of individuals throughout the world. These records have been contributed by thousands of people and are organized into family group sheets and pedigree charts. To aid you in collaborating with other researchers, each entry includes the name and address of the person who contributed to the file.

You've already seen how to do a basic search, but did you know you can search for ancestors who are not in your lineage, such as your great-grandfather's siblings? From the Ancestral File search form, type in the father's full name and at least the mother's first name. The search will return a list of their children. Click on each name to go to each child's individual record, which can contain vital statistics and marriage data. There are also links from each individual's page to a downloadable pedigree chart or family group sheet.

International Genealogical Index (IGI)

The IGI contains 285 million names of deceased persons worldwide, as well as information on births, marriages, and christenings. It includes people who lived after the early 1500s to the early 1900s. The names come from three sources: Half have been extracted by volunteers from original records like civil and church sources, including some death and burial records; other records were submitted by members of the Latter-day Saints church and include information from Family Group Records, Marriage, and Individual entry forms; still other records are names of deceased members of the Church of Jesus Christ of Latter-day Saints. To search the IGI, click on the Search tab, then select IGI on the left column.

My IGI search was prompted by a family member's comment that her grandfather, James, had been married prior to his marriage to her grandmother. When I searched the IGI, I entered James's first name and surname, as well as the region (you must enter a region such as North America for an IGI search). My initial search returned more than 200 hits—too many for me to narrow down. I next added a filter, asking for information on James from the state of Missouri.

Of the thirteen results, one was for a James Hendrickson's marriage in Cass County, Missouri. Because I'd once found James on a Cass County census, I suspected this marriage could be the one I was searching for. My suspicions grew when I saw his wife's name was Susan L. Strange. I already knew of several marriages between the Hendrickson and Strange families. An e-mail to a Hendrickson-Bird-Strange cousin helped me pin down Susan's ancestry, and there was a high probability that this was the marriage my family member had heard about. Using a little-known technique, however, I confirmed my suspicions even further. Here's how: At the bottom of the Web page showing James Hendrickson's marriage to Susan Strange is a batch number. Using my cursor, I highlighted the number, right clicked the mouse and clicked on Copy. (See figure 4-10 on page 80.) Next, I returned to the search form, clicked my cursor in the Batch Number box, right-clicked again, and selected Paste. I typed Hendrickson in the surname box and chose North America as the region. When I clicked on the search button, the system returned three results. The results were all Hendrickson marriage records from Cass County, Missouri **(Click on Source Call Number to see the exact source of this data).**

One of the results was for a marriage that took place the day following James and Susan's ceremony, and was between Anna Hendrickson and William Groves. This entry caught my attention because on the 1870 census, James was living in the same household as William Groves [Graves], and next door to Susan Strange! The pieces began to come together. Of course,

Reminder

Figure 4-10
You can sometimes find "hidden" information by doing a batch number search in the IGI.

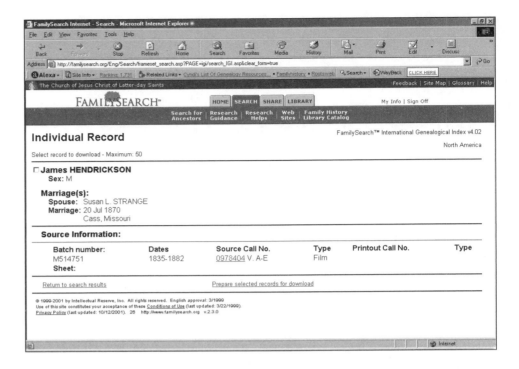

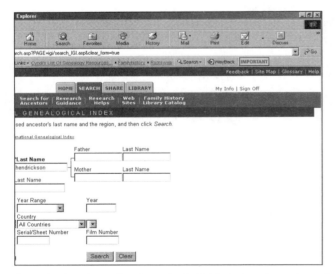

Enter the batch number from the individual record search to discover other records.

these clues do not prove the connection, but they sure point me to where to delve into vital records.

If you've found an ancestor in the IGI, be sure to do a batch number search. You never know what you'll find.

Note: Records can be batched together for various reasons. In this case, they were together because they were found together in the marriage records of Cass County, 1818–1836. At other times, individuals are batched together because the person submitting the information submitted them at the same time. It's possible they may not be related.

Pedigree Resource File

The Pedigree Resource File contains name, birth, marriage, and death information for millions of people. Names are added to the file at a rate of more than one million each month. Use the Pedigree Resource File to find lineage-linked records and obtain reference numbers telling you where to find the complete record on FamilySearch compact discs at most Family History Centers. The Pedigree Resource File records are submitted by users and are sent via the Web site or are gathered from family histories and other sources. Records appear in the file as originally submitted.

I used the Pedigree Resource File to try and find more about an ancestor named Polly Moore. I knew she married Aaron Hendrickson, but had no further information about the Moore family. Using the search form, I entered her first and last names, and the surname Hendrickson in the space for spouse. Two records were returned, both for my Polly. Her individual page gave me the number of the compact disc at the Family History Center (FHC) her records are on, as well as her personal identification number (PIN). The page also contained links to more information on her husband and her parents.

Because I wanted to know more about my female lines, I followed links to Polly's mother, Mary Barnett, and grandmother, Rebecca Holcomb. Along the way, I discovered that Polly's grandfather, John Barnett, was an officer in the Continental Army (Revolutionary War) and that Mary was mentioned in the will of her half-brother, John.

As I followed the family lines back through the generations (just keep clicking on the links related to parents), I ended up in 1600 Scotland. The contact information (name and address) of the person who submitted this information was located near the bottom of the Web page. Again, I found more information than I dreamed existed. However, I used another little-known search technique to find even more. It's called the Submission Search.

SUBMISSION SEARCH

Once you have located an ancestor using the Pedigree Resource File, click on her name to display the individual record page. Near the bottom of the page you will find a section called Submission Search, with a long number written to the right. If you click on the number, you'll be returned to the search form, and the number will automatically be entered into the submission number blank. Next, type in your ancestor's surname and click the search button. You will get a list of all of the people with your surname whose records were submitted by the same individual.

In the case of Polly Moore, the Submission Search returned a list of twelve Moores who were sent in by the same Indiana researcher who submitted Polly's data. More than half the names were unfamiliar to me, but again opened up new avenues of research.

TAKE ANOTHER BREATHER!

Once you've searched FamilySearch and WorldConnect, chances are good that you'll have discovered a GEDCOM containing several generations of

Important

(what you think is) your family. Isn't it tempting to download file after file, reveling in the years of research you won't have to do? But wait a second. **If the information you found has source citations, you need to check the accuracy in original documents** (see Final Thoughts, page 208). And, remember that you build a family file by working from the known to the unknown. That means working from yourself backwards—not trying to make the downloaded GEDCOM fit where you want it to. If you've checked the sources and the information you found is accurate, then what? You assess and analyze the results.

ASSESSING THE FACTS

In the case of the Robert Hume search, here's a list of the unproven facts, according to FamilySearch and WorldConnect:

Robert Hume

- Robert Hume's middle name was Marion
- Birth date: April 18, 1815
- Birthplace: New Lexington, Perry County, Ohio
- Death date: about 1883
- Death place: Cowley County, Kansas
- Buried at Widener Cemetery, Rock, Cowley County, Kansas
- Married April 1, 1841, Van Buren County, Iowa
- First spouse named Nancy Corns, who died after 1860? (birth of last child) and before 1865 (Robert's second marriage)
- Names of children
- Father named John Hume
- Father's birth: 1786, Fauquier County, Virginia
- Mother named Sarah McClelland
- Mother's birth: 1792, Mason County, Kentucky
- Mother's two oldest siblings born in Pennsylvania
- Mother's parents were Robert McClelland and Margaret Howe
- Robert Hume's second marriage to Josephen Gheen
- Second marriage date August 29, 1865, Perry County, Ohio
- Several generations of Hume ancestors going back to Scotland

ANALYZING THE CLUES

When you reach this point in a search, it's time to jot down any thoughts you have, any odd facts that stand out, anything you think is curious, and anything you question. This doesn't have to be rocket science—just a few basic questions that the facts have prompted. From a detective standpoint, we're looking for clues. (Remember, the facts remain unverified until you double check them in original records). My questions went something like this:

- Marion seemed like kind of an odd middle name for Robert and I wondered if it was a family name—maybe a name from his mother's McClelland or Howe lines.

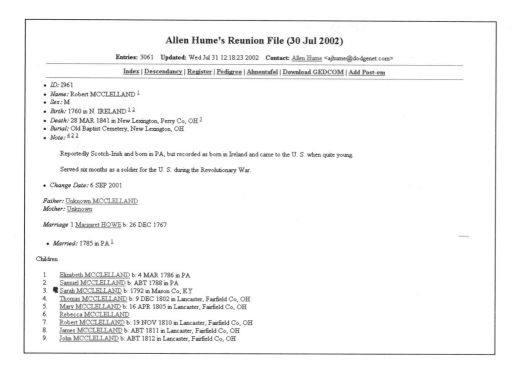

- I also noticed that Robert Hume's second marriage took place in Perry County, Ohio—his own birthplace. We know that Robert had been living in Iowa with Nancy Corns, so why did he return to Ohio? Is is possible his parents or siblings were still there?
- Since Robert's father was born in Virginia and his mother in Kentucky, I was curious how close their counties of birth were to one another.
- The only clue I have about Nancy Corns is where she was married and the approximate date of her death.

WHAT WOULD YOU DO NEXT?

Based on the information you found, what comes next? It depends on what you want to accomplish. If your goal is just to add more generations to your pedigree chart, download the GEDCOMs that go back the most generations and import them into your genealogy software in a separate database or family file from your proven lineage. That way, you have the GEDCOM, but it doesn't clutter up your database with potentially erroneous data, which is time-consuming and frustrating to weed out and eliminate later. If you want to open up new lines of research, concentrate on the lines you know the least about—in the case of my search, probably the Howe or Corns line.

Do you want to join a lineage society like the Daughters or Sons of the American Revolution? If so, you could go into the GEDCOM and pick up the people whose age makes them likely candidates for Revolutionary War service. The same holds true for Civil War or War of 1812 ancestors. Then you can use those clues to find proof of your lineage in original records, since these organizations do not accept GEDCOM files as proof.

What type of research would you do if you're interested in tracing migration patterns? More than likely you'd get a modern-day gazetteer (list or description of places) to compare to a period map (see chapter two for map sites); then try to pinpoint birth, marriage and death locations. For example, I'd look for a map that shows the relationship between Mason County, Kentucky, and Fauquier County, Virginia, and Pennsylvania, where the McClellands were from.

What could I do about all those generations of the Hume family that were found on the WorldConnect site? Well, since someone has already done the research, right now there is no point in my retracing their efforts—that is, until I'm ready to start documenting in original sources. I would, however, download the Hume GEDCOM and place it in a separate "unproven" database file, contact the submitter, and exchange whatever information I have that they don't. I would also ask the submitter if he or she would be willing to exchange source information so that we both could be assured of an accurate lineage.

I'd like to know more about Robert Hume's maternal line, which includes Margaret Howe, mother of Sarah McClelland. If Robert's middle name of Marion was a family name, I'd look for someone with the surname Marion who might have married a Howe. I could also try to track down more on Robert McClelland, but he wouldn't be my first choice; because it would be fruitless to tackle a Northern Ireland ancestor when I know nothing more than his name and date of birth. Because of his 1760 birth date, however, I might look for him in the Revolutionary War.

Next, I know that Sarah Howe and Robert McClelland were married in Pennsylvania and both died in Perry County, Ohio. Accordingly, I would begin an Internet search of Perry County (see chapters five and six). I would look for information regarding the cemetery in which they were buried. Perhaps someone has posted an online transcript of the cemetery, or maybe I could locate someone willing to go to the cemetery and take a photo, or someone could do a look-up for me. I would also try to find someone who has already started researching the Howe family (see chapter five).

Going back over the information I found and the information I need, it looks like I've outlined a pretty ambitious research plan, haven't I? Obviously, I can't search for the Howe, McClelland, and Corns lines all at once. For now I'll pick one and see where it leads—still using only the Family-Search and WorldConnect databases.

HOWE (SWEET) IT IS!

Okay, I couldn't resist poking around for Margaret Howe. Why don't you get back online and do the search with me, starting back at FamilySearch?

Entering Margaret Howe as my search criteria, nothing came up but SSDI hits. That was quick, wasn't it? I tried the same search over at WorldConnect—and while the results weren't overwhelming, they were interesting. The WorldConnect search showed a marriage between a Robert McClelland and a Margaret Howe. It showed Margaret's date of birth as

1764 (the first Robert Hume file I found had her birth as 26 December 1767); however, both files showed a date of death of 1 November 1856. Obviously, it will take further research on my part (and probably done offline in microfilmed records) to discover which, if either, of these dates is correct. The interesting tidbit, however, was it showed Margaret's father, James Howe, as having been born in 1745 in Northern Ireland. Did the Howe and McClelland families know each other in Northern Ireland?

As I read further it got even better. The person who submitted this file had documented information about James's arrival in America and his service in the Revolutionary War. The GEDCOM also included information on Margaret's siblings: Mary, Joseph, Robert, David, and James Jr. In addition, the submitter listed his source as the *Howe Family Book of Clark County, Illinois*, a book I will try to track down. James's death is listed as 19 January 1808, in Fairfield County, Ohio, which (according to the map) is right next door to Perry County.

Obviously, I could return to both FamilySearch and WorldConnect to run down more on the McClelland and Howe lines—particularly when I start doing research on siblings. For now, though, let's leave the search where it is and explore other strategies.

ASSESSING THE SNOW/CAVE/EASLEY SEARCH

Since the Cave connection is not part of my lineage, I'm going to table further research on them for the time being. Since another researcher supposedly has tracked the Easley line back to sixteenth-century Switzerland, and I will need more time to verify that, I will turn my attention to the Snows.

The Snow family presents a variety of research challenges. Chief among them is the surname itself. It's difficult to search the Internet for Snows without getting weather reports. On a positive note, one of my ancestors had a good sense of humor. He named his children Frost &, Ice &, Hail &. While this makes searching for those particular men less challenging, it still brings up page after page of weather reports.

As you may remember, my search on this family turned up information on John Snow's paternal line (the Ballards) back many generations. This branch of the family is of particular interest to me because I noted that one of my ancestors was born in Williamsburg, Virginia. I've visited Williamsburg and loved it. Knowing that family was from there makes it doubly interesting to me now. Although I know far more about the Ballards than the Snows, I'd like to poke around a bit in the Ballard history in early Virginia. To do that, I'll need to use the search techniques in chapters five and six. Remember, too, that I haven't even run the Snow search through RootsWeb.

Chapter Four Checklist
- Gather your pedigree and family group sheet for one ancestor.
- Search for that ancestor on FamilySearch and WorldConnect.

- If you get too many hits, refine your search.
- If too few hits, broaden your search or vary search options.
- Record the searches and results, along with the date.
- Try the advanced search techniques at FamilySearch on at least one of your ancestors.
- Make a list of the facts uncovered by your chapter four search.
- Are there other lineage-linked database searches you can conduct to help in this particular search? If so, do them.
- Analyze the information and construct a list of questions.
- Based on the facts and your questions, decide on which ancestor you want to focus.
- Devise a game plan for researching your ancestor; include types of information you'd like to find, like military records, maps, histories, etc.

WHAT'S NEXT?

How to connect with other family researchers.

FIVE

Search Strategy #2: Networking

NEWS FROM A COUSIN

John Chapman was born about 1635 in Stanhope, England. As a young man he converted to the Quaker faith, and for years suffered persecution for his beliefs. Finally, in 1660, he was confined in York Castle for refusing to take an oath.

On 21 June 1684, Chapman and his wife Jane, along with their five children, left Stanhope and boarded the ship *Shield of Stockton*. Four months later, the family landed safely in America, although a violent storm off the Virginia coast nearly dismantled the *Shield*. After a brief stay in Maryland, the family made its way to Bucks County, Pennsylvania, where Chapman had purchased five hundred acres on the furthest reaches of the frontier. From then until his death ten years later, he enjoyed the religious freedom denied him in England.

The story of John and Jane Chapman came to me from an unexpected source: Nancy McEwen, an Internet cousin who'd read a query I'd posted online. "Hello cousin!" her e-mail began. "Bet you didn't know we had Quaker ancestors, did you?"

E-mails flew fast and furiously as Nancy and I brought each other up to speed on our research finds and speculations. Without her help, I'm not sure I would have ever made the leap to the British life Chapman left more than three hundred years ago.

My online success was not an unusual one. Every day, distant cousins make connections that lead to new family lines, fresh evidence is uncovered, and brick walls are scaled. How? By networking.

BENEFITS OF NETWORKING

The rewards of sharing data are obvious. Genealogists researching different lines of the same family can help each other clarify dates, fill in missing names, and share digital family photos and documents. Comparing notes

Reminder

87

also helps catch decades-long errors. For those of us who are searching our female lines, Internet cousins frequently have the one missing link we've been looking for. I didn't have a clue about my third-great-grandmother's maiden name until an Internet cousin casually mentioned that she had Grandma's marriage record. And while you're sharing data, don't miss the chance at turning Internet cousins into research partners. With "so many ancestors, so little time," I need all the help I can get.

In the case of Nancy McEwen, our third-great-grandfathers were Dimmitt brothers; she followed them back to the Chapmans, while I spent time gathering records from the brothers on down. Once we connected, we were like kids showing off our new bikes. But even more special was the friendship we developed: I cherish the e-mails about our Dimmitt bad boys and the nightmares they must have caused their Quaker in-laws.

Unfortunately, networking can have a downside. You're certain to receive information that has never been confirmed in original sources. And, you may get e-mails from someone who only wants to grab all your data and run, or worse, pry into your personal life. But for the most part, Internet cousins are like the ones you know in real life. There are a few you avoid at family reunions, but the rest are ones whose company you enjoy.

In the years I've networked, I've added many names to my family tree, uncovered more possible Revolutionary War ancestors than I know what to do with, and have enough clues to fill up my research notebook for the next several years. For the first time in my life I've seen photos of my ancestors as adults who were born two centuries ago. All through connecting with my favorite Internet cousins.

Networking Methods

Finding and contacting Internet cousins is done through several routes:
1. Message boards
2. Mailing lists
3. Surname sites/personal Web pages
4. Newsgroups

Let's try all of them, using Nancy Corns (from our chapter four search) as our search goal.

MESSAGE BOARDS
(Also Known as Forums)

The queries you post online are just like the ones you may have posted in a genealogy magazine or society newsletter. They let people know which family member you're looking for and how readers can contact you. Years ago the number of people who saw your query was limited to the readership of a specific publication. Today, an online query has the potential of being seen by tens of thousands of readers. Does posting queries work? You bet. I got exceptionally lucky. Within twenty-four hours of posting a query about my Snow family, I received a digital file that contained more than three hundred pages of text, compliments of another Snow researcher.

Part of your success with queries is based on how well you write them. If your query reads like this—"Looking for anything you have on the Casey family of Michigan"—it's guaranteed you won't get the networking results you want. A successful query is a brief, well-worded, tightly focused request for specific information. Here's a sample:

> Looking for information on the parents of Henry JACKSON, who was born abt. 1715 in Albemarle County, Virginia. He married Sarah LEE in 1735. Their children were Joseph, Henry, Mary, Virginia, John, and Caroline.

Tip

When posting on forums or bulletin boards, make sure you use the subject line of the post wisely. In other words, instead of "Looking for JONES," how about "Looking for Jeffrey JONES, Bracken Co KY." To read more about writing good queries, visit CousinConnect.com and read "How to Post a Query" <www.cousinconnect.com/query_help.htm>. Don't miss the links at the bottom of the page; they lead to other "how to write effective queries" articles.

Once you've decided which ancestor to track down and you've written the perfect query, what do you do with it? Begin by visiting the query sites suggested on page 90. Once your query is posted, take the time to read the other queries. It's very possible that someone in your line has already posted a query—a perfect opportunity for immediate networking.

Hint: Remember the computer file you started for each of your surnames? Open the file and note which query was posted to which sites, along with the date. Then, be sure to go back to those sites every month or so to read new posts. Can you imagine how frustrating it would be to know that the message you've waited years to find had been posted the day *after* you were there, but you had never returned!

MAKING THE CONNECTION

After you've been reading and posting queries, one of three things will happen.

1. You'll find a post that relates to your family.
2. Someone who's read your post will contact you.
3. You won't get any response.

Then what?

If you find a family-related post, click on the person's e-mail address, and send a note telling him where you saw his post, and how you think you are connected. Let him know what information you're trying to find, and tell him how you can help in the search. If the post is on a bulletin board, respond there so others can learn, too.

Most online genealogists are incredibly generous, but no one likes to feel used. Imagine how you would feel if someone answered your post with a message like this one: "I saw your post about the Adams family. I'm pretty sure we're related. Send me everything you have on the family."

The most frequent exchange between two researchers is sharing a GED-COM file (see chapter ten for sending and receiving GEDCOMs), or an attempt to fill in each other's blanks. If you are contacted by someone reading your post, respond as soon as possible; you know how frustrating it can be to wait weeks for a reply. Again, let the other researcher know what you have to share and ask him questions about his data.

QUERY SITES

USGenWeb

<www.usgenweb.com>

If you're a United States researcher who hasn't used USGenWeb you're missing some major networking opportunities. Many of our nineteenth-century ancestors lived in rural America, and their lives revolved around their farms, their neighbors, and their small community stores and churches. Women in one family married men from a neighboring family, and close friends or in-laws witnessed wills or other legal documents. What better place to find Internet cousins than posting queries in the counties where these close-knit families lived? If Great-great Granny Sarah and her eight siblings lived and died in Lincoln County, Kansas, you can bet your Internet cousins will be hanging out there too. Or the descendants of Sarah's in-laws or neighbors. A post on a county page of the USGenWeb can also get you a "howdy!" from an "allied family" cousin—someone whose ancestor migrated with, lived next door to, or married into your family.

When you search county queries, look beyond your immediate family and also search for the surnames you saw on Grandpa's will or as neighbors on a census. It's possible people searching for those surnames have run across your family too. And don't forget to look for alternative surname spellings. To maximize your networking success, visit every USGenWeb county your ancestors lived in to post and read queries.

GenForum

<http://genealogy.genforum.com>

Yvonne Clingerman is one of the many genealogists who struck gold on GenForum's surname bulletin boards. After years of dead ends, she found a message from another Clingerman family genealogist. "He didn't know the names of the Clingerman parents either," she said, "but he knew the names of other siblings and was in contact with several researchers."

Through e-mails and forum messages, Yvonne and others eventually formed a group of about ten researchers and together discovered a family link that had eluded Yvonne for years. "I'm convinced that without a way to connect to others looking for the same families," she said, "we would have spent years amassing the information we managed to gather in a few short months." (See figure 5-1 on page 91.)

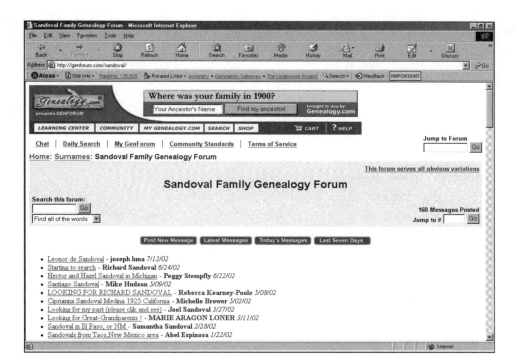

GenForum contains thousands of bulletin boards, or forums, where researchers can post queries and connect with Internet cousins. **Some of the forums are monitored by expert family historians who generously help newcomers untangle confusing family lines.** One of them, Mike Gregory, helped me find my way through 250 years of perplexing Gregory lines. Of course, Mike warned me that not all of his data was confirmed, but he left me with enough clues to track down the records on my own.

GenForum's bulletin boards are categorized by surname, state, county, country, and research topic. For the greatest chance at successful networking, post your query on every applicable forum. For example, if you're looking for the Jamieson family of Shelby County, Indiana, post in the Jamieson surname forum, the Shelby County forum, and state of Indiana forum.

GenForum does not archive messages; every one of the millions of posts is left online. You can search each forum separately or the entire system. Want a little inspiration? Visit the Success Stories Forum.

CousinConnect

<www.cousinconnect.com>

This newcomer to the world of query sites has lots to offer. Steve Johnson, Webmaster of Interment.net, created the site so researchers could search and post "pure" queries. When you enter a surname in the search box, the system only searches the surname field of posted queries, not the body text. That means you won't get irrelevant hits from junk messages or off-topic threads.

A unique feature of CousinConnect is the control it gives visitors over managing their queries. Once you go to the site and post your query, you

Reminder

can go back at any time to change or delete it. This feature is particularly useful if your e-mail address has changed, or if you want to correct a name or date in your original post.

Surname Helper
<http://surhelp.rootsweb.com/srchall.html>

Although this isn't a site to post queries on, it's one where you can search for your surname in other people's queries. In fact, this system searches more than fifteen thousand sites including the USGenWeb.

Surname Helper has detailed search capabilities that allow you to search for the exact spelling of a surname, its Soundex equivalent or a surname using wildcards. Additionally, you can specify the type of site to search, the type of post, or location.

Types of posts include Bible records, biographies, census files, court records, military service, queries, and obituaries. Sites searched are personal Web pages, surname pages, the USGenWeb, and WorldGenWeb. Search parameters can be changed to search a single state, country, or worldwide.

Try varying your searches if you get too many or too few search results. When I searched the entire system for the surname Snow, I got back nearly five hundred hits. When I specified the system search for queries only from the state of Virginia, I got back eleven. One of them was from a researcher who was looking for my line. A connection!

Ancestry/RootsWeb
<http://boards.ancestry.com/mbexec?htx=main&r=rw>

When Ancestry acquired RootsWeb in June 2000, one of the major changes to both systems was a launch of new message boards to replace the MyFamily and GenConnect systems. At that time, the new boards represented the largest collection of genealogy and family history messages on the Internet, offering free access to more than eighteen million postings.

Notes

If you used the old boards but were frustrated by their less than user-friendly interface, it's time you went back and searched again. **The new message boards have a cleaner appearance, use slick search technology, and are a breeze to navigate.** The more than 100,000 boards are divided into surname, locality, and research topics, and can be accessed from either Ancestry.com (click Share, then Message Boards), or RootsWeb.com.

Although you'll probably jump right into a message search, don't miss out on the built-in extras that can reduce research time. For example, you can add any board to My Notifications if you want to receive an e-mail whenever a reply to your message is posted. You can also add any board to My Favorites, which is a list of quick links to your most frequently visited boards.

Another unique feature of the system is its "gateway" to mailing lists. Some (but not all) of the message boards are set up so that every posted message is automatically added to a mailing list of the same topic. This is great news for researchers, as it increases the number of people who will see your message. You'll know which boards have gatewayed messages by the notice posted at the top of the board.

Although anyone can post or read any board message, only registered users can access the My Notification and My Favorites features. If you're a MyFamily.com user, just use the same ID and password you use to access your MyFamily.com Web site. If not, register by choosing a user name and password, along with providing your name and e-mail address.

One of the handiest features is the on-site search engine. Use it to wade through millions of messages to locate other family researchers or ferret out clues for further investigation. You can confine your search to any one board, such as your surname board, or broaden it to search the entire system. If your surname has several variant spellings, use the Advanced Search option to search by Soundex.

Although your first searches will probably be by surname, be sure to give the locality boards a spin. They are divided globally by geographic area with the United States divided by county. If your ancestor lived in a small town, there's a good chance of finding a post about in-laws or neighbors on one of the county boards.

Topic boards can also be of great help if you're just getting started or are jumping into a new branch of research, such as immigration or military records. These boards contain messages ranging from questions about Revolutionary War pay vouchers to opinions about genealogy software products. To leave a message, click the Post a New Message link. If you don't want to check back on the Web site for replies to your message, check the box "Send me an e-mail when anyone replies to this message." You can reply to any message by clicking the Post Reply link. Be polite in your posts, as other users can report abuses, such as obscenities, spam, or personal attacks.

Message boards are one of the quickest ways to network with other family researchers. With the tens of thousands of boards at Ancestry/RootsWeb, you're sure to find the one that will open up even your most perplexing dead end.

RootsWeb Surname List (RSL)
<http://rsl.rootsweb.com/cgi-bin/rslsql.cgi>

Although the RootsWeb surname list is not a place to post queries, it is an excellent resource for locating other family researchers. Basically, this is a surname registry with one million surname entries on file. All surnames in the RSL are actively being researched, so any connection you make could be The One.

To locate other family researchers, just enter your surname, and the RSL search engine will return a matching list in table form. The table includes the surname, the dates the researcher has information about the family, any known migration, and the name tag of the submitter. (See figure 5-2 on page 94.) For example, if you search Hendrickson, one of the listings reads:

Hendrickson 1600 now AR>MO>KS   birdbaby

This means that a researcher with the name tag "birdbaby" has informa-

Surnames matching hendrickson

New entries are marked by a +, modified entries by a *, and expiring entries by an x. Clicking on the highlighted code wo researcher who submitted the surname. (If no names are listed below this line, then none were found.)

Alternate Surnames (Click for a detailed list of alternates)

See the hendrickson resource page for more searches

You might have to scroll left or right to view all of the information

Surname	From	To	Migration	Submitter
Hendrickson	1560	----	HOL	rajack
Hendrickson	1600	now	AR>MO>KS	birdbaby
Hendrickson	1600	now	??	leeclw
Hendrickson	1643	1950	HOL>ManhattanCo,NY>NassauCo,NY,USA	lyle
Hendrickson	1660	1700	NLD>NY	RaeLynn
Hendrickson	1662	----	SWE	gini
Hendrickson	1670	1750	SWE	babbs
Hendrickson	1700	now	NY	SteveAMD
Hendrickson	1737	1916	NOR>DEU>PA>VA>NC>KnoxCo,KY>Monroe,IN>CookCo,IL	audreym
Hendrickson	1749	now	MercerCo,KY>IN>KS>Cass,JacksonCo,MO,USA	stjoemo
Hendrickson	1750	now	LongIsland,NY,USA	lyle
Hendrickson	1750	now	UlsterCo,NY>LucaCo,OH,USA	joynick
Hendrickson	1750	1800	DEU>SC>TN,USA	bobdixon

tion about Hendricksons from 1600 to present day. Additionally, this Hendrickson family migrated from Arkansas to Missouri and then Kansas. Click on the name tag for the researcher's e-mail address, as well as a list of other surnames that person is researching.

Tip

If you have a common surname, check the researcher's other surnames to get an idea of whether this family line is yours. You don't want to inundate a Jones family researcher with e-mails when it's obvious he isn't in your line. Other sites to search are Surname Origins <www.digiserve.com/heraldry/surnames .htm> and Surname Web <http://surnameweb.com>.

MESSAGE BOARD SEARCH: NANCY CORNS

Remember back in chapter four, when the FamilySearch site had a link to the Corns Family Forum? Why not go there and see what else can be found regarding Nancy Corns and Robert Hume?

Note: Nothing is perfect. Although the link from FamilySearch led to the Corns Family Forum, the message in question had vanished. Thankfully, I had already written the information down in EditPad Lite. I did, however, manage to find a related post on the Corn message board, which read:

Nancy Corns, age 17 m Robert Hume, age 26 in Van Buren County, Iowa on April 1, 1841. Nancy was b in PA per the 1860 census of Putnam County, MO. Her children: Sarah Hume b June 30, 1842, Mariah Hume b July 30, 1844, Charles Hume b abt 1847, William Hume b abt 1849, Margaret Hume b abt 1853, Caroline Hume b abt 1854, and Augustine or Augustus Hume b abt 1859. Nancy was m in the home of Henry Corns and Henry Corns and Margaret are also living in Putnam County, MO in 1860. Does anyone know anything about this family?

What does this information suggest? Make your notes here:

_____

_____

_____

_____

My thoughts are
- If Nancy was 17 in 1841, she was born about 1824.
- She was married in the home of Henry Corns, her father? brother?
- Do you remember from chapter four that Robert Hume had a second marriage in 1865? Does that mean that Nancy died sometime after 1860 (the birth of her last child) and before 1865?
- She died after the 1860 census, according to the information in this post. But if you look more closely, it says, "Nancy was b. in PA per 1860 census." It doesn't say she was listed. This person may have gotten the birthplace from the kids' information. To help narrow her death date, I'll need to see if she was alive in the 1860 census.
- Are Henry and Margaret Corns her parents?

That message board post had a lot of information, didn't it? Where do you think we should go next? How about searching the Corn and Corns boards to see if we can find any more information on Henry or Margaret? But because we know nothing about them, it's hard to know if any of the posts relate to them, isn't it? How about trying the Hume message board?

A search of the Hume board, using the search word Robert returned seventy-nine hits. To narrow it down a bit, I changed the search word to Putnam, since we know Robert spent time in Putnam County, Missouri. This time there were thirteen hits. One of them, a post by Andy Hume, listed the children of Nancy Corns and Robert Hume, along with the children's spouses and their own children.

Another post by Andy noted that Robert M. Hume's middle name was probably McClelland (his mother's maiden name), not Marion. He also said Robert was an original land owner in Putnam County, Missouri. Other posts on the forum contained information about deaths, burials, and land records.

I tried other message boards for the Corns; however, the information I found was primarily on the Hume family. Can you think of another message board I should search? How about the Iowa and Missouri boards on Gen-Forum? Or the Van Buren County, Iowa, and Putnam County, Missouri, boards at Ancestry/RootsWeb? And, of course, both surnames and places on the other message board sites. Why don't you give them a whirl and see what you find? Meet you back here.

Ready to share what you found? My most valuable clue was one I found in the Van Buren County, Iowa, board when I searched for Hume. It read:

> I am descended from George W. Hume, brother of your Robert M. Hume, both of whom moved from Athens County, OH to Van Buren County, IA ca. 1840 and on to Putnam County, MO ca. 1852 at the same time as John and Sarah Hume. The latter are assumed to be their parents on the basis of locality and ages of children with John and Sarah on old OH census records, etc. I have been communicating with several descendants of both George and Robert who join me in this assumption in the absence of proof. Do you know of any, such as old family Bible, etc? Please contact me by e-mail so we can share knowledge and sources.

Now, we have an Athens County, Ohio, connection, and the name of Robert's brother and probably his parents. (Remember, none of this has been verified.) What message boards would you search next and for which names? Write down your thoughts.

_____

_____

_____

_____

I'd head for the Ohio and Athens County boards, as well as back to the Hume message boards, looking for mentions of John, Sarah, and George. If Robert moved to Iowa in 1840 and married Nancy in 1841, is it possible they met in Ohio? Maybe. That means I'll be looking for Corns in Ohio as well.

Reminder

As you go through the message board searches, be sure to record the names and e-mail addresses of the people who posted the messages. For example, from the brief search we just did, there were at least a half-dozen names of other family researchers. Once you've found and responded to the messages left on the boards, send an e-mail to each researcher, stating your possible connection and what information you have to share.

MAILING LISTS

Although most people see technology as part of the future, for genealogists it often brings us an important part of the past. That's what happened to genealogist Carolyn Meek Nelson when she received the 182-year-old Bible that belonged to her great-great-grandfather, thanks to an Internet mailing list.

The story of Carolyn's Vandyke family Bible began in the 1950s, when Bert and Ethel Dawson purchased it at a Goodwill store in Missouri. Although the Dawsons weren't connected to the Vandykes, they bought the Bible in hopes of finding descendants of the original owners. In June 2000, a friend of the Dawsons placed a notice on the Vandyke mailing list, stating that "a neighbor" was seeking information on this family, and listed the names recorded in the Bible. "We found the posting and quickly replied, showing our direct-line connection to this J. H. Vandyke," said Nelson.

On 31 July 2000, after fifty years of guardianship, the Dawsons returned the family Bible to Nelson. "It's amazing that the powers of the Internet could do this," Nelson said.

Carolyn Nelson's story is only one of many networking successes achieved through Internet mailing lists. A mailing list allows someone to send a message to a single e-mail address that relays the message to the many others who have subscribed. There are different types of mailing lists, with the most common being announcement and discussion.

Announcement lists are used by a list owner to send notices to everyone on the list. No one but the list owner can post to the list. A common use of an announcement list is an e-mail newsletter.

With discussion lists, everyone can participate. When one person on the list sends an e-mail it is automatically sent to everyone else on the list. When you receive an e-mail from the list, you can read it, respond to it, or post a new message. Discussion lists are the kind most often used in genealogy research.

There are thousands of mailing lists just for genealogists. These include lists for surnames, locations, states, counties, countries, software, beginners, and research techniques. If you are researching your Kennedy family, for example, join the Kennedy family mailing list. Introduce yourself and the Kennedy family you are researching, along with research problems you're trying to solve. Since everyone else on the list is also researching the Kennedy surname, you may be able to combine research efforts or research results.

Once you subscribe to a mailing list, you'll start receiving a copy of all the e-mails sent to the list by its members. If you subscribe to a "small" list, you may receive one or two pieces of e-mail a week; with larger ones, you can get several pieces a day. **When you subscribe, you'll have the option of receiving the e-mails via "mail mode" or "digest mode."** In mail mode, you will receive each message as a separate e-mail. In digest mode, separate e-mails are batched together and sent as one large e-mail.

\di'fin\ *vb*

Definitions

Your chances of networking success via surname mailing lists are excellent; however, don't forget to subscribe to county lists. People who have subscribed to this list are researching in the same county where your family lived. Who knows, they may be related. You can find mailing lists here:

RootsWeb (more than twenty-four thousand lists)
http://lists.rootsweb.com/

Genealogy Resources on the Internet
www.rootsweb.com/~jfuller/gen_mail.html

MAILING LIST SEARCH: NANCY CORNS

At this point, let's join the appropriate surname and locale mailing lists to see if we can learn more. (See figure 5-3 on page 98.) Right now, the best lists are:

- Hume
- Corns (Corn and other variants)

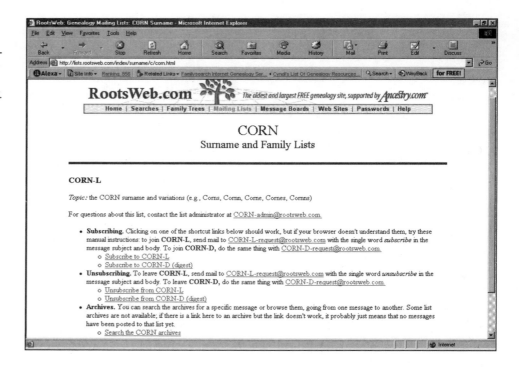

- Athens County, Ohio
- Van Buren County, Iowa
- Putnam County, Missouri

Keep in mind that although we are searching for more information on Nancy Corns, it's possible we may have to use a sidedoor-type approach, which means searching for McClelland, Knox and any other associated families that are uncovered. Once you've joined, it's a good idea to get a feel for the list and how it's run. Then introduce yourself and the lines you are researching.

PERSONAL PAGES

Did you know there are thousands of personal Web sites devoted to surname research and data compilation? You might have an ancestor on one of them. Personal Web sites are the pages posted online by individuals or groups of individuals who are compiling GEDCOMs, photos, or historical information about a specific surname or branch of a family.

Sites may contain photos of the family homestead, an online database, a query board, favorite music, or a scrapbook. The Hume Family Home Page <http://homepages.rootsweb.com/~hume/> for example, features pictures of Scottish castles near and dear to the Hume/Home family. There are also links to the Hume message board at RootsWeb and another at The Gathering of the Clans. In addition, you'll find a bibliography of books containing Hume references, as well as Webmaster Jim Hume's database of thousands of individuals and families, many of of them with the Hume/Home surname. (See figure 5-4 on page 100.)

ABOUT SURNAMES

William Shakespeare was no genealogist—else he wouldn't have asked "What's in a name?" Instead, the bard would have spent his off-hours searching for the "spear-brandishing" forebear who gave the family its name.

Although surnames are the backbone of genealogy research, the irony is they haven't been around all that long—only since the eleventh or twelfth century in Europe. Before that time, a name like "Richard of Middlebury" was identification enough. As the population grew, however, so did the need for surnames.

Surnames are generally derived from four sources: places (Hill, Brooks), occupations (Bishop, Miller), personal characteristics (Little, Smart) or patronymics—father's name—(Johnson, O'Brien). Of the four, patronymics can present a research challenge because different cultures employed different methods of naming.

In Welsh patronymics, for instance, children took their surname from their father's given name; James, the son of Terrence Gregory would be called James *ap* Terrence while James's son Michael would be Michael *ap* James. In Denmark, the surname was derived from the father's given name followed by "sen" for son or "datter" for daughter. Therefore, Hans Nielsen's daughter, Johanne, would be Johanne Hansdatter.

If wading through patronymics wasn't enough, **we also have to contend with more variations in spelling than thorns on a cactus.** Those who wrote about explorer William Clark(e) thought nothing of adding (or subtracting) a final *e* to his name. In my own family, a South Carolina deed index carries on its rolls Faulkenberry, Fortenbery, Faulkenbury, Falkenberry, and Falconbury. And you Smiths thought you had it tough.

Whatever challenge your surname brings—and we all have one—one thing's for sure: We're all proud of the name we bear. And we want to find the family who carried it down through time.

Reminder

The Wickwire/Wickware Family page <www.wickware.com> contains a unique online "museum"—a collection of photos of family history and memorabilia. The Webmaster of Kassell Connections <www.geocities.com/Heartland/Estates/4375/kassell.html> has uploaded information about the Cassell/Kassell families of the St. Louis and Chicago areas from the mid-1800s to the present. Their pages include family census, cemetery and city directory listings, and links to other Kassell researchers.

Locating Personal Pages

Search Engines. The quickest way to locate surname sites is to use one of the major search engines such as Google <www.google.com> or AltaVista <www.altavista.com>. Yes, you'll get thousands of hits if you have a common surname (Smith genealogy turned up 282,000), but the top half-dozen

Figure 5-4
This Hume family member posted more than 46,000 names on his personal home page. *James R. Hume*

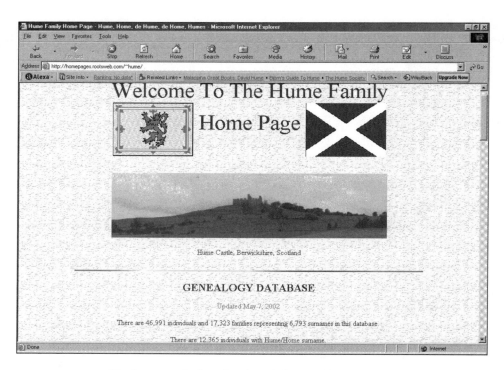

or so are most likely to include a lead. I did a quick run-through on Google for "faulkenberry genealogy" and got only 501 results. Wouldn't you know it, one of them actually had land records relating to one of my ancestors. (See chapter six for more information on using search engines).

Cyndi's List. From Cyndi's home page <http://cyndislist.com> scroll down to the category Personal Home Pages. Then click on the letter of the alphabet for your surname. If you don't find any pages with your name, it doesn't mean it isn't there. Unfortunately, Cyndi's Personal Home Pages are listed alphabetically by the name of the Web page. That means if someone named a Web page Genealogy of the Rutherford Family, that site will be listed with the G pages.

You can work around this problem by going to the top of Cyndi's main page, clicking Search Cyndi's List and entering your surname. This technique will also help you pick up surnames that are listed as allied families but are not the main surname on a Web site. For example, the Law, Bruce, French, Parks, Rogers, and Hollister lines are listed under a Taggart page; however, the on-site search engine will find them.

Genealogy Resources on the Internet
<www-personal.umich.edu/~cgaunt/surnames.html>
You can search for surnames on this site either alphabetically or by using the on-site search engine. If you opt for the search engine, it will return any occurrence of the surname including personal Web sites and surname-specific mailing lists.

GenCircles
<www.gencircles.com>
Search through information on thirty-two million people with this

genealogy-only search engine. The site's designer developed a SmartMatching method that links ancestors in your file with the same ancestor in other people's files.

Gengateway
<www.gengateway.com>

Gengateway is a portal site to thousands of surname-related Web sites. It contains more than 200,000 listings, and ninety thousand different surnames. In all, the total number of surnames found within entries on the site are more than 500,000. After entering your surname in the search box, a results page is generated with links to personal Web pages, surname bulletin boards, and researchers. The site also contains its own searchable query forum.

Genealogy.com

The folks best known for selling Family Tree Maker software host a virtual online community for personal Web pages. The pages are searchable by surname or keyword. Enter your search terms at <www.genealogy.com/community.html> and the system will pull out all of the family home pages with that name.

If the search results seem too good to be true, they may be. A search of Hume returned 4,302 matching documents. However, several of the hits were generated from the same Web site. The same thing happens on Google.

SURNAME SEARCH: NANCY CORNS

I went through the surname sites without a lot of luck. After doing a global search of Cyndi's List, however, I did discover a couple of sites with information on the Corn family. Apparently the Corn lineage has been well-researched, with at least three books written about the surname. But I have no way of knowing if my Nancy Corns is included until I find copies of the books.

I also found a Hume family page with information on Robert Hume and Nancy Corns, including a 9 May 1824 birth for Nancy in Pennsylvania and a notation of her death in Putnam County, Missouri. Additionally the site had property records for Hume in Iowa. More clues!

What's been found on these personal sites?
- There is a well-researched Corn line; is it possible to connect Nancy?
- Robert was involved in several land transactions in Iowa; perhaps those will uncover more clues.
- Nancy has been reported as being born in Pennsylvania and Illinois. Is it possible to find someone of her age on a Pennsylvania or Illinois census? What did she likely report as her birthplace in 1850 and 1860?
- If Nancy died in Putnam County, Missouri, is it possible to find a death record or possibly an obituary that would provide more family information?

Case Study

In addition, I've gathered the names of several Corn/Corns researchers to contact. The next step on the networking front is to e-mail other researchers to let them know who I am researching, what information I'm looking for, and how I think we might connect. Don't forget to contact the researchers you found on FamilySearch and WorldConnect.

NEWSGROUPS

Another way to network is by using newsgroups. These are forums on specific topics, where anyone can post messages and reply to other users. To read or post to newsgroups, you once needed special newsreader software, a newsgroup-capable browser (like Netscape Navigator or Internet Explorer), or mailing programs like Outlook Express.

Recently, however, Google.com archived all of the Newsgroup messages dating back to 1981. Messages can now be read and replied to through Google's Group Home Page <http://groups.google.com>.

To use Google's Web-based newsgroup features, just go to the Group Home Page and type in the name of the newsgroup you're interested in reading (there's a complete list on the site), like alt.genealogy. A list of all the messages will pop up. Follow the directions to post a new thread or reply to an old message. You can even use Google's Group feature to do a keyword search in any or all of the newsgroups.

For a list of genealogy-specific newsgroups, go to <http://rootsweb.com/~jfuller/gen_use.html>.

Chapter Five Checklist
- Pick one or two people you want to find and begin searching for them on message boards.
- Read and post queries on the USGenWeb counties where your ancestor lived.
- Leave queries on the other message boards.
- Register with the RootsWeb Surname List.
- Join the appropriate surname and locale mailing lists.
- Create e-mail file folders for your mailing lists.
- Search for personal home pages containing your surname.
- Contact the researchers you think you are connected to and be prepared to exchange GEDCOMs or other family information.

WHAT'S NEXT?

Become a power user of Internet search engines.

SIX

Search Strategy #3: Search Engines

HOW SEARCH ENGINES WORK

When you use a search engine, you are asking it to search the World Wide Web and show you the pages that contain one or more of the keywords you entered. Each search engine is designed a bit differently from the others and will not return the exact same results, even when the same search terms are entered. That's because the formula used to determine the relevancy of sites varies from engine to engine. For example, some engines give a higher relevancy rating to the sites with "link popularity"; that means sites such as Amazon.com, which many other sites link to, will receive a higher rating than other book sites without as many links to them.

Search engines do not find every single Web page on the Internet. In fact, each engine has indexed only a small percentage of the Web—but amazingly this translates to billions of Web pages. Google, according to its 2002 statistics, indexed 2,073,418,204 Web pages, AlltheWeb at a little more than two billion, and Wisenut came in third at 1,571,413,207. Don't let the size fool you; according to a survey done in 2002, the Web pages found by Wisenut were nearly a year old. Compare this to updates at least every eleven days by AlltheWeb.

Warning

Currently, the engines with the highest number of indexed pages are

- Google <www.google.com>
- AlltheWeb <www.alltheweb.com>
- Wisenut <www.wisenut.com>
- Northern Light <www.northernlight.com>
- AltaVista <www.altavista.com>
- Hotbot <www.hotbot.com>
- MSN Search <http://search.msn.com>

BOOLEAN, DEFAULT, AND SEARCH ENGINE MATH

When I went to Google.com and entered the search phrase of *Mayflower genealogy*, the engine found 23,500 pages. When I entered the phrase "May-

REV UP YOUR ENGINES

When SearchEngineShowdown.com did a test to see how much overlap existed between results using various search engines, surprisingly there was little. Using four small searches on ten engines, the results returned 141 specific Web pages. Of those 141, seventy-one were found by only one of the ten search engines while another thirty were found by only two. What this means for genealogists is to use more than one search engine.

\di'fin *vb*

Definitions

flower genealogy," it found 281. Why the difference? The quotation marks. (See figure 6-1 below.)

Boolean searching is the term used to describe how multiple terms are combined in a search. Boolean "operators" are the words used to instruct the engine how to deal with multiple terms. Some search engines use all of the operators, some use only a few. Check the Help or Advanced Search options on your favorite search engines to see which operators are supported. The most common operators are:

- and
- or
- not
- +
- –
- " "
- ( )

Figure 6-1
Caleb Johnson's *Mayflower* Web ranks high in the search engines because of its highly relevant content. *Caleb Johnson*

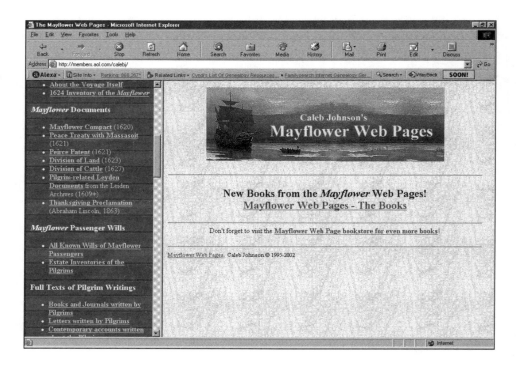

Here's how each operator works:

and The Web page must contain both terms. For example, if you enter *lewis and clark*, the search engine will look for pages that contain both words. That means you may get a page describing how well Fred Clark did at the Lewis Golf Tournament. When you use *and*, the search engine does not look for the words in any specific sequence. Generally, the default operator for handling multiple search terms is *and*.

or The Web page must contain at least one of the search words. If you enter *lewis or clark*, it will return pages with either of those words, not necessarily both. *Or* is particularly useful when one of your search terms has synonyms, e.g., *"georgia brown" and (marriage or engagement or betrothal)*.

not This term excludes documents containing specified words or phrases. For example, if you know that your ancestor, Jacob White, never lived in Kentucky, although many Whites did, you can use *not* to exclude the word Kentucky. Be cautious in using this operator; you don't want to exclude a page that may have your information.

+ The plus sign is equivalent to the *and* operator.

− The minus sign is equivalent to the *not* operator, but some engines that recognize the minus sign don't recognize the operator *not*.

" " Using quotes around words forces the engines to look for the words as a search phrase. If you search for *"lewis and clark"* the engine will return Web pages containing that exact phrase.

( ) This is probably the most underutilized operator because of its resemblance in looks (and action) to high school algebraic formulas. The parentheses allow you to "nest" search terms and create complex searches. If you remember back to that algebra class, tasks inside the parentheses were performed before functions outside of it, e.g., $(10+3)\times(14-5)$. Search engines perform their functions in the same way. Here's an example: The search phrase *("jacob dearing") and land not (Iowa or Ohio)* will return Web pages containing *Jacob Dearing* and *land*. However it will not return any *land* pages with the words *Iowa* or *Ohio*. Note: Not all search engines use the ( ) operator.

\di'fin\ *vb*

Definitions

Hint: Use all lower case letters, even when searching for proper names. Generally (depending on the engine), if you capitalize the first letter of a surname, it will not find Web pages where the surname is written in all capital letters. A search term in all lower case, like *snow*, or mixed case, like *Snow*, will find pages containing *snow*, *Snow* and *SNOW*. All upper cased search terms, like *SNOW*, don't always find pages containing mixed-case words (*Snow*).

Every search engine has certain features that determine how the engine will handle your search words and phrases. For example, on Google, if two or more words are entered in the search box, the engine's default is set to *and*. That means each of the words you entered must be on a Web page for it to be included in your search results, but not in any specific order.

To discover the default setting for your favorite search engine, click on its Help or Advanced Search link. At Google.com, for example, go to <www .google.com/help/basics.html> for information on basic searches, then follow the links to Advanced Search. Some search engines allow you to choose the default settings—just click on the Help or Advanced Search links for more information.

A SIMPLE SEARCH

What do you think three of the leading search engines will do with a simple genealogy-related term? Let's see. Pretend that you've heard you descend from a *Mayflower* family, and you want to know more about tracing lineage to the *Mayflower* passengers. Let's plug the phrase "mayflower genealogy" into the search box and see what happens.

Google: A search for the phrase "mayflower genealogy" (remember, put a phrase in quote marks) returned 281 results. The top three results were

- The *Mayflower* Web Pages
  <http://members.aol.com/calebj/mayflower.html>
- Scott McGee's Other GenWeb Databases
  <www.genealogy.org/~smcgee/genweb/other_db.html>
- *Mayflower* Genealogy Books
  <www.genealogy-books.com/books/mayflower.html>

WiseNut: 132 results
- The *Mayflower* Web Pages
  <http://members.aol.com/calebj/mayflower.html>
- Geneology [*sic*]
  <http://home.adelphia.net/~church/geneolog.htm>
- *Mayflower* Genealogy Books
  <www.genealogy-books.com/books/mayflower.html>

AlltheWeb: 192 results
- *The Mayflower Genealogy of Tod Marshall*
  <http://bocasource.com/todmar/mayflow.htm>
- *Mayflower* Genealogy Books
  <http://genealogybooks.us/books/Mayflower.html>
- International Black Sheep Society—Genealogy Hall of Shame
  <http://blacksheep.rootsweb.com/mayflower.htm>

It's no wonder the *Mayflower* Web Pages comes up first because it is an excellent resource for everything *Mayflower*. It includes a passenger list, Pilgrim documents, wills, and links to *Mayflower* lineage societies, such as the *Mayflower* Society. If you click to the Society site, you'll find a membership section with suggestions for tracing your lineage. The sites that came up second and third are both commercial sites carrying *Mayflower*-related books.

At this point, don't stop searching and just use the information on the *Mayflower* Society site. See if there's a way to change the search phrase to get more information.

Using Google, I typed in "tracing *mayflower* lineage"; one of the results was a CD-ROM compilation of The Complete *Mayflower* Descendant, Volumes 1-46 <www.genealogy.com/203facd.html?Welcome=1037573486>. That sounds promising, doesn't it? Other results included an article on tracing *Mayflower* lineage written by Rhonda McClure, author of *The Genealogist's Computer Companion* (Cincinnati: Betterway Books, 2001) <www.GenealogyMagazine.com/finmayfam.html>. (McClure mentions that at least forty million people can trace their descent from the first Pilgrims!).

I changed the search again to *"mayflower ancestors."* This search linked to an audiotape on finding *Mayflower* ancestors, which I thought would be helpful <www.audiotapes.com/product.asp?ProductCode='SLC-62'>. The best hits from this search were personal Web pages published by people who are *Mayflower* descendants. If you know the name of the Pilgrim you think is your ancestor, use these personal pages to track down another descendant and exchange notes.

HOW TO STRUCTURE YOUR SEARCH

The one thing you probably noticed from this first search was how important it is to restructure search phrases. As you could see, the three search terms all brought different hits, and each of the searches returned pages with potentially useful information. What other terms could we use? (See figure 6-2 on page 108.)

- *"mayflower* lineage"
- *"mayflower* descendants"
- "pilgrim genealogy"
- "pilgrim ancestors"
- "pilgrim lineage"

Next, if you thought you were descended from *Mayflower* passenger Thomas Rogers, for example, how would you structure your search? A Google search for "thomas rogers" returned 8,440 hits; however, many of the top twenty were relative to the *Mayflower*'s Thomas Rogers.

If you changed the search to *"thomas rogers" and mayflower*, the results dropped to 1,040, with almost all seemingly relevant to the search. Results contained biographical information about Thomas Rogers, the *Mayflower* Compact, and the *Mayflower* passenger list. It's great to get so many relevant results, but hard to wade through so many, particularly if you're trying to find some clue about whether you're descended from Thomas Rogers.

What about changing the search term to *"thomas rogers" and descendants and mayflower*. Oops! That one was even worse: 2,120 results. Why? Because the search engine picked up pages with Mayflower descendants and Thomas Rogers, but not necessarily Rogers' descendants! Let's try that again.

Searching for *"thomas rogers descendants" and mayflower* resulted in two hits. One of them contained a link to the Thomas Rogers Society, a Web page for the descendants of Thomas Rogers. Now, *that's* a find.

Just for fun, I tried one last search. My phrase was *descendants "thomas rogers" mayflower*. The search resulted in 497 hits. Some dandies among them were message boards discussing *Mayflower* descendants, a biography of Thomas Rogers, and a link to the Frequently Asked Questions (FAQ) file for the *Mayflower* mailing list.

If you are following along with this search, you'll see that some of these searches found the same Web sites and some found entirely different ones. **If you type in a phrase in only one search engine, examine the results, and then consider the search completed, you're apt to miss some gems.** Restructure, rephrase, and rework your searches!

Notes

ADD ONE MAGIC WORD TO YOUR SEARCH

Search engines are particularly fun when you're searching for your surname, regardless of how unique or common it is. When I searched for Faulkenberry (a fairly unique name), there were 4,640 results; when I searched for Snow, there were nearly eight million. The Faulkenberry results included a bunch of living people; the Snow hits were all about the weather. Neither of these searches helped. By adding a single "magic" word, the number of returns were drastically reduced, and the number of relevant ones skyrocketed. The word was "genealogy."

The search for *faulkenberry and genealogy* found 388 results; *"faulkenberry genealogy"* returned ten. Of those one was an 1815 deed which involved one of my ancestors—and included new information. The results of this search were excellent, but I could possibly find even more by trying the same search with variant spelling of the Faulkenberry surname, e.g., Faulkenbury, Falkenberry, Falkenbury, and Falkinbury.

What about the Snow search? The phrase *snow genealogy* turned up 85,800 hits, but "*snow genealogy*" reduced the hits to a manageable 121. But why stop there? Structuring some creative search terms might ferret out another genealogy-rich page.

Let's try looking for Frost Snow. If I searched for *frost and snow* I'd get more of those weather reports. When I changed the search to "*frost snow*" I still got more than two thousand hits, primarily because of the Web pages with sentences like "Frost, snow, ice, and hail all hit XYZ City!"

How can I structure this search to weed out the weather reports? How about "*frost snow*"-*weather*. That came back with 1,490 hits, but the tenth result on page one was family information. Okay, I'm still not satisfied with these results. How about changing the search to "*frost snow*" *and* "*north carolina*." Oops! More than sixteen thousand hits because I forgot to add the -*weather* operator.

At this point I moved from Google to AltaVista, primarily because I prefer AltaVista when structuring more complex phrases. When I searched for "*frost snow*" *and* "*north carolina*"-*weather* I only got six hits. One of those six, however, was priceless. It was a digital transcription of the book *Fisher's River Scenes and Characters*. When I searched the text it contained several anecdotes about my ancestor, Frost Snow. The stories about him (and other family members) were precious.

Hint: If the search of "*your surname and genealogy*" doesn't pan out, try "*your surname and family*," e.g., "*fite family*."

BACKDOOR SEARCHES

As you can see from above, searching for the Snow surname is a challenge. If you have a common surname, you'll face this challenge, too. **There is a way around getting eight or ten million hits, however. It's by structuring a "backdoor search."**

Tip

Here's how it works. If you're trying to track down Joseph Smith, instead of searching for "*joseph smith*" or even "*joseph smith genealogy*," search for Joseph Smith and someone else in his family with a more unusual name. Follow this search on AltaVista.com:

I wanted to find more about John Snow. Since John and Snow are both common names, I knew I would get thousands of search hits. I knew that John Snow traveled to Missouri with two brothers-in-law, Galen Cave and Warham Easley. I constructed this search: "*galen cave*" *and* (*snow or easley*). The search yielded five results and all were keepers.

I conducted the same search on Google.com. I only got three results, but the first one was a humdinger. It listed four generations of the descendants of one of my Snow ancestors. How else could you use the backdoor method?

- surname 1 and surname 2 and town name
- surname 1 and surname 2 and state name

- surname 1 and surname 2 and wife's name
- surname 1 and surname 2 and record (e.g., land, will, probate)

Can you think of more?

AltaVista Hint: If the search engine you like to use features the operator *near* (such as AltaVista), you can use it to find pages where your ancestor's name may be listed with a middle name or initial. For example: If you use AltaVista and type in the search phrase *john near worthington*, the engine will find pages in which the word "john" is within ten words of the word "worthington." This will pick up items such as John R. Worthington. AltaVista also has another operator term: *and not*. If you have a surname like England, this is an especially useful operator, e.g., *england and not british, england and not britain*.

SEARCHING FOR TRANSCRIBED RECORDS

You know you can find Web pages that mention your surname, but can you find more detailed information, such as a will or deed? Maybe, if the document you want has been transcribed or digitized and uploaded to the Web. But let's take a look. Since we're familiar with the Snow challenges, why not stick with them? I concocted this search phrase: *"frost snow" and virginia and deed*.

Believe it or not, I got countless hits for Robert Frost and his poetry. The second result on page one, however, was a personal Web site with timelines, deeds, and land records!

Using the search *"frost snow" and "north carolina" and census* I found several relevant records, including federal and agricultural censuses.

SEARCH ENGINE TIPS AND STRATEGIES

- If you're looking for the name of an individual, place it between quotation marks or use the *near* Boolean operator: *"john worthington"* or *john NEAR worthington*.
- If you anticipate search results containing many terms you don't want, use *and not* (although not all search engines support this). If you are searching for the surname "England," use *and not* to exclude as many references as possible to the country England, e.g., British, Britain, UK, and United Kingdom.
- If your search contains many common words use *and*: *john and worthington and virginia and deed*.
- If you are searching for a common surname, try searching for it in conjunction with the word "family" or "genealog*" (use asterisk as a wildcard if the search engines allows).
- Does your search term have synonyms or spelling variations? If so, try *or*: *"sally west" and (marriage or wedding or engagement or betrothal)*.
- Use multiple search engines. Because of its design, each engine will return different results.

- Be creative in constructing search terms and terminology.
- Use the asterisk as a wildcard whenever needed.
- Read the search engines' help files.
- Use variant spellings, synonyms, and word combinations.
- If you get disappointing results, rephrase your search.
- Use as keywords both the surname and a place name where your ancestor lived.

WHERE TO FIND SEARCH ENGINES

Search engines include
- AltaVista <www.altavista.com>
- Google <www.google.com>
- Northern Light <www.northernlight.com>
- Infoseek <www.infoseek.com>
- Fast Search <www.alltheweb.com>
- Excite <www.excite.com>
- Hotbot <www.hotbot.com>
- Webcrawler<www.webcrawler.com>

META-SEARCH ENGINES

A meta-search engine uses multiple search engines at one time. When you enter your keywords into the search box of a meta-search engine, it sends your search to several individual search engines and returns a compilation of results. **Using a meta-search engine saves time, but it only retrieves about 10 percent of the results in any of the databases queried.** Additionally, the search terms default to whatever the default of the search engine is.

Timesaver

Meta-search engines are most effective when used for a "simple" search, e.g., a search containing a unique name or phrase. Two of the best meta-searchers are
- **Dogpile** <www.dogpile.com>. Dogpile can be configured for a customized search. It includes Fast, About, Ask Jeeves, AltaVista, Look-Smart, Infoseek, Lycos, Yahoo, and a few directories. Dogpile does not rank results. Ranking is done by the individual search engines. If you find a result you find promising, click on the link to that engine and use its advanced search capabilities. Default is *and*. Using Dogpile to search for "*frost snow*" *and virginia and deed*, I found two links to several generations of Ballard family history (Frost Snow married a Ballard), as well as a 1789 deed that Frost Snow witnessed.
- **MetaCrawler** <www.metacrawler.com>. Complex searches are not supported. You can, however, choose all terms (*and*), any terms (*or*), or phrase. MetaCrawler searches AltaVista, Excite, Infoseek, Lycos, WebCrawler, and Lycos. It can be configured for custom searches.

Other meta-searchers include
- **HotWords** <www.hotwords.com>

- **Mamma: Mother of All Search Engines** <www.mamma.com>
- **ProFusion** <www.profusion.com>
- **Web Taxi** <www.webtaxi.com>

NEW KIDS ON THE BLOCK

Although Google and AltaVista are longtime favorites, new search engines are springing up every day. When you have time, why not run a few searches through them just to see how they stack up?

- **Kartoo** <kartoo.com>. This nifty engine splashes search results over a blue background with color-coded links suggesting how the results interconnect. Although beautiful, Kartoo will never win any competition for speedy searches.
- **Teoma** <teoma.com>. Teoma tries to figure out if you want to find "snow" the person or "snow" the weather report by breaking your query into categories, and then grouping them by themes.

NANCY CORNS AND THE SEARCH ENGINES

Although we've picked up a lot of clues about Nancy Corns and Robert Hume, we don't have much solid data. In fact, we don't even know the names of Nancy's parents or where she was born. This makes the search much tougher because when we do find Corns Web sites, we won't know for sure if they're part of the family.

I started the search engine phase by going to Google.com, then the other major engines and meta-searchers and simply typing in *"nancy corns."* A bust. A search for *"henry corns"* at AltaVista turned up a list of Corns people in Muskingum County, Ohio, but there wasn't enough information to know if I made a connection. I did, however, write down the name and e-mail address of the researcher and sent her a note about my line.

A similar search on Google found two Corns marriages in Mason County, Kentucky. Hmm. Does Mason County sound familiar? Yes, it was the birthplace of Nancy's mother-in-law, Sarah McClelland. I also found a list of Corns/Korns Ohio marriages, <http://freepages.genealogy.rootsweb.com/~corn/cornohio.htm>, which I'll keep tucked away for a rainy day.

How about trying *corns and genealogy*? The first hit was a great Corns family Web site that was loaded with records. Unfortunately, no sign of Nancy. Here's another approach: corns + *"van buren"* + *iowa* (See figure 6-3 on page 113.) This turned up early Van Buren County Marriages, Book A, which listed Robert and Nancy's marriage. I also found an 1878 biographical listing for Ira Corns, millwright and farmer. Could this be one of Nancy's relatives? Possibly, but it needs to be verified. Next, a link to Corns burials in four Van Buren County cemeteries: Bentonsport, Bonaparte, Farmington, and Vernon. I liked the search results so much I ran it on the other major search engines, but didn't learn anything new.

Again, the same search, but *hume* instead of *corns: hume* + *"van buren"* + *iowa*. The results were not helpful. I did, however, discover one tantaliz-

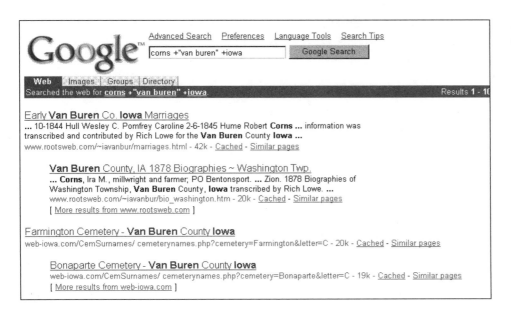

Figure 6-3
A successful complex search.
Google.com

ing page from *Portrait and Biographical Album, Polk County, Iowa 1890* <www.usgennet.org/usa/topic/historical/1890polk_10.html>. The page had a listing for a lawyer named Thomas C. Dawson of Des Moines, a partner in the law firm of Hume and Dawson. What stood out was a line noting that Thomas Dawson's mother was "Anna Cleland, a sister of the mother of Mr. Hume, and is now a resident of Enterprise, Fla." Doesn't Cleland seem awfully close to McClelland? The book's index also had listings for James C., John T., and W.Y. Hume, but unfortunately none of those listings had been transcribed. But more clues to ponder, a major one being to include Cleland when I search for McClelland, as well as Florida and Des Moines. Here are my suggestions for more search terms:

- hume and corns and genealogy
- hume and putnam and missouri
- corns and illinois
- corns and putnam and missouri
- "hume family" iowa
- "corns family" iowa

What search terms would you use?

_____
_____
_____
_____
_____

CASE STUDY: THE BALLARDS OF WILLIAMSBURG

In chapter four, while searching for John Snow, we uncovered his Ballard maternal line. Although another researcher has already climbed this branch

Case Study

of the family tree, let's see if we can use search engine strategies to discover more about the Ballards of Williamsburg.

From information at FamilySearch, we learned that John Snow's grandmother was Elizabeth "Betsy" Ballard. Betsy was descended from a long line of Ballards, some of whom were involved with the early days of Williamsburg, Virginia. According to the GEDCOM downloaded from FamilySearch, Betsy's fourth-great-grandfather was Thomas Ballard, born in 1630, died in 1689. With that information, let's see what we can turn up using a search engine. Entering *thomas ballard williamsburg*, the first hit was a whopper: the Thomas Ballard family history. Interestingly enough, the file was stored on the Web site of the Kansas Heritage Server <www.ku.edu/heritage/cousin/ballard.html>. Good thing we used the search engine, because not in a million years would I have searched a Kansas Web site for a Williamsburg family.

The online family history contained seven pages of printed material. That was certainly a find, but there was even more. A gentleman named Vaughn Ballard had compiled seventy-five pages of Thomas Ballard history, including "his descendants and possible ancestors." Among the gems in the file was information on Thomas, the founder of the American branch, including his

- membership in the Governor's Council
- land holdings
- involvement with the Nathaniel Bacon rebellion
- position with the Bruton Parish Church in Williamsburg

In fact, the Ballard family was associated with several historic events in the Williamsburg area.

Another search for *thomas ballard virginia* took me to a biography of Thomas Ballard <http://users.legacyfamilytree.com/EvaGremmert/2/24258.htm>.

MORE EASY SEARCH ENGINE PROJECTS

A lot of family connections were untangled during the chapter four search for Cave, Snow, and Easley. Could I find more with a search engine? Let's see.

Using the search term *easley cave snow*, I found a page with information similar to the pedigree charts at FamilySearch. I had hoped to find something more than a chart, however. My next search was structured + *cave* + *easley* + *snow* + *"lone jack."* Of the five results, one link led me to a personal Web site called "Tangled Web." What an appropriate name given the three families' relationships. The site's owner, Judith Mohr, had uploaded the GEDCOM file for the family, along with several obituaries. In addition there were "scrapbook" pages displaying photos of family tombstones and tombstone inscriptions. What a great idea for sharing photos that otherwise wouldn't be seen. (See figure 6-4 on page 115.)

Scrapbook Page for John Snow

John Snow

"Sacred To the memory of John Snow who departed this life June 23rd 1851. Aged 61 yrs 3 months 11 days." ~~ "Remember friends as you pass by, As you are now so once was I. As I am now so you must be. Prepare for death."

Figure 6-4
Create an online scrapbook page for your ancestors.
Judith M. Moore, <http://freepages .genealogy.rootsweb.com/ ~ramblin/index.htm>

Chapter Six Checklist
- Decide which line or person to search.
- Make a list of what you know.
- Make a list of your assumptions.
- From your lists, construct a variety of search terms.
- Conduct your searches on the various search engines.
- Keep track of the URLs you visited.
- Note the e-mail addresses of the Webmasters (see glossary) of pertinent pages.
- E-mail the Webmasters to whom you believe you are connected to, introducing yourself and your research.

WHAT'S NEXT?
Searching online databases.

SEVEN

Search Strategy #4: Online Databases and Transcripts

WHERE ELSE TO LOOK?

Our ancestor-hunt began back in chapter four when we explored lineage-linked databases. From there, we expanded the search using networking and search engines. Along the way we found a lot of family and even more clues. Now, it's time to delve into the other online databases and transcript sites that don't fall neatly into other categories. The types of sites included are

1. cemetery
2. census
3. immigration
4. land
5. marriage
6. military

CEMETERIES

If you live close to your ancestral home, you're lucky. Our mobile society has taken most of us hundreds or thousands of miles away from the towns and villages of our early ancestors. Because of that, doing on-site cemetery research is difficult unless you have the means to travel. But thanks to online cemetery databases, there's a good chance you can find an ancestor's grave, and along with it the dates of birth and death.

As mentioned in chapter two, Internet research won't help with those wonderful clues we can obtain through on-site cemetery research. As you know, it's not unusual for an old tombstone to contain a Bible verse, a maiden name, or place of birth. The carvings on the stone—something we won't find in a database—can contain clues to religious beliefs or reflect the family's expression of grief. But thanks to a couple of online projects, there is a chance of obtaining a tombstone photo. Start your cemetery research with these sites:

Find a Grave
<www.findagrave.com>

Search the largest database of online cemetery records. Just enter the name you want to find, and let the system search its 3.6 million records. If you find the name of an ancestor, click on the name for information on where he was buried and the name of the cemetery. If you do want to visit, just click on the name of the cemetery and an area map will be displayed, along with Global Positioning System (GPS) coordinates. A fun part of the site is Find Famous Graves. You can search by name, location, or claim to fame (e.g., explorer, author, president, royalty).

If you want, you can register for a free membership on this site. This allows you to leave virtual flowers or upload a photo.

GPS AND GENEALOGY

Global Positioning System (GPS) is a satellite navigation system which provides real-time positioning information from anywhere on earth. This means you can turn on your GPS unit, acquire a signal from the satellite system, then read out your current latitude and longitude. GPS was originally designed by the Department of Defense, who still maintains control (along with the Air Force) of the system.

Genealogists can use GPS to mark the exact location of family homesteads, "lost" cemeteries, or any site relevant to their family tree search. Many GPS units are capable of downloading coordinates to topographic or mapping software, so you can accurately pinpoint your location on a map for future use.

Cemetery Records Online
<http://interment.net>

Cemetery Records Online started as a single Web page in 1997 and has grown to close to three million records from more than five thousand cemeteries worldwide. You can use this site by browsing cemeteries by locale or performing a surname search of the entire site. You can also browse by U.S. state to the county level or internationally by country.

Volunteers provide the transcripts, so what you'll find is dependent on what was transcribed. Some volunteers will include burial records, a cemetery history, and photos. Others will provide only the basic name-date facts. The site also has records from some national cemeteries, such as the 71,608 records from Fort Rosecrans in San Diego, California.

When you search by surname, the results page will display the number of cemeteries with burials by that surname along with a link to the transcription page. (See figure 7-1 on page 118.)

Cemetery Junction
<www.daddezio.com/cemetery>

Trying to locate a cemetery? This site contains links to more than forty-

Figure 7-1
Search Interment.net to find the burial site of your ancestor. *Steve Johnson*

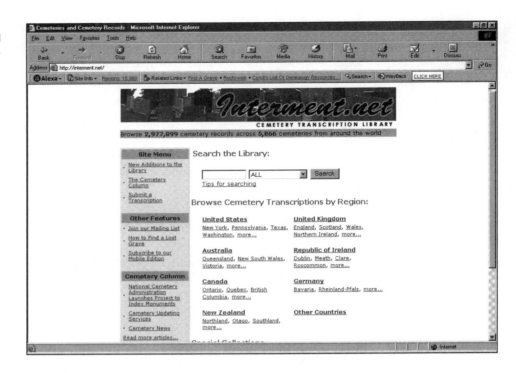

five thousand cemeteries in the United States, Australia, and Canada. Sites are alphabetized by location. Some links go to sites with cemetery histories, others link to transcripts of burial records. Of particular interest to those of us with rural ancestors are records from twenty-one thousand family cemeteries.

I know at least one instance of my ancestors being buried in a small cemetery on the family farm. Frequently these burial grounds have been plowed under or overrun with weeds, so being able to access these records is a bonus. (Few of these small family cemeteries are online, but many have been transcribed by local Daughters of the American Revolution chapters and are available on microfilm through the Family History Library in Salt Lake City, Utah.) I ran a quick search on Hendrickson and found mention of four cemeteries in Bell County, Kentucky. Since I know part of my family came from Kentucky, just finding this Bell County mention is a clue for me.

The Tombstone Transcription Project
<www.rootsweb.com/~cemetery>

This is one of the USGenWeb transcription projects. Volunteers sign up to transcribe various cemeteries' headstones, then upload the results to this site. U.S. cemeteries are organized by state and foreign cemeteries by country. There are even a few transcripts from military cemeteries. From the home page, click View the Registry, then click on your state of interest, then the county. You'll find a list of cemeteries that have been transcribed.

GeneaSearch Cemetery Records Online
<www.geneasearch.com/cemeteries.htm>

This site links to more than thirty cemetery Web sites, including specific cemeteries (with transcripts) and listings of cemeteries by locale. Click on GeneaSearch Cemetery Index at the bottom of the page. A new page will pop up with links to online transcriptions for the United States and worldwide.

Locating An Old Cemetery

<http://mapping.usgs.gov/www/gnis/gnisform.simple.html>

What if your ancestor was buried in a cemetery that is no longer displayed on a map? Use the United States Geological Survey's Geographic Names Information System (GNIS) to pin it down. In the Feature Type Box, type cemetery, then the name of the cemetery in Feature Name. Because this database contains historical names, it's possible to locate a historical cemetery.

OTHER CEMETERY-RELATED SITES

African-American Cemeteries Online
<www.prairiebluff.com/aacemetery>

Cemeteries from the U.S. Civil War Center
<www.cwc.lsu.edu/cwc/links/hist.htm#Cemeteries>

Cemetery Iconography
<www.ancestry.com/library/view/columns/george/868.asp>

Cemetery Links
<www.totentanz.de/cemetery.htm

Cyndi's List Cemeteries and Funeral Homes
<www.CyndisList.com/cemetery.htm>

Past Endeavours
<http://members.attcanada.ca/~catworld/PastEndeavours.html>

Tombstone Meanings
<http://homepages.rootsweb.com/~maggieoh/tomb.html>

Yahoo's Cemetery Listings
<http://dir.yahoo.com/Society_and_Culture/Death_and_Dying/Cemeteries/>

Photos From Afar

Want a photograph of your ancestor's tombstone, but can't make the trip across country to get it? Fortunately, there are people all over the United States (and some in other countries) who have volunteered to shoot photos at local cemeteries. Here are some Web sites where you'll find people who'll help:

Cemetery Photos
<www.rootsweb.com/~cemphoto>

The Cemetery Photos project grew out of amateur genealogist Paula Easton's quest to find someone to photograph her ancestors' tombstones, that were thousands of miles away. The project, which began as a mailing list in May 1999, was so popular that within three days the list's membership grew to 850. You can search the site for a volunteer photographer who lives near the cemetery in question or post a query to the site's bulletin board. Cemetery Photos also contains tombstone photographs that have been uploaded.

Per the regulations of this project, volunteers may only charge you for the cost of film, developing, postage, and any copy costs. No fees may be charged for mileage, time, gasoline, or wear and tear to a camera. In fact, many volunteers charge nothing for their services. If you are interested in taking cemetery photos in your location, the site provides valuable tips on getting good tombstone shots.

HeadstoneHunter
<www.headstonehunter.com>

This free service helps link up photo requests with volunteer photographers. If you want to request a photo, just fill out a request form and it will be posted online. Then you'll need to wait until a volunteer reads it and offers assistance. A second option is to search the database of the more than twenty-five hundred volunteers (categorized by locale), and e-mail a volunteer in the area of the cemetery you're searching, requesting assistance. This option is often the quickest way to get your photo.

Virtual Cemetery
<www.genealogy.com/vcem_welcome.html>

The Virtual Cemetery Project is a collection of digitized tombstone photographs and a searchable archive of headstone transcriptions. Although you can't request photos from this site, you may be lucky enough to find a headstone photo already uploaded to the site. You can search the database by surname only, or add a first name, date of birth or death, and location. If someone has taken a photo of the headstone you're searching for, you can see the photo, read the inscription, and correspond with the person who contributed the photo. You can right-click on the image and save it to your hard drive as well (but you should ask the uploader's permission first).

Important

Although cemetery research on the Internet is not a replacement for on-site work, it is a preliminary step in your research. Once you've found a burial site, go to one of the tombstone photo sites and place a request. When you find a volunteer, ask her to photograph not only your ancestor's tombstone, but several stones around it, just in case other family members are buried nearby. You'll be surprised at how willing most volunteers are to help you; after all, they're searching for photos of their family, too, and you may be just the one to help.

CENSUS

If you're trying to discover the place of birth of one of your ancestors, do you know the date of the first census to contain this information? Or, do you know the first census denoting if an individual's mother or father were foreign-born? If not, go to <http://amberskyline.com/treasuremaps/uscensus .html> to see which questions were asked on every census from 1790 to 1920.

Because the census includes vital information (name, age, place of birth), it is a major tool for American genealogists. The census is frequently used to advance research from one generation to the next. **The census is also a great tool for tracking a family's movement.** For example, if the parents were both born in Pennsylvania and the first three children were born in Pennsylvania, Ohio, and Indiana, you know where you need to be researching.

The federal census was first taken in 1790 and has continued to be taken every ten years, although the majority of the 1890 census no longer exists. Early reports listed only the name of the head of household and the number of people living there, broken down by gender, age, free, and slave. Starting in 1850, however, the census taker (enumerator) wrote down the name of every free person living in the household (slaves were enumerated on a separate schedule, but not by name). Census reports are held as confidential

Research Tip

HOW TO OBTAIN CENSUS RECORDS

If you can't locate an online transcribed copy of a census, you'll have to obtain the record through another source. Your choices include subscribing to a commercial service, asking an online genealogist to do a look-up, viewing the microfilm at a Family History Center, ordering a copy of the microfilm from the National Archives, or asking the interlibrary loan division of your local library if it participates in the National Archives microfilm rental program.

For detailed information on using *The 1790–1890 Federal Population Censuses: Catalog of National Archives Microfilm,* and ordering microfilms from the National Archives, go to <www.archives.gov/research_room/genealogy/census/using_c ensus_microfilm_catalogs.html>. Lookup-sites include

Genealogical CDs
<http://loricase.com/CDs/cdlist.html>

GenSwap
<www.genswap.com/free.html>

GeneaSearch
<www.geneasearch.com/research.htm>

Locate a Family History Center near you using this interactive search form <www .familysearch.org/Eng/Library/FHC/frameset_fhc.asp?PAGE= library_fhc_find.asp>.

for a period of seventy-two years in order to protect privacy. The long-awaited 1930 census was released on 1 April 2002. To learn more about this census, what it contains and how to search it, go to <http://1930census.archives.gov>

Currently, online commercial services such as the ones below are the only places you can find the majority of the federal census records. There are ongoing volunteer projects that are transcribing and posting the census on the Web. They are

Ancestral Findings
<www.ancestralfindings.com>

Free look-ups in a variety of subscription and CD-ROM databases, including digitized census record databases.

Census Finder
<www.censusfinder.com>

Directory of census links to help you locate free census records online.

Census Links
<http://censuslinks.com>

Links to digitized census record sites and census indexes in the United States and beyond.

Census Online
<www.census-online.com>

Census CDs for sale, links to online census transcriptions, and tools for census research.

Historical United States Census Data Browser
<http://fisher.lib.virginia.edu/census>

Census data that describe the population and economy of U.S. states and counties from 1790 to 1960.

USGenWeb Census Project
<www.rootsweb.com/~census>

All-volunteer project to transcribe census records and make them available free to online researchers.

IMMIGRATION

From the first exploration to the last great flood of twentieth century immigration, our ancestors came by ship. They paced the decks of the *Snow Squirrel*, *Friendship*, *Two Brothers*, and *Adeline*, their eyes on a new horizon. We know they came, but often our knowledge ends on American shores. As genealogists, finding when and where they landed in the New World is often *our* first step in the long journey back home.

In the past, chronicling our family's arrival in America has been a task confined to microfilm, CD-ROMs, or library searches. **But now, some ship passenger lists are finding their way onto the Internet.** Try these five sites in your search:

Immigrant Ships Transcribers Guild

<http://istg.rootsweb.com>

The Immigrant Ships Transcribers Guild, founded in 1998, is a volunteer organization that transcribes and uploads ships' passenger lists to the Internet. To date, the ISTG has transcribed lists for more than three thousand ships and 1.5 million passengers.

To find out if your ancestor is in an ISTG database, just use the on-site search engine. In seconds, the engine will comb all five volumes posted online and return a list of results. The site is updated once monthly, so be sure to check back frequently. Also, researchers are encouraged to check for every possible surname spelling; transcribers may have had to make a spelling judgment when transcribing a poor quality record.

If your family arrived in the early twentieth century, you may hit the jackpot. In many instances, the name and address of the nearest living relative in the old country is given, along with the name and address of the person the immigrant is joining in the United States. Although these names are not those of official passengers, they are included in the database.

While on this site, be sure to check out the links from the home page to the Bremen and 1903 projects. The Bremen Project is a joint effort of the ISTG and the Die Maus Genealogical Society of Bremen, Germany, to transcribe ship manifests departing from Bremen and Bremerhaven, Germany, in the nineteenth and twentieth centuries. The 1903 Project links to records, transcribed by another group, of 1903 arrivals in New York.

The ISTG Web site also includes The Compass, a separate section with links to other ship-related sites, including basic immigration and naturalization information, maritime resources, passenger ships, ship types and descriptions, historic maps and charts, ship captains, and ship images.

If you'd rather browse the site, you can search by dates of sailing (seventeenth, eighteenth, nineteenth, and twentieth centuries), ship names, port of departure and arrival, captain names, and surnames. If you're unsure of your ancestor's date of arrival or country of origin, try searching for your surname alone and see what pops up.

The Olive Tree Genealogy

<http://olivetreegenealogy.com/ships/index.shtml>

This searchable site includes passenger lists as well as information on the captain, the ship, and miscellaneous data about passengers. Lists range from the 1492 voyage of the *Santa Maria*, *Niña* and *Pinta*, to the *S.S. Groote Beer* crossing of 1957. Links are included to passenger lists both on and off this Web site. The information you'll find is always dependent on what's on the original list. For example, you may find that David Usilie, a farmer from Calais, was traveling with his wife and nursing child, or that the passenger list of *The Love* included Wiggert Reinders, a farmer from Ter Gouw, Maritje Jansen, a maiden, and Cornelis Davitsen Schaets, a wheelwright.

Digitalarkivet
<http://digitalarkivet.no>

Did your great-uncle Olaf travel to the United States from Norway? If so, you may find him on this Norwegian site. This free, searchable site has databases of censuses, tax lists, military rolls, church registers, emigrants, probate registers, fire assessment registers, and more.

American Plantations and Colonies
<http://englishamerica.home.att.net/>

This site contains more than eight hundred passenger lists and the names of more than twenty-five thousand passengers. Indexed alphabetically by ship name, many of the entries include dates and ports. Nearly every ship that sailed to the American plantations is on this Web site. Some also include lists of known passengers and other information. Ships names are included, even if passenger information is not known. If a passenger list is given, it frequently includes the source of the information. The site also includes links to other Web pages with passenger lists.

One caution: The information on this site isn't from original passenger lists; it's from published classics, such as *Cavaliers and Pioneers*, *Of Plimoth Plantation*, *Planters of the Commonwealth*, etc.

National Archives of Canada
<www.archives.ca/02/020118_e.html>

The National Archives of Canada holds immigration records from 1865 to 1935, including the names of immigrants on passenger lists. Most entries are arranged by date and port of arrival and include the names of all passengers. They also include references to people who landed at American ports and indicated that they were proceeding directly to Canada. This searchable database contains more than 500,000 records. The search screen contains five search fields: Surname, Given Name, Year of Arrival, Port of Arrival, and Ship. The results screen will give the name of the passenger, age, sex, nationality, date of arrival, port of arrival, and the name of the ship.

TheShipsList
<www.theshipslist.com>

TheShipsList is a link site with a twist. In addition to passenger list links, it contains tutorials, photos of ports of the world and ships, period narratives, nineteenth-century magazine articles, and information about shipping lines.

Not sure which port Great-great-grandpa Harold sailed from? Click on Pictures of Maps to see the major European ports of the 1800s. Wonder what the 1870 fare was from Hamburg to New York? Check out the Trivia section for an answer that may surprise you. If your immigration research

SHIPS AND PASSENGER LISTS ON THE INTERNET

Emigration/Ship Lists and Resources
<www.geocities.com/Heartland/5978/Emigration.html>
Portal site with more than 120 ships links.

GenSwap Passenger Lists and Immigration Records
<www.genswap.com/immigrate.html>
Links to over seventy-five passenger list sites.

Immigrant Ships Descriptions
<www.fortunecity.com/littleitaly/amalfi/13/ships.htm>
Description of ships, owners, and voyages.

Immigrants to Canada And Ships They Came On
<www.dcs.uwaterloo.ca/~marj/genealogy/thevoyage.html>
Link list to voyage accounts, ships sailing to Canada, and ports of arrival and departure.

Immigration and Ships Passenger Lists Research Guide
<http://home.att.net/~arnielang/shipgide.html>
Excellent research guide from the Genealogical Society of Bergen County, N.J.

Magellan—The Ships Encyclopedia
<http://208.249.158.172/magellan>
Encyclopedic entries, some with photos.

On The Trail of Our Ancestors
<www.ristenbatt.com/genealogy/shipind.htm>
Includes seventeenth- and eighteenth-century passenger lists to Pennsylvania and New Jersey.

Passenger Lists, Ships, Ship Museums
<www-personal.umich.edu/~cgaunt/pass.html#SHIPS>
Portal site to researching passenger lists.

What Passenger Lists Are Online?
<http://home.att.net/~wee-monster/onlinelists.html>
A link list to online passenger lists.

has turned up the puzzling phrase "Declaration of Intent," you'll find a complete explanation under Q&A.

This site also maintains its own mailing list to help you find information on the vessel that brought your ancestor to a new land. This is an international list and useful to subscribers regardless of what country their ancestors settled in. Another feature of this site is its query board. Click on The-ShipsList Searchable Archives Database to leave a message about your ancestor. You can also search the message board or browse the archives.

ELLIS ISLAND, WITHOUT TEARS

By Sharon DeBartolo Carmack, originally published in *Family Tree Magazine* (December 2002): 24-31.

Sharon DeBartolo Carmack is a Certified Genealogist who served on the Statue of Liberty–Ellis Island Foundation's History Advisory Committee for the American Family Immigration History Center. She is the author of *A Genealogist's Guide to Discovering Your Immigrant and Ethnic Ancestors* (Cincinnati: Betterway Books, 2000).

Some seventeen million immigrants passed through Ellis Island between 1892 and 1924, but those "huddled masses yearning to breathe free" are far outnumbered by their millions of ancestors logging on to the Ellis Island Web site to look for them. Since the site <www.ellisisland.org> launched in 2001, it's recorded more than 2.5 *billion* hits and sixty thousand users visit every day.

For some researchers, finding their immigrant ancestors in Ellis Island's massive database of passenger arrival lists proves to be a snap. But for others, Ellis Island's sobriquet of "Island of Hope, Island of Tears" takes on new meaning. You know your ancestors are in that giant computer file somewhere—but *where?* And why can't you find them? Or you do find them—you think—but the records don't show what you thought they would. You're tired, you're poor, and you're yearning for some answers.

Don't give up! Ellis Island's records can still open a golden door into your past— if you know some essential strategies for turning those tears into hope. First, it helps to understand how passenger records were created, how immigrants were processed at Ellis Island, and how the records were preserved, which in turn will help you figure out why you might be having trouble finding your ancestors.

THE NAME'S THE SAME

Ellis Island officially opened its doors as an immigration receiving station on 1 January 1892, and the arrival records created from about 1891 to the 1950s are referred to as immigration passenger lists. These lists were printed in the United States, but completed at the port of departure, and then filed in America after the ship docked. The information provided in immigration passenger lists varied over the decades. As the influx of immigrants became greater, more details were recorded. For example, in 1893, passenger lists contained twenty-one columns of information; in 1906, twenty-eight; in 1907, twenty-nine; and in 1917, thirty-three. All of these details are valuable to your research, but in particular, items such as last residence, final destination in the United States, relative's name and address (if the passenger was going to join a relative), personal description, place of birth, and name and address of closest living relative in the native country will give you information you may not find anywhere else.

When immigrants arrived on Ellis Island, they went through a number of screening tests, many of which were medical examinations. But at one point, each immigrant—whether traveling alone or with a family—had an "interview" with a registry clerk. These clerks, who spoke several different languages, questioned arrivals in the immigrant's native tongue, asking them the same questions from the passenger list that the immigrants answered when they left their homeland. Armed with the passenger list that was compiled at the port of departure, clerks merely compared the answers the immigrants told them. If an immigrant's answers produced any discrepancies, the clerk could detain the person. But the clerk had instructions not to change any of the information on the passenger list, unless the inspection revealed the original information contained an error.

That means, despite popular belief, names were not changed on Ellis Island. As Immigration and Naturalization Service historian Marian L. Smith's article "American Names/Declaring Independence" <www.ins.usdoj.gov/graphics/ab outins/history/articles/nameessay.html> explains, "the Ellis-Island-name-change-story . . . is as American as apple pie," but the facts of immigrant processing just didn't allow for names to be changed on Ellis Island.

Important

So, in order to find your ancestors on passenger lists, you need to know your ancestor's *original* name back in his or her ancestral homeland, which may not be the name your ancestor later adopted in America. The name your ancestor gave when he or she purchased the ticket to America is the name that you'll find on the list. Of course, just as with any document, the name could have been accidentally misspelled or appear to be spelled a different way because of the clerk's handwriting—an *a* looks like an *o* or an *e*, for example.

PATHS TO PASSENGER LISTS

After the original passenger lists for the Port of New York during the Ellis Island years were microfilmed, they were destroyed. **You can get prints of microfilmed passenger lists in three ways:**

Microfilm Source

1. **By mail from the National Archives** for a fee, using NATF Form 81. You can request forms by e-mail at inquire@nara.gov or by writing National Archives and Records Administration, Attn: NWCTB, 700 Pennsylvania Ave. NW, Washington, DC 20408. (You may also find copies of National Archives request forms at its regional records services facilities—see <www.arc hives.gov> for a complete list.)

    The National Archives will not do research for you, however. The minimum information required for a search of the index is the full name of the person, the port of arrival, and the month and year of arrival. Additional facts, such as the passenger's age and names of accompanying passengers, are also helpful. If the list isn't indexed, NARA needs more specific information, such as the exact date of arrival and the name of the ship, to look up your immigrant.

continued

2. **By visiting a repository and searching the microfilmed lists yourself.** Passenger lists on microfilm are available for researchers not just at the National Archives in Washington, DC, but also through the Family History Library (FHL) or its local Family History Centers (FHCs) <www.familysearch.org>. A number of public libraries with large genealogy collections also have some of these microfilms. Or check with a National Archives regional records services facility that would have films for its corresponding port, such as NARA's Northeast Region in New York City for the Port of New York passenger arrival lists.

3. **By finding the list on the Ellis Island database** at <www.ellisisland.org> and ordering a print of the list from the American Family Immigration History Center. You can also view an image of the passenger list right on your computer screen.

DATABASE SEARCH STRATEGIES

The Ellis Island database includes the digitized passenger lists of more than twenty-two million passengers and crew members who entered through the Port of New York between 1892 and 1924—the peak years of immigrant arrival. Among them are records of seventeen million immigrants. Supposedly, finding your immigrant ancestor online is as easy as typing in a name. But for many of us, it's a bit trickier than that. To demonstrate, let's look for someone I know is on an Ellis Island passenger list.

In the days before the database, I found Angelina (Vallarelli) Ebetino the old-fashioned way, using microfilmed indexes and lists. Angelina arrived on the *Verona*, which left the Port of Naples on 5 February 1910, and arrived at the Port of New York on 18 February 1910. In the new Ellis Island database, I typed in the name Angelina Ebetino. The results: "No records in the archive match the name Angelina Ebetino." According to the site, my choices are to

1. Widen the search by using the last name with only a first initial. I tried that and still no matches for an A. Ebetino.

2. Widen your search by using only the last name. This found only one record, and it was for Salvatore Ebetino, Angelina's husband. He came in 1906, but Angelina and their children came in 1910.

3. Search on alternate spellings of the last name. There were six alternate spellings, and still no Angelina.

I guess it's not so easy, is it? That shouldn't be too surprising, and it's not the fault of the zillions of volunteers and programmers who built this amazing database. After all, we're talking about *millions* of *handwritten* records here.

So let's take a deep breath and stew on this a minute. Obviously, I'm doing something wrong. I *know* she's there. But remember, I said that you need to know the original name the immigrant went by in the old country. One of the problems is I haven't been searching under the original name Angelina used in Italy. Back in Italy, as in some other Catholic countries such as France, women were recorded in all legal documents by their maiden names, not their married names. Let's try Angelina *Vallarelli*. Nope. Still didn't get a match. What if I broaden the search to just A. Vallarelli? Ah-ha! There she is, but recorded as *Angela* Vallarelli. (Research in Italian records revealed that this was in fact her original name.)

WHEN YOU'RE STUMPED

Clearly, you sometimes need to get creative when searching for an ancestor in the Ellis Island database. But what do you do if you still can't find your ancestor? **Here are five key questions to ask when you're stumped:**

Notes

1. **Did your ancestor actually come through Ellis Island?** Because Ellis Island was the leading immigrant receiving station of its day, many people think their ancestors came through the Port of New York, when they might have come through one of the other major U.S. ports or Canada. Going back to Angela Vallarelli, she had six siblings who all immigrated to America, presumably through Ellis Island. I could find all but one. After wearing down my teeth from grinding them each time I'd get a negative search result on the Ellis Island database, I began to wonder if he might not have come through another port. Sure enough, he came through the Port of Boston, not New York.

2. **Did your ancestor arrive during the right time span?** Remember that the database covers only 1892 to 1924—after the largest influx from Germany, Scandinavia, Great Britain, and Ireland. If your ancestor came before Ellis Island opened, you'll need to search the National Archives microfilms.

3. **Are you checking for immigrant women under their maiden names?** While this custom was more prevalent in Catholic countries, it never hurts to try this strategy even if your ancestor wasn't Catholic. Regardless of whether the woman was traveling alone, with her spouse or with her children, she might be recorded on the list by her maiden name. Don't know what her maiden name was? If she did travel with her children, they should be recorded under their father's surname. So look for the kids.

4. **What age were they when they arrived?** To avoid latching on to the wrong immigrant in the database—another person with the same name or initials, for example—you'll need to know your ancestor's approximate age when she came to America. It's also helpful to know the town of origin. Any other identifying information can help find the right immigrant.

5. **Have you checked for transcription-related spelling variations?** Keep in mind that you're at the mercy of the transcriber who looked at the microfilmed copy of the passenger list and tried to interpret the name to enter it into the database. A transcriber unfamiliar with the German clerk's script

continued

may convolute a name or place name you'd find easy to read because you've looked at records with that type of script before. Take, for example, Angelina Vallarelli from Terlizzi, Italy: The transcriber had problems reading *Terlizzi* because the clerk's *T* looked like a *C*. So the transcriber wrote the place of residence as "Cerlizzi." If that happened to your ancestor's name, you won't have a prayer of finding your ancestor on the database. But all is not lost— you can still do it the old-fashioned way.

MICROFILM VS. COMPUTERIZED IMAGES

Anyone who's used both microfilm and Web sites knows it's far faster to crank through a roll of microfilm than it is to download computer images of passenger lists, one page at a time. Sometimes the lists span two pages, so it takes several minutes to view your ancestor's full list. And some of the pages, for whatever reason, were filmed out of order! So you might land on the second page of information, then you need to figure out whether to click on Next Page or Previous Page. The images of pages that don't include passenger information were also digitized, making it time consuming to view the whole ship's list.

Microfilm also makes it easier to see things in context. Passengers traveling in first and second class were recorded in a separate section of the same list for that ship. So on microfilm you'll find a page or two for the first class passengers first, then a few pages for the second or saloon class, then multiple pages for the steerage or third class.

Microfilm Source

Perhaps the biggest disadvantage I've found in using the computerized images is that it takes forever to get to the end of that ship's list. Why would you need to see the end of the ship's list? That's where some more good stuff is hiding.

THE END OF THE LIST

Beginning about 1903, the passenger arrival lists began to include a supplemental section for detainees. Many immigrants were detained for short periods of time at the port of arrival until relatives came to claim them; this was particularly true of unescorted women arrivals, whether or not children accompanied them.

Detainee lists, or Records of Detained Aliens, that have survived were microfilmed with their corresponding passenger lists at the end of the lists of arrivals. They contain each detainee's name, the cause for detention and the date and time of discharge. The number of meals the detainee was fed during detention was also recorded. If the emigré was deported before being released from the immigrant receiving station, these records stated the reason and the deportation date. The abbreviation LPC meant "likely public charge" (that is, likely to wind up on the public dole), and LCD signified "loathsome contagious disease," two main causes for deportation.

Check subsequent passenger lists and indexes for aliens who were deported; they might have entered the country later when they were able to pass inspection. Another common way for aliens to re-immigrate was to save enough money and re-enter as a first- or second-class passenger, who underwent less stringent exams aboard ship.

Following the Record of Detained Aliens will be a page or pages of the Record of Aliens Held for Special Inquiry. This form noted the cause of the detention or rejection, along with actions taken by the Board of Special Inquiry, the date of hearings and the number of meals eaten during detention. For deportees, you'll find the date and the name of the vessel and port from which they returned to their native land. If a rejected immigrant was waiting for someone, the form will also include the name and address of the American contact.

Don't get me wrong—the Ellis Island database is a good starting place and perhaps the greatest thing to come along since reduced-fat cookies. For those who hit the nail on the head, instantly finding their forebears, the database is a dream come true. But if you're having problems tracking down your Ellis Island immigrants, the Island of Hope and Tears can be just as challenging for you as it was for your ancestors. Not to worry. You still have ways to trace your Ellis Island ancestors. And the worst of 'em is cranking a roll of microfilm.

For more, see Searching the Ellis Island Database in One Step <www.avotaynu .com/ellis.html>: Stephen P. Morse's handy page lets you skip the step-by-step walk-through of the Ellis Island site and dig right into the database from one super-search page.

For More Info

LAND RECORDS

You'll find most of your ancestors' land records in a county courthouse and not online. Or, they may have been microfilmed by the Family History Library in Salt Lake City, Utah. To learn how to obtain land records, consult Patricia Law Hatcher's *Locating Your Roots: Discover Your Ancestors Using Land Records* (Cincinnati: Betterway Books, 2003).

See Also

LAND RECORDS

On 5 August 1834, the federal government transferred title of eighty acres of public land to Aaron Hendrickson. Aaron's acres were located in Shelby County, Indiana, just southeast of the land owned by his brother, William. I found a record of the transfer at the Bureau of Land Management's (BLM) Land Patent site <www.glorecords.blm.gov>. The site serves as a repository for over two million General Land Office (GLO) title records for Eastern public land states issued between 1820 and 1908. The free, searchable database also contains Western patents issued after 30 June 1908, with more to come.

Unlike some online databases, the GLO records are far more than an index. They contain the name of the person the land was transferred to (patentee), the legal land description, the land office that had jurisdiction over the title transfer, and the congressional act or treaty under whose authority the land was transferred. If that's not enough to send you running to your computer, this will: The site also contains scanned images of the original patent.

Dividing the Land

Public lands were surveyed using a rectangular survey system, unlike the metes and bounds system (see Glossary) of the original thirteen states. Instead of describing ownership by "ten paces from the black oak tree," the rectangular survey system divided each township of thirty-six square miles into thirty-six sections of one square mile each. The section was then divided into quarters or halves, which were named by their location within the section. For example, Aaron's land was the east one-half of the southwest quarter (E½ SW¼) of Section 35.

Figure 7-2
Within each township there are 36 sections, each one mile square. The sections are numbered from 1 to 36.

6	5	4	3	2	1
7	8	9	10	11	12
18	17	16	15	14	13
19	20	21	22	23	24
30	29	28	27	26	25
31	32	33	34	35	36

Each section contained 640 acres, which means each quarter of it contained 160 acres. Aaron owned half of a quarter, which was 80 acres. If you don't want to do the math, click on the scanned image of the patent and it will tell you how many acres your ancestor owned. If you're interested in learning more about the terminology of the land patent system, there's a dandy glossary at <www.glorecords.blm.gov/visitors/glossary.asp>.

Step By Step

How to Search the Database

From the BLM home page, click on Search Land Patents. You'll be asked to enter your zip code (for demographic tracking purposes).

Your first step will be to do a basic search by clicking the Basic tab, choosing a state, and at least the last name of your ancestor. The basic search will return all instances of your surname in the state, regardless of county. From the search results screen you can view and print a copy of the document (be sure to follow the directions on how to improve the quality of your print-out).

If you click on the person's name, the next screen will show when and where the title was transferred, the size of the property, the file numbers, a legal description of the land, as well as information on how to obtain a certified copy of the document.

Next, you can try a standard search by clicking on the Standard tab. Once the standard search screen appears, select a state, then fill in at least one of the search fields, such as the patentee's first and last names. If you're certain of the county your ancestor lived in, select it from a pull-down list, otherwise let the system search statewide. If you don't find your ancestors in this database, don't despair. Most of your ancestors' land was recorded in a county courthouse.

If you don't get the results you expected, read the Search Tips or broaden your search criteria by using wildcards in the name. The wildcards used on this site differ from the standard asterisk (*) on other sites, but there's a simple tutorial on their use at <www.glorecords.blm.gov/FAQ.asp#5>.

When searching for Aaron's records, I went to the Indiana screen and entered Hendrickson and chose Shelby County. Within a few seconds I had a list of twelve Hendrickson land patents. After using wildcards, I found another handful. Be liberal with using wildcards and alternative spellings.

Once your search returns a patent of interest, click on the Details button. The next screen shows the general patent description. The Legal Land Description tab gives an exact description for the land, including the Section, Range, Township, and Meridian (see Glossary). In the Land Patent Details section, look for the Authority section. While many are Sale-Cash Entry, if the authority lists anything else, you should order the land entry file using NATF Form 84 from the National Archives. Homestead and bounty authorities often have valuable information tucked away in the entry file.

The Document Image tab takes you to the scanned images of the patent. To print the image, choose a TIFF or Adobe Acrobat (PDF) format. If you're unsure which format will work best for you, check out the detailed chart at <www.glorecords.blm.gov/help/image_formats.asp>. The graphic may show the county and/or state from which your ancestor came. For two dollars, you can order a certified copy from the BLM, with your choice of plain or parchment paper.

Note: If you're looking for land records from the original thirteen states or the seven state-land states (Maine, Vermont, Kentucky, Tennessee, West Virginia, Texas, and Hawaii), you won't find them on this Web site. The BLM records are only for public lands. However, this site does include a resource list for those states <www.glorecords.blm.gov/Visitors/stateresearch.asp>. Also, credit sales in public lands prior to 1820 are not included.

Bonus: Advanced BLM Land Exploration

Now that you've found your ancestor's land patent, the search is over, right?

Wrong. Now the real fun begins. (See figure 7-3 on page 134.)

If you know who owned land around your ancestor, you're going to have more clues about your own family than you'll know what to do with. Fortunately, you can use the search form to discover who owned the surrounding property and where it was located.

Research Tip

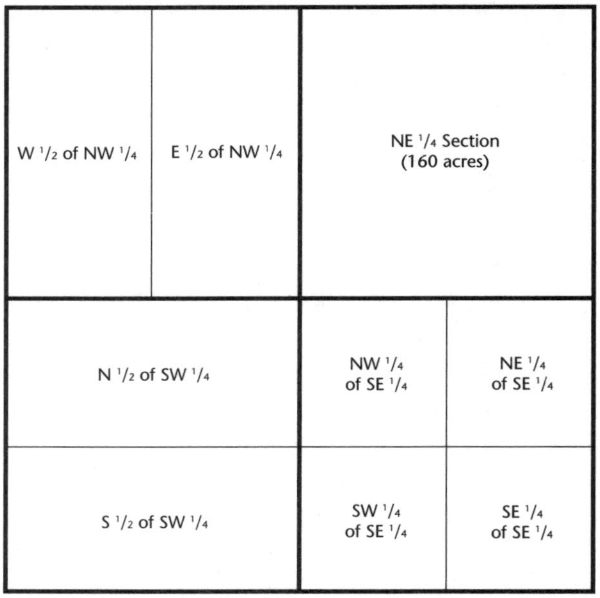

Figure 7-3
Each section contains 640 acres. Within each section, divisions are called half and quarter sections.

W ¹/₂ of NW ¹/₄	E ¹/₂ of NW ¹/₄	NE ¹/₄ Section (160 acres)
N ¹/₂ of SW ¹/₄		NW ¹/₄ of SE ¹/₄	NE ¹/₄ of SE ¹/₄
S ¹/₂ of SW ¹/₄		SW ¹/₄ of SE ¹/₄	SE ¹/₄ of SE ¹/₄

Go back to the Legal Land Description screen and write down the aliquot part (that's the E½ SW¼ notation), the Section, Township, Range, and Meridian of your ancestor's land. Next, return to the search form and hit the Clear button. Choose the county, but instead of filling in names, go to the

OTHER LAND RECORDS DATABASES

Arkansas Land Records Interactive Search
<http://searches.rootsweb.com/cgi-bin/arkland/arkland.pl>

Illinois Public Domain Land Tract Sales
<www.sos.state.il.us/departments/archives/data_lan.html>

Indiana Land Records
<www.state.in.us/icpr/webfile/land/land_off.html>

Land Office Patents and Grants, Library of Virginia
<http://image.vtls.com/collections/LO.html>

Louisiana Land Records Interactive Search
<http://searches.rootsweb.com/cgi-bin/laland/laland.pl>

North Dakota Land Records
<http://pixel.cs.vt.edu/library/land/nodak/>

South Dakota Land Database
<www.rootsweb.com/~usgenweb/sd/land/sdland.htm>

Wisconsin Land Records Interactive Search
<http://searches.rootsweb.com/cgi-bin/wisconsin/wisconsin.pl>

bottom of the form and fill in the Section, Township, Range, and Meridian fields. One click and you'll get the names and land descriptions of everyone who owned land in that Section. Pretty nifty, huh? But don't stop there because it gets even better.

Becoming a Map Maker

Get a blank piece of paper and draw a square, then divide the square into quarters. Label the top right NE, the top left NW, the bottom right SE, and the bottom left SW. Click on the land description of each person who owned land in that particular section, then divide each of the quarters you drew according to the legal land description. You now have an accurate section map.

N W		N E	
Steven Smith	John Adams	John Adams	
Jack Clark	Benjamin Clark	Charles Adams	
S W			SE
		Charles Adams	Aaron Hart
		Charles Adams / Thomas Hart / John Carter	Thomas Hart

Figure 7-4
Draw a simple square divided into quarters, then begin filling in names of property owners.

When you fill in your section map, be sure to write down the names of *all* the land owners. You never know what name is going to turn up carved in the family tree. In my search for Aaron, I found that in Section 35, in addition to Aaron's eighty acres, there were five other land patents belonging to William Hendrickson, John Moore, and Thomas Moore. Since I knew that Aaron's daughter-in-law's maiden name was Moore, this got my attention. I decided to explore the neighborhood. I returned to the search form and changed the section number from 35 to 34 (the section immediately west). Guess what? There were three more patents for Hendrickson and Moore. And in Section 27 (the section just north of Section 34), every single patent belonged to someone related to Aaron either by blood or marriage.

Two hours after I began my search, I had plotted the ownership of nine sections. In all, there were forty-three separate land patents belonging to four different branches of my family. Without plotting the surrounding sections, I would never have realized the number of extended family members living in the area. Why? Because I wouldn't have entered surnames in the search form for people like the husband of Aaron's daughter-in-law's

Tip

Looking for a great range map? It's here <www.root sweb.com/~ilmaga/ landmaps/ range_map.html>.

aunt. But he was there, too. As they say, a picture is worth a thousand words, and the picture that emerged from my maps depicted how my family intertwined through both time and space.

MARRIAGE RECORDS

Did you know that several states have posted searchable marriage databases to the Web? One state, Illinois, posted their Statewide Marriage Index, 1763–1900 <www.library.sos.state.il.us/departments/archives/marriage.html> and to date, records for more than one million marriages have been entered into the database.

The sources for the index include original county clerks' marriage records (marriage registers and licenses), and publications of genealogical societies and private individuals. The index includes the names of the bride and groom, the date of the marriage (or issuance of the license), the name of the county as well as a citation of the original record, when available.

Data input is performed by state archives staff and volunteers. Although the goal is to include all marriage records up until 1900, some volunteers have transcribed records up to 1920. Follow the link from the Index home page for information on obtaining copies of the original marriage records.

Performing a search is as simple as entering a surname and choosing a statewide or specific county search. For example, a statewide search for brides with the surname Dimmitt returned the entries below.

Figure 7-8
It's possible to find your ancestors' marriage record in a state index, like this one posted by the state of Illinois.
Illinois State Archives

Illinois Statewide Marriage Index 1763 - 1900

Click here for information about how to obtain copies of original marriage records.

GROOM	BRIDE	CNTY	DATE	VOL/PAGE	LIC
VONELSNER, HUGO	DIMMITT, AMANDA CATHARINE	MC LEAN	05/09/1855	C/ 192	
DUNLAP, EDWARD J	DIMMITT, BETSEY ANN	FULTON	07/02/1857	00B/0357	00000159
HOBSON, JOSEPH R	DIMMITT, CARINTHA	PIKE	04/04/1879	/	00000420
MCILVAIN, MOSES E	DIMMITT, CARRIE J	MC LEAN	06/01/1868	00E/0461	
RIDLE, IRA	DIMMITT, ELDANA CARRY	FULTON	12/25/1895	00F/0188	00000379
RIDLE, IRA	DIMMITT, ELDORA CARRY	FULTON	12/25/1895	00F/0188	00000379
HOOSIER, HARVEY	DIMMITT, ELSIE	FULTON	12/17/1899	G /36	335
SWAIN, JAMES C	DIMMITT, EMMA	MACON	02/22/1884	/	
MATTHEWS, JOHN C	DIMMITT, HELEN MAY	MC DONOUGH	11/27/1889	/	00003277
WETZEL, THOMAS EDWARD	DIMMITT, JOANNA REBECCA	MC DONOUGH	11/18/1891	/	00000270
WINN, CHARLES G	DIMMITT, LURA E	MORGAN	07/23/1896	D/ 132	6869
BENTLEY, ASHLEY A	DIMMITT, MARY ANN	PIKE	11/18/1855	I/ 221	
SMITH, JAMES A	DIMMITT, MARY C	MC DONOUGH	04/29/1869	/	00003705
SMALLEY, ISAAC	DIMMITT, MARY G	FULTON	11/11/1874	00E/0014	00000266
WALTER, HENRY J	DIMMITT, SUSAN	PEORIA	10/02/1872	4 /111	338

Although none of the brides' names are familiar, do you remember that the volunteers from Calvin Dimmitt's 65th Illinois Regiment came from Boone and McDonough counties? Knowing that, wouldn't the three McDonough County marriages catch your eye? Always be thinking like a detective.

In addition to state-maintained databases, some marriage records posted are those transcribed by individual researchers. For example, Brenda Jordan Raymond transcribed marriage records from Rutherford County, Tennessee <http://ftp.rootsweb.com/pub/usgenweb/tn/rutherford/vitals/rutcotn.txt>, Teresa Lindquist from Anderson County, Kansas, <http://skyways.lib.ks.us/genweb/anderson/library/vital/marriages.htm> and other volunteers are

TYPES OF MARRIAGE RECORDS

By Sharon DeBartolo Carmack

Several different types of marriage documents are generated before a couple says "I do." While all of these won't exist for any one couple, they are worth looking for.

CHURCH RECORDS

- **Banns:** Custom dating back to colonial America. Banns of a couple's intention to marry were posted or read on three consecutive Sundays.

- **Marriage Returns or Registers:** Ministers and justices of the peace sent to the town hall or county courthouse a record of the marriages they performed. They were recorded in books called returns or registers. Unfortunately, some marriages were never recorded beyond what the minister or J.P. kept in their private journals or ledgers.

- **Certificate:** The document given to the couple after the ceremony and may be found among family papers. It may not have all the personal detail that can be found on a license. Copies of certificates may be recorded in the church or with a town or county clerk.

TOWN OR COUNTY RECORDS

- **Intentions:** Similar to church banns, only filed with the county or town-clerk.

- **Bonds:** Common in Southern colonies and states. A bond was posted before the marriage license by the groom and usually the father of the bride or some other close relative. The bond carries a monetary amount to defray costs in the event the marriage did not take place. Usually recorded in the bride's county of residence.

- **Licenses:** These applications to marry usually contain the most genealogical information of all marriage documents, giving personal information on both the bride and the groom, but licenses may not have been required in all states or have survived. They are most common after the Civil War and re-place banns and bonds.

- **Prenuptial Contracts:** Most common in the South, where the bride brought substantial real or personal property to the marriage that was to remain in her family and not become part of her husband's property. "Prenups" are more common prior to a second marriage, where the widow wants to ensure that her property passes to her first husband's heirs. Look in deed books and in other court documents.

continued

- **Marriage Returns or Registers:** Ministers and justices of the peace sent to the town hall or county courthouse a record of the marriages they performed. They were recorded in books called returns or registers. Unfortunately, some marriages were never recorded beyond what the minister or J.P. kept in their private journals or ledgers.

- **Certificates:** The document given to the couple after the ceremony and may be found among family papers. It may not have all the personal detail that can be found on a license. Some copies of certificates may be recorded in the church or with a town or county clerk.

Reprinted with permission from the June 2000 issue of *Family Tree Magazine*.

contributing to the Missouri Marriage Project <www.rootsweb.com/~usgen web/marriages/missouri/jackson.htm>. These are just a few of the online marriage records. More on finding transcribed records in chapter six.

MILITARY

Online military records are difficult to find; in fact, they probably exist only if someone (like you) transcribed and uploaded them to the Web. Although there are thousands of sites devoted to America's wars; they include rosters, battle descriptions, historic overviews, biographical thumbnails of major participants, causes of the conflict, and maps. **If you want to order copies of your ancestors' actual records, visit the National Archives' Web site for a full description of what's available and how to order copies <www.archives.gov/research_room/obtain _copies/veterans_service_records.html>.**

Library/Archive Source

Because of the popularity of the Civil War, this will be the easiest conflict for online research. However, this doesn't mean you won't discover something about your Korean War or War of 1812 veteran.

Here are some of the most outstanding military sites:

The Civil War

Money Saver

Our Civil War ancestors tramped across an American landscape ripped apart by sectionalism. As a family historian, locating your ancestor, and tracing his long march can bring you to a closer understanding of the most significant event of his lifetime. For most researchers, searching military records in the National Archives isn't always a possibility. Thanks to online databases, however, you can often locate your Civil War grandpa by a quick trip to your own computer. **Here are eight free sites and one commercial database where you can begin your Civil War ancestor search.**

The Civil War Archive
<www.civilwararchive.com>

A good site for locating a regimental history. How detailed is the information? Very. The 18th Missouri, for example, chronicles the regiment's

MAKING THE CONNECTION

If your ancestor served in the Civil War, and you can prove the lineage, you may be interested in joining one of these organizations.

Daughters of Union Veterans of the Civil War
<www.suvcw.org>

Sons of Confederate Veterans
<www.scv.org>

Sons of Union Veterans of the Civil War
<www.suvcw.org>

United Daughters of the Confederacy
<www.hqudc.org>

involvement in the siege of Corinth, Mississippi, its guard duty of the railroad, skirmishes at New Albany, the Battle of Atlanta, operations against Hood in Georgia, Sherman's March to the Sea, the campaign of the Carolinas, and its final march in the Grand Review. For a broader scope of the regiment's role in the war, note which corps your ancestor's regiment belonged to. Then, go to the Corps History to read about troop movements. For example, the 18th Missouri was assigned to the 16th Corps toward the end of the War. The history of the 16th details its various assignments and commanders throughout the War.

This site links to hundreds of regimental histories—so grab a map and start tracing your ancestor's wartime movements.

American Civil War Home Page
<http://sunsite.utk.edu/civil-war>
This is one of the largest collection of Civil War links on the Internet. The site's resources are divided into twelve general categories:
- Battles and Campaigns
- Biographical Information
- Civil War Reenactors
- Civil War Round Tables
- Documentary Records
- General Resources
- Histories and Bibliographies
- Images of Wartime
- Other Military Information
- Rosters and Regimental Histories
- The Secession Crisis and Before
- State/Local Studies

It's unlikely you'll find specific data on your ancestors here; however, you will learn about the poetry of his day, his songs, what his money looked like, and the books he may have read. Don't miss the information on becoming a Civil War re-enactor.

Civil War Rosters
<http://geocities.com/Area51/Lair/3680/cw/cw.html>

Here you'll find rosters of many, though not all, Civil War regiments. The site is arranged by state, then by regiment. Click on any regiment to see a list of all the men who belonged to it.

Occasionally you will find a complete list of a state's Civil War rosters. For example, the link to Wisconsin will take you to a page of the State Historical Society of Wisconsin, containing the *Roster of Wisconsin Volunteers, War of the Rebellion*, 1861–1865. The volumes reproduced on this site list all soldiers known to have participated in Wisconsin's Civil War regiments. You'll see actual scanned images of the volumes, and can browse by regiment or by soldier's name.

Civil War Soldiers and Sailors System
<www.itd.nps.gov/cwss>

This site is maintained by the National Parks Service and contains a computerized database of basic facts about many people who served in the Civil War. The facts are taken from records in the National Archives. The site also includes links to descriptions of major battles and regimental histories. The entry of 5.4 million records is complete, but the records are being edited first, then added to the database on a continual basis. Currently, there are five million records available from more than thirty states. The site is searchable by name, state, and regiment.

Civil War Resources
<www.libraries.rutgers.edu/rul/rr_gateway/research_guides/history/
 civwar.shtml>

If you're a little fuzzy on the causes of the Civil War or how it progressed, be sure to visit this Rutgers University Library site. Its linked categories include

- Abolitionism
- Bibliography
- Civil War Related Listservs (Online discussion groups)
- General Sites
- Leading up to the War
- Military Histories
- MSS Collections: Diaries, Letters, Papers
- Reconstruction Documents
- State Studies
- Online Bibliographies
- The War Years

An interesting link is to newspaper and social commentaries of the period, including one by James Russell Lowell. In 1861, Lowell wrote, "It is time that the South should learn, if they do not begin to suspect it already, that the difficulty of the Slavery question is slavery itself—nothing more, nothing less. It is time that the North should learn that it has nothing left to compromise but the rest of its self-respect. Nothing will satisfy the extremists at the South short of a reduction of the Free States to a mere police for the protection of an institution whose danger increases at an equal pace with its wealth."

Check out the link to the site The Valley of the Shadow: Living the Civil War in Pennsylvania and Virginia. Through newspaper transcripts spanning the war years, you'll learn the story of two neighboring communities, Chambersburg, Pennsylvania, and Staunton, Virginia.

Cornell University Library
<http://library5.library.cornell.edu/moa/browse.monographs/waro.html>

Several years ago, I saw a multivolume set of Civil War books that cost close to one thousand dollars. Although you could always access them for free at a major library, today you can access those volumes for free using the Cornell University Library's digitized collection. The volumes are *The War of the Rebellion: A Compilation of the Official Records of the Union and Confederate Armies*. This massive compilation done by the U.S. War Department contains the official records of the Army and Navy during the Civil War. You can search the entire collection using either a simple or advanced search, as well as searching for keywords or names within a specific volume.

CivilWar.com
<www.civilwar.com>

This site will give you a detailed account of the people, places, and events of the Civil War. For example, click on Timeline for a chronological list of all Civil War events. Or, select The Battles for a chronological list of engagements. Battle descriptions include the dates, principal commanders, number of participants, and casualties. If you're interested in seeing images of battlefields, forts, parks, monuments, or cemeteries, follow the link to The Places. The Music section of this site offers a peek into the musical life of everyday soldiers. Listen to favorites of the North and South, including "Do They Miss Me At Home?" and "Green Grow the Lilacs."

The United States Civil War Center
<www.cwc.lsu.edu/cwc/civlink.htm>

This site was established to promote the study of the Civil War and contains an index of sixty-five hundred links. Links are organized alphabetically, from Abolition to Vendors, and include almost every Civil War topic you can think of. Click on Casualties, for example, to read about the ten most costly battles of the war, or on Flags for dozens of links to flags of the war. If any of your ancestors were wounded in battle or fell ill to disease, you'll probably want to click on the link to Medicine. From there, you can visit other sites devoted to Civil War-era disease, amputation, wounds, and field hospitals.

American Civil War Research Database
<www.civilwardata.com>

The American Civil War Research Database is one of the most comprehensive, fully searchable sources of soldier and regimental data on the Internet. For an annual fee of twenty-five dollars, you can search more than 2,665,000 Union and Confederate records. The site's dynamic links will take you into several layers of information, ranging from the names of other hometown enlistees to those who died in any given battle.

Important

Locating your ancestor is as easy as entering a surname and launching a search. **Be sure to follow search tips, though, as many records identify soldiers only by an initial for a first name.** In addition, many soldiers joined a neighboring state's military unit, so you may not find them if you specify the state where they lived. Once you've located an individual, you can click on the name to read his history including dates of enlistment, age at enlistment, and rank achieved, along with source citations. Because a large amount of information in the database is from state rosters, you'll find data previously unavailable to the public. As a bonus for researchers, you can follow the link to your ancestor's place of residence (if known) and see names of other soldiers in town. If you're lucky, you may even find your soldier in one of the fifty-five hundred photos on the site.

If you know what regiment your solider served in, use the Regiment Lookup screen to dive into battles fought, regimental assignments, and a graphical view of the unit's combat experience. From the casualty analysis screen, you can view the dates and places where soldiers were killed, wounded, captured, or reported missing, along with the names of the individual soldiers in each of those categories.

For researchers who want a deeper understanding of how the losses in one regiment compared with others, use the Regimental Dynamics screen to sort statistics by several options, including the percentage of men who were killed, wounded, disabled, or captured. Sorting can also be done by unit type, state, and length of enlistment. For example, in sorting Union regiments by percentage of deserters, you'll see that of 257 men in the 154 Pennsylvania Infantry, nearly 44 percent went over the hill. These statistics lead, of course, to questions about the ability of the officer corps, camp conditions, or recruiting techniques.

Although the American Civil War Research Database is available in various Ancestry.com databases, the dynamic links on this site make it a far more valuable resource. If you're only interested in locating your Civil War ancestor and don't want detailed regimental information, you can purchase a seven-day pass to the personnel database for ten dollars. In either case, a subscription to CivilWarData.com is one of the best bargains on the Net.

REVOLUTIONARY WAR

Valley Forge Muster Roll Database
<www.nps.gov/vafo/mropening.htm>

This searchable database contains information on more than thirty thousand soldiers who served with General Washington at Valley Forge. The information includes the soldier's name, state, rank, regiment, division, brigade, ethnicity, and monthly status data. Don't miss the links to more details on the brigades and divisions as well as Washington's staff.

Revolutionary War Pensioners Living in Ohio, 1818–1819
<http://php.ucs.indiana.edu/~jetorres/ohiorev.html>
   Scan this alphabetical list of pensioners containing name, state, and rank.

American Revolution on the Internet
<www.lineages.com/military/Links.asp?war=rw>
   This site links to several Revolution-related sites, including battles, parks, historical texts, campaign maps, and lineage societies.

Indiana Revolutionary War Burials
<www.geocities.com/sdfranklin_1999/inssar_cem-project.html>
   Look for your veteran's name, state of service, county of burial, and cemetery. Some names include biographical data.

South Carolina Revolutionary War Letters, Diaries, and Orders
<www.schistory.org/displays/RevWar/archives-online>
   Search by date, keyword, or name, e.g., Lord Cornwallis or General Greene.

Revolutionary War Bounty Warrants
<http://eagle.vsla.edu/rwbw>
   This searchable index covers documents used to verify dates and length of service of officers, soldiers, and sailors in a Virginia or Continental unit during the Revolutionary War. Some entries have links to scanned images of the documents.

WAR OF 1812

Roster of Ohio Soldiers, War of 1812
<www.ohiohistory.org/resource/database/rosters.html>
   The Ohio Historical Society offers this searchable database containing records from the roster from the Adjutant General records of 1,759 officers and 24,521 enlisted men. Search results include name, rank, company, and company commander.

Illinois War of 1812 Veterans
<www.cyberdriveillinois.com/departments/archives/war1812.html>
   Search names of Illinois militiamen listed as having served in the War of 1812. Information is provided on how to obtain copies of records. Name, rank, and company are listed, along with place of enlistment, if given.

Historical Overview War of 1812
<www.rootsweb.com/~canmil/1812/1812view.htm>

This is an excellent overview of one of America's "forgotten wars." Be sure to follow the link on the left side of the page to War of 1812; you'll find databases, Canadian muster rolls, and a list of widows.

Library of Virginia War of 1812 Pay Rolls and Muster Rolls
<http://eagle.vsla.edu/war1812>

Approximately forty thousand names are contained in this searchable database of *Pay Rolls of Militia Entitled to Land Bounty Under the Act of Congress of Sept. 28, 1850*, and *Muster Rolls of the Virginia Militia in the War of 1812.*

OTHER MILITARY

American Battle Monuments Commission
<www.abmc.gov>

Searchable databases of people interred at American military cemeteries overseas and those missing in action from World War I, World War II, Korea, and Vietnam, as well as those who died in Korea.

World War I Draft Registration Cards
<www.genexchange.org/draftcard.cfm>

More than twenty-four million male citizens born between 1873 and 1900 completed draft registration cards. The cards include name, age, home address, citizenship, birthplace, and more. Approximately 13 percent of cards have been transcribed and uploaded to this searchable site. All records are available through a subscription to Ancestry.com. These cards are also available on microfilm through a Family History Center.

Vietnam Casualties Database
<www.lineages.com/military/mil_vn.asp>

Search by exact surname or Soundex. The information in this database contains a wealth of information, including name, date of birth, race, hometown, marital status, religion, service, grade, age, place of death, cause of death, and location of name on Vietnam Memorial wall. Database is also searchable by hometown.

POW-MIA Korean War Casualties
<www.aiipowmia.com/koreacw/kwkia_menu.html>

Casualties are listed alphabetically by state, including date of death, rank, and branch of service.

Chapter Seven Checklist
- Search the cemetery sites for at least one of your ancestors.
- If you know your Civil War ancestor's regiment, find its history.
- Locate a regimental history of the 54th Massachusetts Infantry.

- Begin searching immigration sites for one of your ancestors.
- If you have an Ellis Island ancestor, locate her and the ship on which she arrived.
- Locate at least one online census record for your ancestor.
- Find a Web site with information on the ship *Snow Squirrel*.
- Locate land records for one of your ancestors who lived in a public land state.
- Go to Cyndi's List and find where to write for vital records for at least one of your ancestors (hint: look under United States/States).
- Order (by snail mail) at least one vital record.

WHAT'S NEXT?

Even more online resources, including sites for history, maps, photographs, state resources, and books.

EIGHT

Peripheral Resources

Reminder

Although the four search strategies in the previous chapters will get you a long way down the ancestral trail, there are some sites that may not pop up near the top of a search list. That doesn't mean they aren't valuable—just that they may not be optimized enough for search engines to find them. Many of these sites are a little off the beaten genealogical path, but are great "peripheral resources." These include

- state resources
- maps
- photographs
- history
- books

STATE RESOURCES

No matter which state your ancestors lived in, you're sure to find helpful state-related online resources. For example, the Handbook of Texas Online <www.tsha.ut exas.edu/handbook/online/> contains twenty-three thousand articles on Texas history, people, places, and events. Being aware of the online resources for the state you're researching is a key ingredient to successful Internet genealogy. In fact, you'll probably want to spend some of your initial online time just getting familiar with state resources.

If you live in or can visit the state you're researching, it is well worth your time to visit the state archives and libraries. Often these facilities are the only place on earth where certain resources exist. For example, a state library may be the repository for original pioneer diaries, local railroad employee records, or microfilmed copies of statewide newspapers.

Many of the state archives and libraries have Web sites, and some have posted genealogical information on the site. The Indiana State Library, for example, has a pre-1851 Indiana marriage database, as well as an Indiana cemetery database. You can locate the Web site for most state libraries and archives (which will include their address and phone number) by using your favorite search engine. Just type in "yourstate state library" and then click Search. This is not a comprehensive list, but merely a suggestion for getting started.

MAPS

I spent an embarrassing number of years searching Jackson County, Missouri, records for one of my ancestors. After unsuccessfully pouring through church memberships, cemetery inscriptions, and census microfilms, I did something I should have done long before. I pulled out my Missouri atlas and scrutinized the area surrounding the family farm. Guess what? The boundary lines of two other counties were within spitting distance of the farm. And, on my next trip to the library, I found my ancestor in less than an hour. In 1900, at the age of seventy-seven, he was living with a daughter less than twenty miles from the town I'd spent years searching.

How Maps Can Help

I don't know about you, but after that experience I don't do much research without my maps at hand. Besides, my ancestors were an itchy-footed bunch, and tracking their movement means tracing old roads and rivers. And that means using old maps.

Look at a map and you'll get a real understanding of migration routes and patterns. Clearly, the easiest routes were along coasts or up and down rivers. Pull out a present-day atlas, and try to imagine it without roads. You'll quickly see how your ancestors traveled and why they ended up in certain locales. If you ever "lose" a generation, you can use maps to help speculate on a possible new home.

Research Tip

Since most early birth and death records, and most land, tax, and court records were kept at the county level, knowing the county your ancestor lived in is essential for tracking down those records. Thanks to the detail in this family footnote—"he lived at Wilson Creek on the Chaplin Fork of the Salt River, on the border of Mercer and Washington Counties in Kentucky"—I knew without a doubt that my search would take me to both counties. Some researchers aren't so lucky.

Old maps show old place names. Although your ancestor may have lived in the same location for generations, the name of the place and the county in which it was located may have changed numerous times. It's possible that your search for the family who *didn't* move may lead you to more county courthouses than tracing the ones who migrated with every generation.

Fortunately, the *Map Guide to the U.S. Federal Censuses, 1790–1920* (Baltimore: Genealogical Publishing Company, 2002) will help with the changing boundary problem. It shows all of the U.S. county boundaries, and on each map, old county lines are superimposed over modern ones to highlight boundary changes at ten-year intervals. Both Ancestry's *Red Book*

(Salt Lake City: Ancestry, 1989) and Everton's *HandyBook for Genealogist* (Draper, Utah: Everton Publishers, 2002) will provide you with state maps showing current county boundaries.

If you just want an idea of the geography of your ancestor's surroundings, a period map will probably help more than a visit. Thanks to modern engineering and Mother Nature, the topography of a place may have changed so much that your ancestor wouldn't recognize his favorite fishing hole. Period maps will depict the landscape as it was, including the rivers your family forded and the forests they helped clear.

WHERE TO FIND MAPS

You can use search engines (see chapter six) to find specific maps, or surf over to these sites.

Library of Congress
Map Collections 1544–1999
<http://memory.loc.gov/ammem/gmdhtml/gmdhome.html>

The Geography and Map Division of the Library of Congress has digitized a small portion of its 4.5 million items and placed them on the Web. The images you'll find on this site cover the wide expanse of America history and in general include maps and atlases not covered by copyright protection. You may not find a map of your ancestor's property in this collection, but you may find a map he knew during his own lifetime.

The collection is divided into seven categories, and all contain potentially valuable images for your genealogy research. Check each category to determine copyright restrictions, if any. The categories are

Cities and Towns
Some city and town maps may show individual buildings as well as panoramic views of cities. The collection included an 1868 "bird's eye view" of my hometown, Saint Joseph, Missouri, in amazing detail. The panoramas are handdrawn artists' images of cities as if viewed from a bird's perspective. Although not drawn to scale, they do show street patterns, buildings, and landscape features in perspective.

Once you find a map of interest, you can zoom in or out on any section. There are currently panoramic maps available of towns in every state except Mississippi. The collection also includes maps from the Canadian provinces of British Columbia, Nova Scotia, Ontario, and Quebec.

Cultural Landscapes
This collection includes large-scale topographic maps, land surveys, and atlases. There are several maps of Native American lands. Sample maps include an 1849 image of a Shaker village in Canterbury, New Hampshire, 1887 Oklahoma Indian Territory; and 1848 California gold fields. My favorite in the collection is a 1766 "plan of my farm on Little Huntg. Creek & Potomk. R" drawn by George Washington.

Transportation and Communication

These are the maps that will show how your ancestor traveled and the route they took. Transportation maps depict canal and river systems, railway lines and roads. Communication maps show the location and distribution of telegraph routes.

If your ancestor traveled the rails, you'll find his rail routes here. Railroad maps include progress report surveys for individual rail lines, government surveys, maps showing land grants and right-of-ways, and route guides. To locate maps in a specific state, choose Geographic Location, then click on your state of interest. A typical map is "New enlarged scale railroad and county map of Tennessee showing every railroad station and post office in the state, 1888." You can also search by keyword. Another "don't miss" map in the collection is the 1851, "Disturnell's new map of the United States and Canada showing all the canals, rail roads, telegraph lines and principal stage routes."

General Maps

These maps show areas larger than towns or cities. For example, you'll find a 1706 "new mapp of East and West New Jarsey" or an 1867 image showing the Alaskan territory ceded by Russia to the United States.

This is the section to search if you want to visualize a larger picture of your ancestor's world. You'll frequently find these maps are large scale and contain an exceptional amount of detail. For example, the 1751 map of the "most inhabited part of Virginia, containing the whole province of Maryland with part of Pennsylvania, New Jersey and North Carolina" includes not only rivers, but a large number of creeks and other small landscape features.

Conservation and Environment

Although you wouldn't think this category of maps would be helpful in genealogy, conservation and environmental maps are an excellent source for detailing changes in the landscape, including natural and man-made features, geology, wetlands, and wildlife. Maps of specific conservation projects, such as the growth of the U.S. National Parks, are included in this category.

Want to see how things have changed over a hundred years? Look at the twenty maps of Yellowstone National Park, dating from 1871 to 1988. You'll also find an 1880 report on the geology and resources of the Black Hills, an 1814 map of the Great Smoky Mountains, and a 1904 image of Bar Harbor, Maine, which includes the names of property owners and the streets they lived on.

Discovery and Exploration

Want to travel with an explorer? A portion of the discovery and exploration maps and manuscripts reflect the European explorations of America dating from the late fifteenth century. Here you'll find detailed maps of coastlines and outlines of continents. The eighteenth- and nineteenth-century maps document exploration of interior parts of the continent, such as the maps of Lewis and Clark, or later government explorers and surveyors.

If you have an ancestor who traveled with Lewis and Clark, or who went west not long after the Corps of Discovery returned to St. Louis, don't miss the handdrawn maps of newly discovered territory. In particular, check out the Lewis and Clark map, with annotations in brown ink by Meriwether Lewis, showing the "Mississippi, the Missouri for a short distance above Kansas, Lakes Michigan, Superior, and Winnipeg, and the country onwards to the Pacific."

Military Battles and Campaigns

A large majority of Americans had ancestors who fought in the Civil War. If great-great-grandpa shouldered a rifle, you'll want to download and print the campaign maps that show battles in which he fought. These maps include troop movements, defensive structures, roads, campsites, and vegeta-

---

OTHER MAP SITES

Antiquarian Maps at Reed College
<http://web.reed.edu/resources/library/maps>

David Rumsey Map Collection
<www.davidrumsey.com>

Hargrett Library Rare Map Collection, University of Georgia
<www.libs.uga.edu/darchive/hargrett/maps/maps.html>

Historic USGS Maps of New England
<http://docs.unh.edu/nhtopos/nhtopos.htm>

Historical Maps of Illinois and the Northwest Territory
<http://images.library.uiuc.edu/projects/historical_maps>

Historical Maps, University of Connecticut
<http://magic.lib.uconn.edu/cgi-bin/MAGIC_HistList.pl>

Military History Maps (U.S. Military Academy)
<www.dean.usma.edu/history/dhistorymaps/MapsHome.htm>

Old Kansas Area Maps
<http://history.cc.ukans.edu/carrie/kancoll/graphics/maps>

Perry-Castañeda Library Map Collection, the University of Texas, Austin
<www.lib.utexas.edu/Libs/PCL/Map_collection/Map_collection.html>

Texas Historic Sites Atlas
<http://atlas.thc.state.tx.us>

The Yale Map Collection
<www.library.yale.edu/MapColl/index.htm>

tion. Some maps were actually drawn on the battlefield. They can also include genealogy clues, such as the location of plantations, small towns, settlements of Native Americans, and names of landowners.

A typical image in this category is an 1861 view of the Mississippi Valley, and "Reconnoissance of the Mississippi River below Forts Jackson and St. Philip: made previous to the reduction by the U.S. Fleet, under the command of flag officer D.G. Farragut, U.S.N."

Geographic Names Information System
<http://mapping.usgs.gov/www/gnis>

GNIS is the official database for place names. It is maintained by the U.S. Geological Survey and is an excellent resource if you know a place name, but aren't sure where it's located. The database contains two million entries and includes the names of places that no longer exist, as well as secondary names for existing places. This is an excellent place to search for old cemeteries and churches. Once the database has located the feature you're researching, click on Show Feature Details and Location. You can then click on options to show the feature on a regular or topographic map.

OFFLINE MAP RESOURCES
Historical Societies

A local historical society is frequently the repository for original maps and documents pertaining to a specific county. The Research Archives of the San Diego Historical Society, for example, owns an extensive map collection that documents

Reminder

LOCAL LIBRARIES

Your local library is a great starting point for hard-to-find historical atlases and maps. However, you'll probably have to do your research on site, since most libraries keep older books in the reference section. The library's collection may vary, depending on where you live, but typically will include

- *Atlas of World History*, by Patrick O'Brien

- *The Historical Atlas of the American Revolution*, by Ian Barnes

- *Historical Atlas of Expeditions*, by Karen Farrington

- *Mapping America's Past: A Historical Atlas*, by Mark C. Carnes and John A. Garraty with Patrick Williams

- *The Routledge Historical Atlas of the American Railroads*, by John F. Stover

- *The Routledge Historical Atlas of the American South*, by Andrew K. Frank

Be sure to ask reference librarians for help, as their library's valuable historical holdings aren't always evident to a casual browser.

the places in San Diego's past. The collection, which is open to the public, contains more than two thousand maps of San Diego County, the Southwest, and Baja California. The categories include four hundred maps of city subdivisions and topographic quadrangles, more than twenty thousand parcel (assessor's) maps for 1957–1958, and a twenty-volume aerial photomap collection. The society also has a set of Sanborn fire insurance atlases updated to 1955.

Fire Insurance Maps

Fire insurance maps were originally produced to assess the risk of fire and the cost of insurance. The maps are extremely detailed, drawn to a scale of 50 feet per inch. They were printed in color and include information about streets, businesses, houses, and utilities. A brief history of the origin of fire insurance maps is at the Web site of the University of Virginia <http://fisher.lib.virginia.edu/sanborn/about.html>, along with an actual Sanborn map of 1920 Charlottesville, Virginia <http://fisher.lib.Virginia.EDU/sanborn/1920/fullindexmap.html>.

The Sanborn National Insurance Diagram Bureau, founded in 1867, is the oldest mapping company in the United States (the company became known as the Sanborn Map Company in 1902). The largest collection of these maps is owned by the Sanborn Library and copies of the collection are offered to the public through Environmental Data Resources (EDR) <www.edrnet.com/reports/historical.html>. The Sanborn maps show titles of businesses, names of owners, building materials used, and structural dimensions.

The Sanborn collection of 1.2 million maps—covering twelve thousand towns and cities—has been digitized and is available through EDR. Costs vary, but the maximum for the search and up to fifteen maps is $125. To order, visit the Web site or call (800) 352-0050.

Also, libraries that subscribe to ProQuest may have access to Sanborn fire insurance maps through Digital Sanborn maps <http://sanborn.umi.com>.

Family History Center

The map you need may be right around the corner at your local Family History Center. **Unlike historical societies, the maps you'll find here are not confined to the same geographic location as the library.**

Holdings at my local FHC fill more than a dozen map drawers and include

- Medieval England
- Central Belfast, 1931
- York County, Ontario, 1860
- Montreal, 1953
- Philadelphia, 1860
- A Map of the Travels of George Washington
- Pennsylvania, 1796
- Rowan County, North Carolina, 1808
- Map of SW Virginia, including Wilderness Road, Boone's Road
- New Jersey, 1778

Important

Because many of the items were donated by library patrons, the selection varies widely from center to center.

IN THE ZONE

<www.topozone.com>

Would you like free access to more than fifty-six thousand topographic maps? TopoZone.com is a fully searchable Web site containing topographic images of the entire United States. Just click on Get a Map, then enter the name of the place in the search box. The system will then return a list of places that match your search criteria.

Click on the name you want and you'll get the topographic map which contains that feature. The default scale is 1:100,000 (small), so zoom in to a larger scale map for more detail. You'll find the zoom selections along the top edge of the map; they are 1:25,000, 1:50,000, 1:100,000 and 1:200,000.

Topographic maps will show vegetation in green, water in blue, and densely built-up areas in gray or red. The wiggly lines are contour lines and represent elevation. Contours that are very close together represent steep slopes. Widely spaced contours, or an absence of contours, means that the slope is relatively level. You can find elevation values written along contour lines.

Read the FAQ and help files for information on displaying and printing the maps, as well as placing them on your Web page.

PHOTOGRAPHS

Don't you just love old family photos? I do, too. Unfortunately, my family didn't end up with many pictures, so the ones I have are precious. Currently, more and more historic photos are being uploaded to the Web. Although your ancestor's photo may not be here, it's possible to find a picture of a hometown, a railroad, or even a Civil War regiment. Many of the photos on the sites below are copyright free, but be sure to double-check before downloading them for your use.

Archival Research Catalog (ARC)
<www.archives.gov/research_room/arc>

Through the online catalog of the National Archives and Records Administration, you can search 124,000 digital images. These include:
- fifteen architectural and engineering drawings
- fifty-eight artifact items
- 308 maps and charts
- 57,786 still pictures
- 15,005 textual documents

You may find digitized images of your ancestor's alien registration affidavit, Dawes Commission application, or Rough Rider military service card. But keep in mind, only 13 percent of NARA's massive holdings are described in the Archives Research Catalog. As more holdings are added (and some digitized), it will become easier to find NARA records online. But for now, if you don't find what you're looking for through ARC, you may have to visit the archives in Washington, DC, or one of its regional facilities yourself—or order copies of records from NARA.

Museum of the Rockies
<www.montana.edu/wwwmor/photoarc>

If your ancestors were early settlers in the American West, search this excellent collection of "Indian Peoples of the Northern Great Plains." The search can be done by subject, name, geographical location, tribe, date, photographer, or artist. For example, a geographical search of Fort Union returned five photographs taken in 1926, while a search of Powder River, Montana, returned the photo of an 1880 drawing of a war raid by Medicine Crow.

These photos are copyright-protected and may be used for educational and research purposes.

Library of Congress Civil War Photograph Collection
<http://memory.loc.gov/ammem/dwphtml/cwphome.html>

This collection includes the work of several photographers, including those of famed photographer Mathew Brady. Brady was one of the first to document the carnage of the battlefield, with his 1862 display of battlefield corpses from Antietam. *The New York Times* said that Brady had brought "home to us the terrible reality and earnestness of war."

The searchable database of about sixteen hundred photographs (1861–1865) can be searched by subject, title, photographer, and format. A sample search using the word "Gettysburg" returned forty photos. Among them were General Lee's headquarters, federal dead on the battlefield after day one of the three-day battle, an image of three Confederate prisoners, and a view of Little Round Top.

Tip

When searching this database, be sure to use a wide variety of search terms. For example, a search of "bridge" returned seventy results; "signal tower" returned seventeen; and "grand review" (the Union parade at the end of the Civil War) returned fifteen. If your ancestor was a sutler (an outfitter) you'll find six photos of sutler tents; if he was an artilleryman, you'll find ninety-eight images of artillery and the men who fired them. The images depict scenes of daily life that your Civil War ancestor would have experienced.

There are no known restrictions on use of these photographs. You can begin your search at <http://lcweb2.loc.gov/pp/cwpquery.html>. (See figure 8-1 on page 155.)

Panoramic Photograph Collection
<http://lcweb2.loc.gov/pp/panquery.html>

This interesting collection contains about four thousand images from

Figure 8-1
Is there a photograph on record of your Civil War ancestor? *Library of Congress, Prints & Photographs Division*

1880 to 1930, featuring cities, landscapes, and group portraits. They focus on the twentieth century, when panoramic photography was at its most popular. Subjects in the collection include agricultural life, beauty contests, disasters, bridges, canals, dams, fairs, and expositions.

Did your grandparents stroll through the Century of Progress Exposition in 1933 Chicago? If so, this collection will show you what it looked like. Did they sail through Bar Harbor, Maine, in 1910? It's here, too.

You can use these materials for noncommercial educational and research purposes; however, you will need the written permission of the copyright holder for any other use.

Daguerreotype Portraits and Views
<http://memory.loc.gov/ammem/daghtml/daghome.html>

This collection of 650 photos from 1839 to 1864 include portraits taken in the Mathew Brady studio, as well as Philadelphia street scenes and early architectural views by John Plumbe. The collection can be searched by keyword or browsed by subject.

You will find exceptional photos in this collection of daily life. Typical images include an 1853 photo of a woman at her sewing machine, an 1850s steamboat, 1879 Niagara Falls and a cooper (barrelmaker) with his tools. Portraits make up the majority of this collection, so if your ancestors lived around Washington, DC, during the this time period, be sure to check for their photo.

Western History Photos
Denver Public Library
<http://gowest.coalliance.org>

The Western History/Genealogy Department of the Denver Public Library has a collection of more than 600,000 photographs related to the history of Colorado and the American West. Tens of thousands of the collection have been digitized for the Web. This photo database can be searched by keyword, author, subject, or title, or browsed by subject. For example, browsing through the subject "cavalry," I found forty-two images of the Colorado Cavalry, 1860–1870, along with twenty-eight pictures from 1900–1920, including Rough Riders at the Battle of San Juan (which goes to show that many collections aren't always limited to the "main focus" of the collection).

Images in this collection span a wide variety of subjects, including Buffalo Bill's Wild West Show, life in Denver at the turn of the century, a Ute woman with a cradleboard, the ruins at Mesa Verde, and the Deadwood stagecoach. The collection reflects the history of the West, so even if your ancestor did not live in Colorado, it's a good site to search for general photos of the frontier.

Each photo in the collection clearly states copyright information.

Canadian National Railway Historic Photograph Collection
<http://collections.ic.gc.ca/cnphoto/cnphoto.html>

If your ancestor visited Canada or lived there, he probably spent time on Canada's Railway system. This site (in French and English) contains photos of the trains from the six companies who eventually formed the Canadian National Railways. These include Canadian Northern, Grand Trunk Railway, Grand Trunk Pacific, Intercolonial Railway, Canadian National, and CN Today. To view the collection, just click on the logo from any of the railway companies. These logos link to photos of locomotives and freight cars of all the lines. Along with the photos is a history of the company. Some pages include images of passenger cars, such as the one that carried the Prince of Wales in 1860.

Alaska Gold Rush
<www.library.state.ak.us/hist/goldrush/table.html>

Gold miners who missed the California boom poured into Alaska in hopes of finding their fortunes. Just behind them came the photographers who developed their images in temporary darkrooms located in tents or covered sleds, or on boats on the Inside Passage or Yukon Rivers. Did your ancestor head for the Alaskan gold fields? If so, search this collection of images. The categories of photos are Juneau, Skagway, People, Transportation, On the Trail, Nome, Other Towns, Mining, and Entertainment.

On the Trail includes the well-known image of a long line of miners heading for the summit of Chilkoot Pass. The Mining section shows a mining camp and a "sourdough" panning a stream, while Entertainment depicts saloons and gambling halls.

Military History Institute

<http://carlisle-www.army.mil/usamhi/PhotoDB.html>

Although this Web site does not contain digitized photographs, I have included it because it is a searchable database of Civil War soldiers, places, and events. Use this database to see if a photograph exists of your Civil War ancestor. Just enter the surname you're searching and the results page will return a list of photos of soldiers with that surname, along with (if known) their regiments.

If you find a photo description of interest, send an E-mail with the photo ID (instructions are on the Web page). The Military History Institute will then send you a free photocopy of the picture, along with instructions on ordering a duplicate photo. When using this database, don't forget to search by place name or battle name. For example, when searching for "Shiloh" (a battle in Tennessee), the three results all included named soldiers who were at that battle.

Photographs bring history to life—and perhaps by searching these collections, you'll find photographs of your ancestors, their towns, their professions, or the events they witnessed. If you can't find photos on these sites, use Internet search engines to look for state archives, historical societies, and state libraries in the locale you're searching.

Notes

DON'T KNOW MUCH ABOUT HISTORY

An online cousin once commented to me that he hated history when he was a student, but once he became interested in genealogy, he couldn't get enough of it. The more research you do, the more you'll agree.

Here are a few of my favorite sites:

Daily Life

When I was a teenager, my grandmother gave me a book of manners that had belonged to her mother. I remember reading it in disbelief and being grateful that I didn't live during my great-grandmother's time! If you want to learn more about daily life for your ancestors, try these sites:

18th Century American Colonies

<http://home.earthlink.net/~gfeldmeth/lec.col2.html>

Did you know that some of the largest immigrant groups in the Middle Colonies were Germans, Dutch, and Scots-Irish?

Burial Customs in American History

<www.cr.nps.gov/nr/publications/bulletins/cem2.htm>

All about colonial and Native American customs, plus rural cemetery information. For more on this subject, read Sharon DeBartolo Carmack's *Your Guide to Cemetery Research* (Cincinnati: Betterway Books, 2002).

OTHER PHOTO COLLECTIONS

Bureau of Reclamation Photography and Engineering Drawings Collections
<www.usbr.gov/history/photos.htm>

California Missions (from as early as 1895)
<www.cmp.ucr.edu/exhibitions/missions>

Digital Archive of American Architecture (includes 17th and 18th century buildings)
<www.bc.edu/bc_org/avp/cas/fnart/fa267>

Florida State Archives Photographic Collection
<http://fpc.dos.state.fl.us>

Historical Wyoming Photographs
<www.cc.whecn.edu/library/photos.htm>

Issaquah Historical Society
<www.issaquahhistory.org/photoalbum/default.htm>

John C. H. Grabill Collection, Frontier life in Colorado, South Dakota, and Wyoming, late 19th Century
<http://lcweb.loc.gov/spcoll/100.html>

New York, NY, Ellis Island-Immigration: 1900–1920
<http://cmp1.ucr.edu/exhibitions/immigration_id.html>

Photographs of North Carolina folklife, 1914–17
<http://lcweb.loc.gov/spcoll/023.html>

For more information about photography and genealogy, pick up two great reads by Maureen Taylor, *Preserving Your Family Photographs*, and *Uncovering Your Ancestry Through Family Photographs*, both published by Betterway Books.

Colonial Recipes
<www.monroehistoricsociety.org/cookies.html>
    Hobnails and applejacks.

Colonial Games and Toys
<www.ctstateu.edu/noahweb/games.html>
    Great site to explore with the whole family.

Colonial Williamsburg
<www.history.org>
    Explore colonial clothing, gardens, and slavery.

Old Sturbridge Village
<www.osv.org>
    Take a virtual tour of a typical nineteenth-century New England town.

Online Conversions
<www.onlineconversion.com>
   For the next time you need to convert a hogshead to a gallon!

Women's Lives, 16th, 17th and 18th Centuries
<http://womenshistory.about.com/cs/lives161718th>
   Everything from marriage to divorce to fashion.

Timelines

I love adding timelines to my genealogy reports. It's fascinating to know which of my ancestors lived when George Fox founded the Quakers or Edmund Halley discovered his comet. There are some great online Web sites for timelines. One of them will even generate a custom report based on the date of your ancestor's birth and death.

AlternaTime
<www2.canisius.edu/-emeryg/time.html>
   Links to several non-U.S. timelines.

American History Timeline
<www.si.edu/resource/faq/nmah/timeline.htm>
   Lots of extra information on this Smithsonian Institute site.

HyperHistory
<www.hyperhistory.com/online_n2/History_n2/a.html>
   Three thousand years of timelines for people, places, and events.

Our Timelines
<www.ourtimelines.com>
   Creates a customizable, color-coded timeline to add to your genealogy reports or Web site.

Timeline of U.S. Presidents
<http://chaos1.hypermart.net/pres/tusp.html>
   Was your ancestor old enough to vote for Millard Filmore? You'll find out here.

BOOKS

It's not uncommon to find published accounts of our ancestors in county histories or anecdotal accounts of everyday life. The books may have titles like *Fisher's River Scenes* or *History of Jackson County*. If you're lucky, there may even be a published account of your family's history. These types of books are often found in local libraries, Family History Centers, or through used booksellers.

   In recent years, many old books have been digitized and their contents uploaded to the Web. Some are on personal sites, others on county pages

Printed Source

of the USGenWeb, and many more in Genealogy.com's Genealogy Library. You can also find published family or county histories by searching online library catalogs. If you find a book and the library participates in an interlibrary loan program, order it through your own library. Check for online catalogs through Libdex.com <www.libdex.com>, a Web site with an index of eighteen thousand libraries.

Some excellent sites for locating used books are
- Advanced Book Exchange <www.abebooks.com>
- Alibris <www.alibris.com>
- Bibliofind <www.bibliofind.com>
- Powell's <www.powells.com>
- Bookfinder <www.bookfinder.com>

Another site for tracking down out-of-print books is eBay <www.ebay .com>. Interestingly, hard-to-find genealogy or family history books often come up for auction on this site.

Chapter Eight Checklist
- Create a timeline for one of your great-grandmothers.
- Go to the Library of Congress site and find a map of Washington, DC, from the dome of the U.S. Capitol.
- Find a map that one of your ancestors might have used.
- Locate at a photo that relates to your family history.

WHAT'S NEXT?
The BIG search—using combined strategies to find your elusive ancestors.

PART THREE

Putting It All Together

ou've come a long way from chapter one. If you've been working your way through the book, you can now:

- fill in basic genealogy forms.
- plan and conduct an interview.
- understand computer basics.
- organize your online records.
- protect yourself from computer viruses.
- use basic and advanced techniques on FamilySearch.
- search WorldConnect, add Post-ems, download GEDCOMs, and generate reports.
- assess and analyze findings.
- create a research plan.
- join and use mailing lists.
- write a successful query.
- find surname sites.
- communicate successfully with other researchers.
- construct complex searches using search engines.
- locate and search online databases.
- begin gathering relevant historical information.

Congratulations!

You've now learned the most important skills of an Internet genealogist. Now it's time to put everything you've learned into practice.

Chapter Nine: The Search: Pull Out All the Stops

We'll walk through an extensive case study that utilizes the four major techniques:

- Lineage-linked databases
- Networking
- Search engines
- Other databases

If you can log on to your Internet account and follow along, so much the better.

Chapter Ten: Sharing Your Research

Learn how to share the information you find online. This will include

- how to split a GEDCOM into family groups.
- how to create text files.
- posting your findings to the Web.
- learning to build your own family site.
- ways to share research.
- how to start your own electronic newsletter.
- using tech-toys in your research.

NINE

The Search: Pull Out All the Stops

T his is it. You've read about and practiced the search techniques. And, being a detective, you've also discovered how to creatively structure a search, how to do search engine math, and how to weave back and forth between search engines and databases. As new clues emerge, you've learned to reassess your goals and strategies. Now it's time to focus these methods on a "real" search. In this chapter, I'll take the Internet search one step further and demonstrate the importance of checking what you find in online databases against original records.

SEARCH GOAL

My goal is to discover more about Rebecca Holcomb and her husband, John Barnett. Back in chapter four, while demonstrating the advanced technique for the Pedigree Resource File <www.familysearch.org>, we found information on Polly Moore's mother (Mary Barnett) and grandmother (Rebecca Holcomb). Let's concentrate this search on Rebecca Holcomb and her husband, John Barnett. Until doing the search below, I knew nothing about either person except what was originally found on the FamilySearch site.

Please log on to the Internet and follow along with this search.

STEP 1: FAMILYSEARCH

I originally found this family by searching for Polly Moore and a spouse with the surname Hendrickson. By following the family line in one of the Pedigree Resource Files (PRF) back a couple of generations, I found the information on page 164.

Wouldn't you know it; a family filled with men named John! To facilitate our search, I'll refer to Mary's father as John, her grandfather as GFJohn and her great-grandfather as GGFJohn. Mary Barnett's father, John, was the first

Step By Step

Pedigree Chart

No. 1 on this chart is the same as no. 1 on chart no. 1

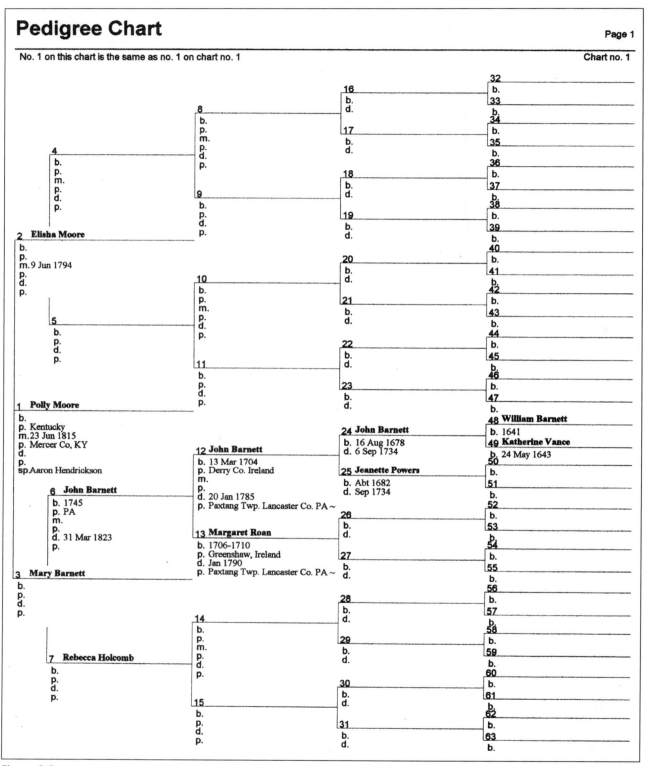

Figure 9-1
Pedigree chart of Polly Moore, showing her Barnett and Holcomb family.

of the Barnett line to be born in the United States. According to the information in the PRF, John was an officer in the Continental Army and served with George Washington in the Trenton Campaign. Other unverified facts

- The rest of the Barnetts were born in Ireland.
- The will of Mary's brother John refers to her as a half-sister.
- There is no information about Mary's mother, Rebecca Holcomb.
- Mary's grandmother, Margaret Roan, was also born in Ireland.
- Mary's grandfather (GFJohn) and grandmother (Margaret) are both listed as dying in Lancaster County, Pennsylvania.
- Mary's grandfather (GFJohn) had a will proved in Lancaster County, Pennsylvania.
- There are several references to Derry Cathedral in Ireland.
- Mary Barnett married Elisha Moore.
- One of Mary and Elisha's children, Polly, married Aaron Hendrickson.

Thoughts

- Because people tended to travel with family members, I wanted a list (if possible) of Rebecca Holcomb and John Barnett's siblings.
- Although there were many tempting Ireland-related clues, the Irish part of the family isn't one of my search goals. Besides, I would want to exhaust all U.S. sources first before jumping the ocean to make sure I have the correct place in Ireland to search and enough information to ensure that I have the right family.
- Since the file said that Mary Barnett was a half-sister, that means her father John had at least two marriages: one to Rebecca Holcomb, one to an unknown person.

Action

- Search for the parents and siblings of Rebecca Holcomb.
- Search for John Barnett's siblings. (To find them, I need to find a file for John's parents that also includes their children.)
- Search for another marriage for John.

Goal: Search for the parents and siblings of Rebecca Holcomb
Results: Zero

I structured several searches trying to locate more on Rebecca Holcomb, without success. If you remember from the chapter four FamilySearch work, you can narrow or broaden a search by adding or subtracting search criteria. Because I knew so little about Rebecca, I tried using a variety of search criteria. My searches included searching for just the name Rebecca Holcomb, Rebecca's name with a Barnett spouse, a Rebecca born in Pennsylvania, and a Rebecca Holcomb with a daughter named Mary. After all those searches, all I know is John was born supposedly in 1745 and was married to Rebecca about 1773. I estimated that Rebecca was born about 1753, plus or minus a few years.

Returning to the main FamilySearch search screen, I tried another approach. This time I asked the system to search for Rebecca Holcomb, event:

birth, date: 1753, year range: +/− 10 years. The results showed nothing definitive: a Rebecca in Connecticut, one in Virginia, another in Kentucky. I then used the same search criteria, except changing the event to: marriage, date: 1773, year range +/− 10 years, but no luck.

Goal: Search for John Barnett's siblings
Results: Found

Returning to the main search screen at FamilySearch, I searched for John Barnett with a spouse named Margaret Roan. The third match in the Ancestral File contained data on the pair and also listed their children. Figure 9-2 depicts John and his nine siblings.

Figure 9-2
Use a descendancy chart to help sort out the various John Barnetts.

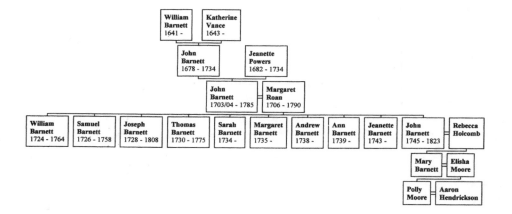

Goal: Search for other marriages for John Barnett
Results: Zero

Since I had no idea who John might have been married to, I entered the search terms John Barnett, with parents John Barnett and Margaret Roan, event: marriage, date: 1765, year range +/− 20 years. Nothing came up but the Rebecca Holcomb marriage.

I tried another search with just John Barnett, marriage 1765, +/− 10 years. There were too many results and not enough information to know if any are the right John Barnett. What do we know so far from the online sources?

- Mary Barnett's father was born supposedly about 1745 in Pennsylvania.
- Mary's grandparents and earlier generations were from Ireland.
- Mary was a half-sister to a brother named John.
- Mary's father was probably married more than once.
- Mary Barnett's grandparents probably died in Lancaster County, Pennsylvania.
- Mary's GFJohn supposedly left a will in Lancaster County, Pennsylvania.

Before moving on, I ran a last search on Mary herself. The search criteria was Mary Barnett with a spouse named Moore. One of the IGI North

America findings showed the marriage on 9 June 1794/1796 in Lincoln County, Kentucky. Remember that there was a Rebecca Holcomb from Kentucky? Is there a connection? Maybe. Let's see if we can find more on WorldConnect.

STEP 2: WORLDCONNECT

Go to the Global Search screen <http://worldconnect.rootsweb.com/cgi-bin/igm.cgi> and search for Rebecca Holcomb with spouse Barnett. One of the nine results showed Rebecca's birth date as about 1755 in Pennsylvania. As good as it was to find that, the third result was a lu-lu. It said that Rebecca was the second of four wives: Rebecca Curie was #1, Hanna Stapleton #3, and Rebecca O'Connel #4. (See figure 9-3 below.)

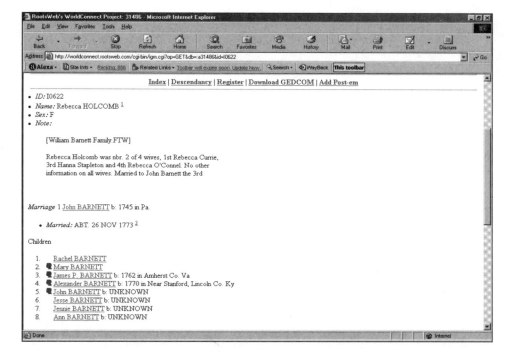

Figure 9-3
The note in this WorldConnect search indicates John had four different wives.
Copyright © 2002 and under license from MyFamily.com, Inc., all rights reserved.

It also showed the eight children of John Barnett and Rebecca Holcomb, along with their marriage date of 26 November 1773. The children are listed as

1. Rachel
2. Mary (married in Lincoln County, Kentucky)
3. James P. (born 1762 in Amherst County, Virginia)
4. Alexander (born 1770 Lincoln County, Kentucky)
5. John (died in Lincoln County, Kentucky)
6. Jesse
7. Jennie
8. Ann (married Lincoln County, Kentucky)

Did you see a problem? Although John Barnett and Rebecca Holcomb's marriage date is listed as 1773, at least two of the eight children were born supposedly prior to 1773. And it appears that the oldest, James P., was born in Virginia. Is this where John's first marriage took place?

Problem:
- I still don't know anything more about Rebecca.
- I don't know the real order of John's other marriages, nor how many there really were.
- I don't know the birth order of the children.
- I don't know why John went from Pennsylvania to Virginia and then Kentucky, which seems like an unusual migration route.

Action:

Search WorldConnect and/or FamilySearch for John's marriages to Rebecca Curie, Hanna Stapleton, and Rebecca O'Connel. If marriages are found, which children belong to which mother?

Searching WorldConnect

Goal: Search for John Barnett's marriage/children with Hanna Stapleton
Results: Found

Staying on the WorldConnect site, I entered the search criteria John Barnett, spouse: Stapleton. There were eight results. From those results, this is what was reported about Hanna

- Born in Virginia.
- Married to John in 1761, in Amherst County, Virginia.
- Father was Charles Stapleton, born 10 August 1734, in Oley, Berks County, Pennsylvania.
- Mother was Sarah Lawson.
- Hanna had five siblings, all born in Virginia.
- Hanna's name was possibly Janna.
- Child: James P. born 1762 in Amherst County, Virginia.
- James P.'s spouse was also listed, along with his child.

Since Hanna's family is not part of my search goal, I'll stop here.

Goal: Search for John Barnett's marriage/children with Rebecca O'Connel
Results: Unreliable

Staying on the WorldConnect site, I entered the search criteria John Barnett, spouse: O'Connel. There was one result. It showed Rebecca O'Connel being the mother of all eight of John's children. Based on what we've learned so far, this is unlikely.

Goal: Search for John Barnett's marriage/children with Rebecca Curie.
Results: Zero

Step By Step

STEP 3: BACK TO FAMILYSEARCH

Goal: Search for John Barnett's marriage/children with Hannah Stapleton.
Results: Marriage found

Using the search criteria John Barnett, spouse Stapleton, I found an individual record for John, noting a marriage to Janna Stapleton about 1761 in

Amherst or Henrico County, Virginia. Her place of marriage suggests that she may be the mother of James P., as he was born in Amherst in 1762.

Goal: Search for John Barnett's marriage/children with Rebecca O'Connel
Results: Found

Of John's eight children, we only know the probable mother of two:
- Mary: Mother was probably Rebecca Holcomb.
- James: Mother was supposedly Hanna Stapleton.

However, we don't know the mothers of
- Rachel
- Alexander
- John
- Jesse
- Jennie
- Ann

When I searched for John Barnett with a spouse named Rebecca O'Connel, the only results I got were in the Social Security Death Index (SSDI). Since SSDI records date from about 1962, they obviously aren't the ones I'm looking for. I then tried another approach: I entered the childrens' names in the main search box, and then entered John Barnett as the father.

Now here's where you have to be like a dog with a bone. **If one search structure doesn't work, try another.** When I entered Rachel Barnett with mother Rebecca O'Connel, I found nothing. When I entered Rachel Barnett with father John Barnett, however, I found a result in the IGI North America—a note of Rachel's 1772 birth in Lincoln County, Kentucky, and mother Rebecca O'Connel. Using the same approach, I found Alexander's 1770 Lincoln County, Kentucky, birth, Jesse's 1766 Amherst County, Virginia, birth, and Jennie Jane's 1768 Lincoln County, Kentucky, birth.

What have we discovered about the children and their mothers from online sources?
1. James, born Virginia circa 1762, Stapleton mother
2. Jesse, born Virginia circa 1766, O'Connel mother
3. Jennie, born Kentucky circa 1768, O'Connel mother
4. **Mary, born Kentucky about 1769, Holcomb mother**
5. Alexander, born Kentucky circa 1770, O'Connel mother
6. Rachel, born Kentucky circa 1772, O'Connel mother
7. John, unknown mother—but since his will says Mary is his half-sister, we know his mother cannot be Holcomb.
8. Ann, unknown mother

Now, unless John was married to two women simultaneously, Mary's birth cannot be 1769 since he hadn't married Rebecca Holcomb until November 1773. Based on this and her marriage to Elisha Moore in 1794, let's estimate Mary's birth around 1774. If this is so, then it appears that Rachel Holcomb was wife #3, not #2.

Reminder

Once again, I found nothing on Rebecca Curie. Whew. Let's take a breather and assess what we've found.

Assessment

Let's restate the original search goal: Find out more about John Barnett and his wife Rebecca Holcomb, parents of Mary Barnett. So far, after searching FamilySearch and WorldConnect, we found the following **(Remember! Everything needs to be verified in original sources. For now, these are just clues.)**

- Rebecca Holcomb was the mother of Mary Barnett.
- Rebecca and John were married in 1773.
- Mary was married in Lincoln County, Kentucky, in 1794.
- Mary was born about 1774.
- John Barnett was married four times.
- John was born in Pennsylvania.
- John's first marriage was in Virginia.
- John was in Kentucky at least by 1768 (Jennie's birth).
- John's last known child with Rebecca O'Connel was Rachel, born in 1772.
- Rebecca Holcomb was probably John's third wife.

What questions do these facts prompt?
1. Were John and Rebecca Holcomb married in Kentucky?
2. Was Rebecca born in Kentucky?
3. Did John really serve in the Revolutionary War?
4. Were many Kentucky settlers in the Revolutionary War?
5. Is Rebecca Holcomb the mother of Ann?
6. What is Rebecca's date of birth? About 1753?

Can any of these questions be answered by further searches on FamilySearch or WorldConnect? Maybe, let's see.

STEP 4: USING FAMILYSEARCH AND WORLDCONNECT TO FIND MORE INFORMATION

Goal: Find a Rebecca Holcomb, born in Kentucky. If found, is it possible she is John's wife?
Results: Questionable

Using the search criteria Rebecca Holcomb, birthplace Kentucky, I found nine matches in the IGI North America. (See figures 9-4 and 9-5 on page 171.) Of those, only one was the right age:

- Rebecca, born 1748, Perry, Kentucky (parents Joseph Holcomb, Leticia Day). However, I question these results because there were several other results for the same person, same parents, but with a birth date of 1854.

There were also three personal Web pages among the results, but none was relevant. The same search on WorldConnect was fruitless. At this point,

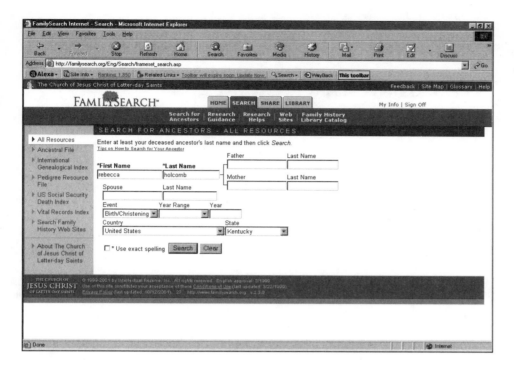

Figure 9-4
Will FamilySearch find a Rebecca Holcomb born in Kentucky? *Reprinted by permission. Copyright © 1999, 2001 by Intellectual Reserve, Inc.*

Figure 9-5
Search results. But is this "our" Rebecca? *Reprinted by permission. Copyright © 1999, 2001 by Intellectual Reserve, Inc.*

I'm not sure much more can be learned from these databases. Let's try some search engine work.

STEP 5: USING SEARCH ENGINES

Current questions

1. Were John and Rebecca Holcomb married in Kentucky?
2. Was Rebecca born in Kentucky?
3. Did John really serve in the Revolutionary War?
4. Were many Kentucky settlers in the Revolutionary War?
5. Is Rebecca Holcomb the mother of Ann?
6. What is Rebecca's date of birth? About 1753?
7. Why did John go from Pennsylvania to Virginia to Kentucky?
8. Can I uncover more about John's Pennsylvania family?

I tried my first search at Google.com:

"rebecca holcomb" + pennsylvania

One of the search results led to a personal Web site of Jesse Barnett <http://freepages.genealogy.rootsweb.com/~jessebarnett>. There is a note referencing William Barnett (born 1679). From the date and other information, it appears that William was the brother of John, (born 1678), who was Mary Barnett's great-grandfather (GGFJohn). In part, the note indicated that William and John (GGFJohn) came to Paxton Township, Lancaster County, Pennsylvania, about 1730 and settled at Barnett's Conquest—a farm within the lower forks of Beaver Creek, northeast of Linglestown, Pennsylvania. Apparently William bought a large tract that extended from the forks of Beaver Creek to the top of Blue Mountains. He built a large loghouse that was still standing in 1882.

This page also included some of the death dates and some of the marriages of John and Rebecca's family:

1. James, born Virginia 1762, died 1835 Lincoln County, Kentucky, married Jane McKinley
2. Jesse, born Virginia 1766
3. Jennie, born Virginia 1768
4. Alexander, born Kentucky 1770, died 1813, Crawford County, Indiana, married Mary Faith
5. Rachel, born Kentucky 1772
6. Mary, born Kentucky aft 1773
7. John, unknown mother—but since his will says Mary is his half-sister, we know his mother cannot be Holcomb; John died 1805, Lincoln County, Kentucky, m. Emma Green. (Note: Because I do not yet have a copy of John's will, I cannot verify that Mary is John's half-sister. Do you think his will has reference to any other siblings being referred to as "half"? On page 181, we'll see what John's will really said.)
8. Ann, married 31 December 1785, Lincoln County, Kentucky to Joseph Hall

There is also a note that a Jesse, John A., and Alexander Barnett were on the 1850 Orange County, Indiana, census.

Just to be certain where William's land was located, I visited the USGS Geographic Names Information System (GNIS) <http://geonames.usgs.gov/pls/gnis/web_query.gnis_web_query_form> and searched for both Beaver Creek and Linglestown. Beaver Creek is still in Lancaster County, but Linglestown is now in Dauphin County. I got the coordinates for both features from the GNIS query, then went to TopoZone <www.topozone.com> to print a map of the area. Next stop: The Dauphin County pages of the USGenWeb (see figure 9-6 below) <www.usgenweb.com>. A search of that site for Barnett found nine documents: Some were 1790 census transcripts, others a link to the Jesse Barnett site above, and another a mention of a John Barnett in a land transaction. There were no documents referable to Stapleton, Curie, O'Connel, or Holcomb.

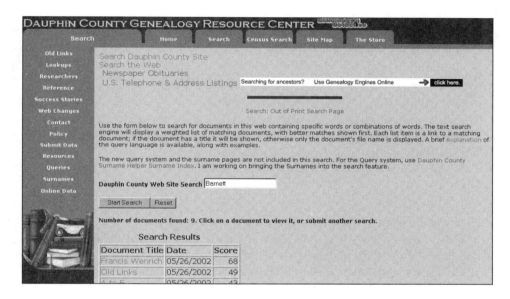

Figure 9-6
A search for Barnett on the Dauphin County, Pennsylvania USGenWeb page yielded nine results. *Copyright © 2002 and under license from MyFamily .com, Inc., all rights reserved.*

When I returned to Jesse Barnett's page, I found the marriage of Rebecca Holcomb and John Barnett, with a note saying the Continental Army information on John was taken from the *Encyclopedia of Pennsylvania Biography*. This reference lists Rebecca as the mother of all eight children and gives birth dates that conflict with those on the FamilySearch site. So which is correct? We won't know until we search the original documents. Conflicting information is common when doing online genealogy. There is an interesting side note, though: A "Mr. Curry" married Sarah Barnett, John's sister.

I bookmarked the Jesse Barnett page because of the tremendous amount of information not only on the Barnetts, but on the Roan family (Mary's grandmother was Margaret Roan). It was tempting to follow the Roan line, but that isn't my search goal today.

Another of the home pages that popped up during the Google search was My Celtic Roots <www.paradoxdesigns.com/celtic/fam00889.htm>. It also listed the John Barnett and Rebecca Holcomb marriage, and it showed all eight children as belonging to John and Rebecca. In skimming through the list of children, however, one thing caught my eye. Although several of the eight children died in Lincoln County, Kentucky, Alexander died in Crawford County, Indiana. The reference to Indiana stood out because it's the first occurrence in all our searches on the family, and I know that Polly Moore and Aaron Hendrickson ended up in Indiana. Is there a connection? Probably.

Next, Google searches for

"rebecca holcomb" +lancaster

"rebecca holcomb" +virginia +barnett

A search for

"rebecca holcomb" +virginia +"john barnett"

turned up a query that had been posted on a Lancaster County query site. It read

> BARNETT, John Looking for a Lancaster Pennsylvania connection to John Barnett, born 1709 in Londonderry, Ireland. Wife was Ann SPRATT. John and his two brothers left Ireland for the US, William Barnett b. 1715, and Thomas Barnett b. 1720. John's father was William Barnett b. ca 1670 in Londonderry, Ireland. John and Ann Spratt had the following children: William Barnett b. 1732, Susan Barnett b. 1761, Ann Barnett, Mary Barnett, John Barnett, Thomas Barnett and Jane Barnett. John Barnett and family eventually moved into Mecklenburg County, NC.

Notes

Yes, there are a lot of similarities, but the dates and some of the children's names don't jive with what we've learned. **But this is a note to tuck away in your research software to pursue another day.**

Another search engine result took me back to the Jesse Barnett "notes" page <http://freepages.genealogy.rootsweb.com/~jessebarnett/Barnett/notes .html>. There were several fascinating notes, which originally had appeared in the *Belfast* (Ireland) *Times* in 1858. They were

- William Barnett (Mary's second-great-grandfather) served in the siege of Derry in 1663.
- The family came to Ireland from Scotland prior to 1634.
- John's uncle, Robert, died in 1773/1774 in Amherst County, Virginia.
- John's uncle, James, died in Albemarle County, Virginia.

There are also pages of Barnett and collateral family information—and enough clues to keep a researcher busy for months.

Did you notice that at least two of John's uncles were in Virginia? Maybe that's why he left Pennsylvania?

Another bust: "john barnett" +"amherst virginia"

And another: "john barnett" +"rebecca holcomb"

And more: "rebecca holcomb" +kentucky

"rebecca holcomb" +virginia

How about "john barnett" +"rebecca o'connel"? This led to another personal page, showing John's death of 1815 in Harrison County, Indiana. Another search of "john barnett" + "revolutionary war" resulted in a page of Revolutionary War soldiers buried in Harrison County, Indiana. John's listing read

> John Barnett was born probably in Virginia. He died in 1816. He was married to an O'Connel. Children mentioned in will: James P. born 1762, Virginia, died 31 March 1834; John; Jesse; Alexander married Mary Faith; Jennie married William Lawrence; Mary married Elisha Hall; Ann married Joseph Hall; Joseph; Polly married Elisha Moore. Source Page 15, *Roster of Soldiers and Patriots of the American Revolution Buried in Indiana*, 1966.

Did you note that the list above contains nine children, compared to the eight we knew before? Joseph is a new name—who is he? And, did you notice that the wife of Elisha Moore is listed as Polly, which is a nickname for Mary? But then, who is the Mary who married an Elisha Hall? Is this a transcription error? And where is daughter Rachel? More questions . . . more conflicts to research.

Time for Another Assessment

- We know some of John's uncles went to Virginia.
- Did John marry Hanna Stapleton in Virginia?
- Why did John go to Kentucky?
- Did John meet Rebecca O'Connel in Virginia or Kentucky?
- Where did John meet Rebecca Holcomb?
- What was John doing in Indiana?
- John had a will, probably in Harrison County, Indiana.
- How many wives and children did John actually have?

Where would you go next? There are many possibilities, aren't there? **Let's think them out:**

Notes

1. The Rebecca Holcomb search has turned up nothing at all. Is it worth continuing looking for her or hoping to find her indirectly? Maybe rely on networking by posting queries about her?
2. If John had a will (as noted above), did it mention a wife? That's something to look for. And does it really name the nine children?
3. Was John living near a Hendrickson, Moore, or Barnett family before his death? Maybe we could find him on an 1810 census.
4. We know that Alexander died in Crawford County, Indiana, and a Jesse, John, and Alexander Barnett were in the Orange County, Indiana, 1850 census. We do not know if they are part of the family.
5. Since John was supposedly married four times, is it possible that we can find a marriage record, or four of them?
6. Since John was out of Pennsylvania by at least 1762 (the date of Alexander's birth), is it worth pursuing more research in Pennsylvania right now? Could there be two John Barnetts; one from Pennsylvania and one from Virginia?

7. Should we look for a Holcomb, O'Connel, or Currie on an early Virginia tax list or state census?
8. If John is living with one of his children in Harrison County, I need to look for the children on an Indiana census or other record. But if he is living with one of the children, he won't be named, so we need to look for a male in his age category living with one of the children.
9. If John married Hanna Stapleton in Virginia, and most of the O'Connel children were born in Kentucky, is it reasonable to assume that Rebecca Holcomb lived in Kentucky?

PLAN OF ACTION

- Visit the surname forums/bulletin boards and post queries regarding Rebecca Holcomb.
- Check for Rebecca's marriage in Kentucky. If we can't find marriage records online, then we'll have to head for the Family History Center and check for records on microfilm.
- Check for Holcombs in Lincoln County, Kentucky.
- Search for Barnett on an 1810 Indiana census.
- Search appropriate USGenWeb county pages for tax lists or census information on Holcomb and Barnett.
- Check Indiana federal land records for Barnetts.

STOP THE PRESS

Goodness. I realized I didn't take my own good search engine advice. So before proceeding with the above plan of action, I went back to the search engines and typed in *"holcomb genealogy."* I thought I'd hit the jackpot when the search results pointed me to the Web site of "Holcombe Family Genealogy." I was doubly sure of my luck when I saw a marriage between Rebecca Holcombe and John Barnett. Unfortunately, this Rebecca was too old to be "our" Rebecca. Back to the plan.

Step By Step

STEP 6: POSTING QUERIES

I visited the message boards and forums mentioned in chapter five, and posted queries for Rebecca Holcomb. I also joined the Holcomb and Barnett mailing lists and the Lincoln County, Kentucky, mailing list. While I'm waiting, I could order the will on microfilm at the Family History Center or from the county courthouse. (See figure 9-7 on page 177.)

Step By Step

STEP 7: A VISIT TO THE USGENWEB

<www.usgenweb.com>
At this point, I'm going to visit the Lincoln County, Kentucky, and Amherst County, Virginia, and Crawford and Harrison counties, Indiana, pages of the USGenWeb and see if I can dig up any census, tax lists, deeds, wills,

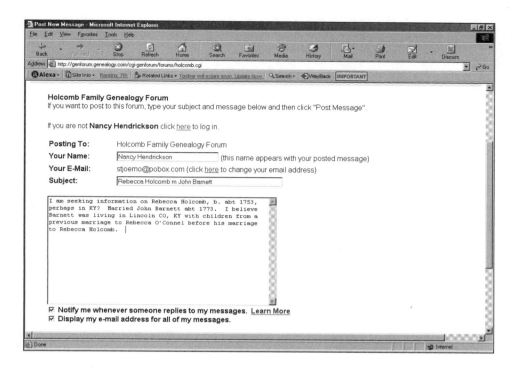

marriages, deaths, or births for Rebecca Holcomb and John Barnett's family.

Just as a reminder, here are the clues and unverified information about Rebecca, John, and the children (marriage and death data taken from the Jesse Barnett page):

1. John was born circa 1745, Pennsylvania (or Virginia).
2. Rebecca was born around 1753.
3. John and Rebecca were married probably in 1773, maybe in Pennsylvania, maybe Kentucky.
4. James, born Virginia circa 1762, married Jane McKinley, died 1835, Lincoln County, Kentucky.
5. Jesse, born Virginia circa 1766.
6. Jennie, born Kentucky circa 1768.
7. Alexander, born Kentucky circa 1770, married Mary Faith, died 1813, Crawford Co., Indiana.
8. Rachel, born Kentucky circa 1772.
9. Mary, born Kentucky after 1773.
10. John, unknown mother (and his birth order is uncertain)—but since his will says Mary is his half-sister, we know his mother cannot be Holcomb; married Emma Green, died 1805 Lincoln County, Kentucky.
11. Ann, married December 31, 1785, Lincoln County, Kentucky, to Joseph Hall.
12. Is there now a ninth child, Joseph?

The Amherst page of the USGenWeb contained a list of Virginia "Head of Families" from 1783. Although John was probably long gone from Virginia at this time, I ran a Barnett search and found a William, Robert, and

John. Are they related? Maybe, but let's save those clues for another search. For the most part, the information on the Amherst site related to events after John's departure. Unfortunately, the Lincoln County, Kentucky, site wasn't a help either. I then decided to search the USGenWeb archives <www .rootsweb.com/~usgenweb/>. My first search was of the Lincoln County, Kentucky archives. I found a brief biography of a Captain Robert Barnett— a person who came to Lincoln County from Virginia. I bookmarked the biography in case I later discovered a relationship.

On the 1810 census, I discovered a James, Robert, Ann, and John Barnett, all listed as heads of household. The 1810 census also showed a Joseph Hall (remember, Ann was married to a Joseph Hall), as well as listings for surnames McKinley and Green (spouses of James and John). Continuing with my search of the Lincoln County, Kentucky, archives, I also found a Robert Barnett as a witness on a 1799 deed. However, I couldn't find one mention of a Holcomb anywhere on the site.

Want to try Indiana? A search of the USGenWeb Indiana Archives for John Barnett <www.rootsweb.com/~usgenweb/in/insearch.htm> in Harrison County and Orange County was another bust. When I searched for early marriages in Crawford County (where Alexander is supposed to have died), I found a listing for

- Jesse Barnett married Elleanore French 23 October 1823.
- John Barnett married Lucinda Wyman 14 January 1824.
- William Barnett married Nancy Clevenger 17 April 1828.
- Elizabeth Barnett married Peter Stalcup 11 February 1819.

I also found Alexander Barnett on the 1820 census and Jesse Barnett on the 1830 census in Crawford County. Do you remember that John's son, Alexander, supposedly died in 1813? Of course, we don't know if the 1813 death is correct, or if any of these Crawford County Barnetts belong to this line. A last try at the Indiana connection will be through federal land records—if they exist.

STEP 8: LAND RECORDS AT THE GENERAL LAND OFFICE

Step By Step

<www.glorecords.blm.gov>

Instead of searching for each Barnett separately, I did a global search for all Barnett federal land records in Indiana. Because the earliest records are from 1820, and we think John died in 1816, clearly he won't be in these records—however, if any of his children had federal land in Indiana, we would probably start checking those counties for John's will (an offline project).

The federal land search for Barnett in Indiana resulted in nine pages of results. Among them were Alexander, Jesse, James, Charlotte, and John in Crawford County. If you look at the legal description, you'll see that Alexander, James, and Jesse's land all border each other. The issue date for Jesse and Alexander's land was August 15, 1838; for James it was 9 January,

1841. There were no matching records for a Barnett in Harrison County.
What do you think?

Here are my thoughts: If the Alexander, Jesse, and James in Crawford County are part of John Barnett's family, why is he in Harrison County and they in Crawford? Is it possible that where Alexander, Jesse, and James farmed was, at one time, part of Harrison County? Or maybe the available land was cheaper to buy in the next county over? I went to a search engine and typed in "indiana map." One of the hits <www.indico.net> displayed a county map showing Harrison and Crawford counties bordering each other, with Orange just north of Crawford.

Next, I searched for "*formation of indiana counties*" and followed a link to a page with <www.rootsweb.com/~inripchs/indiana.html> with county formation dates. Harrison was formed in 1808 from Knox and Clark counties, Orange in 1816 from Washington, Knox, and Gibson, and Crawford in 1818 from Orange, Harrison and Perry counties. Now I needed to find confirmation that Orange and/or Crawford were formed from Harrison. (See figures 9-8 below and 9-9 on page 180.)

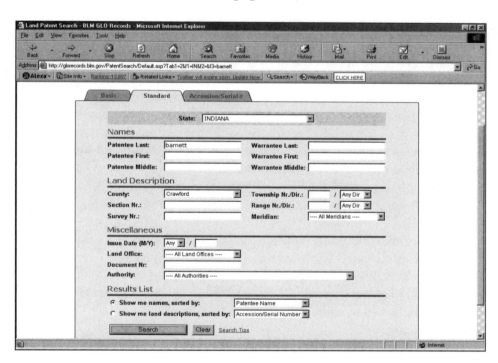

Figure 9-8
Search criteria to find Barnett land holders in Crawford County, Indiana. *Bureau of Land Management, General Land Office Records*

Back to the search engine and the query:

> formation of crawford county indiana

The link I followed <http://home.att.net/~Local_History/Harrison-Co-IN.h tm> had information confirming that the eastern half of Crawford was formed from Harrison County. So there is a possibility that Alexander, James, and Jesse (if they even are related to John) lived close to him in Harrison, but found themselves in Crawford when the boundary lines changed in 1818.

Figure 9-9
Is it possible these people belong to "our" Barnett family?
Bureau of Land Management, General Land Office Records

The Internet Search Draws to an End

If you've been following this search, it's probably evident to you how an effective Internet genealogist goes back and forth across the Net as clues are uncovered. And you've also seen that some searches come to a dead end. In this case it's the Rebecca Holcomb mystery. **By now, though, I have enough information about the family that I can begin searching for her at offline facilities, such as my local Family History Center.**

The other half of the search goal—to discover more about John Barnett—ended with some interesting tidbits and many leads to follow offline, including

Library/Archive Source

- his Virginia-related Revolutionary war service (Note: At the time of the Revolutionary War, Kentucky was part of Virginia.)
- his (?) Kentucky marriage to Rebecca Holcomb
- his Irish heritage—particularly that of his mother's Roan family
- his Virginia marriage
- his Indiana will

If you've discovered more than this, you deserve an A+ in Internet genealogy!

Step By Step

STEP 9: TO THE LIBRARY!

Now that I've done a thorough Internet search, I need to sort out all the conflicts and discrepancies from the online sources. So, it's time to turn off the computer and seek out some of the original records to verify what I've found. Certified Genealogist Sharon DeBartolo Carmack was making a trip to the Family History Library in Salt Lake City, Utah, and offered to look up some records for me on John Barnett and his family. Here's what she found.

Sharon first looked for the book *Revolutionary Soldiers Buried in Indiana* to compare what I had found on the Internet with what the book actually said. She found *Revolutionary Soldiers Buried in Indiana* (1949) with Supplement (1954), compiled by Margaret R. Waters, two volumes in one (Baltimore: Genealogical Publishing Company, 1970), and it gave more detailed information:

> p. 4 Barnett, John   Harrison Co.
>
> d. 1816 (will written 3-22-1815; proved 10-25-1816); m.— O'Connell (living 1815); chn.—James P., b. 1762, Amherst Co., Va., (living 1832 Lincoln Co., Ky.), d. 3-31-1834; John; Jesse; Alexander m. Mary Faith; Jennie m. William Lawrence (& had chn. Rachel & Samuel); Rachel m. Samuel Lawrence; Mary ("Polly") m. Elisha Hall; Ann m. Joseph Hall. Fam. Moved to Guildford Co., N.C., when son James was young; there during Rev. John Barnett qualifies as a Patriot because his son James P. served as a substitute for him. REF: Pens. S12963 N.C. & Va. (son James); Ind. Mag. of Hist. v. 37, p. 93; Thelma Murphy.

So John didn't actually serve in the Revolution! His son, James, did. More on this in a minute.

Sharon also found that John Barnett did leave a will in Harrison County, Indiana. It was recorded in Will Book A, pages 43-44 on Family History Library (FHL) microfilm 1404686. Here's a transcription of that will:

> In the Name of God Amen
>
> I John Barnett of the County of Harrison and Indiana territory being in reasonable health and of sound memory but far advanced in life and knowing that death is the certain lot of all the living do Constitute and ordain this My last will and testament (that is to say) first I do Most sincerely recommend both my soul & body to almighty God that gave it. My body to be buried in A Christian like manner at the discretion of my executors and as touching the things that God in his kind providence has graciously blessed me with in this life to give demise & dispose of in the following manner and form (to wit) to my beloved Son Alexander Barnett I do give the whole and full amount of the piece of my land which is —in the State of Kentucky. I do also give to my son in law Joseph Hall the sum of five dollars. And to my son James Barnett the Aforsd sum of five dollars and further do leave and bestow to Rachael Lawrence & Samuel Lawrence my grand Children by William Lawrence their father the remaining part or balance of my property consisting of Moveable property. I do hereby give my to my [sic] affectionate soninlaw Elisha Moore provided that so much of the aforesaid estate as may be needed for support during life shall be at the disposal of myself or my beloved Wife and I do hereby declare all former wills made by me utterly null & void as though such

wills had never been in testimony whereof I have hereunto set my hand and seal this 22nd day of March in the year of our Lord 1815.

		his	
Test		John X Barnett	
James Rawlins		mark	
William Rawlins			

Indiana Territory
Harrison County

This day James Rawlins and William Rawlins came personally before me Richard M. Heth clerk of the circuit court for said county and made oath that John Barnett Deceased signed sealed & published & declared the within Instrument of writing purporting to be his last will & testament to be his act and deed wherefore I have admitted the same to record in my office in Will Book A pages 43 and 44. October 25, 1816.

Test

Interesting. There's no mention of a son Jesse or a son Joseph. Did they die before father John made his will or did John even have two other sons? John mentions a wife, but doesn't name her. So where did all the other information in *Revolutionary Soldiers Buried in Indiana* come from?

Reminder

Just like the online search, research into original records often raises new questions and leads to follow. Sharon then checked for son James's pension record to see what additional information it contained. It contained details on James's service and battles, plus this from the microfilm of Revolutionary War Pension and Bounty Land Application Files, FHL 970150.

James P. Barnett of Lincoln in the State of Kentucky was a private in the Company commanded by Captain Leak of the regiment commanded by Col. Martin in the North Carolina & Virginia Line for one year from 1780. Pension issued 19 Jan 1833; arrears to 4 September 1832.

On this 22nd day of October 1832 personally appeared before me in open court before the Justices of the Lincoln County Court, State of Kentucky, now sitting, James P. Barnett, a resident of Lincoln County, state of Kentucky, aged seventy years, who being first duly sworn . . . make the following declaration in order to obtain the benefit of the Act of Congress passed June 7th 1832.

That he entered the service of the United States . . . as a substitute for his father John Barnett under the following named officers and served as herein stated. . . . That he was born in Amherst County State of Virginia in 1762. That he was taken to North Carolina to Guilford County when he was young. That he left North Carolina in 1781 and came to Kentucky & directly after the Battle of Guilford Court House, where he has remained ever since. . . . He can prove the greater part of his services by Mrs. Ann Hall, Joseph Hall, Benjamin Briggs and Abraham Estes.

Notice that we now have another locality in which to look for the Barnett family: Guilford County, North Carolina.

Sharon also checked for son John's will to see if it really did say that Polly/Mary was his half-sister. Sharon found the will in Will Book B:272–274, Lincoln County, Kentucky, FHL 192227:

Under and through the perrvision [*sic*] of God Amen I John Barnett Junr of Lincoln county now in a state of lingering indisposition but possessed of my common rational faculties do in the presence of the Witnesses hereto under signed make and declare this Instrument of Writing to be my last Will and testament and do make hereby all other statements Declarations or Writings in the first place it is and I do declare it as my Will that my executors should have me buried at the at the [*sic*] bufoloe [*sic*] Spring meeting house such way and maner [*sic*] as they may think proper and have the same walled in in [*sic*] accordingly. In the second place it is my will that my executors should pay all my Just debts and I do will that all my estate of every description Shall be disposed of in following manner to wit By Executors First I do will to the children of my half of my half [*sic*] sister Polly wife of Elisha Moore my dark bay mare called buff coat and a red and white heifer called Frosty's Heifer to their use and equal proportion. Secondly I do will to Anna Barnett daughter Daughter [*sic*] of Robert Barnett twenty pounds. I do will that my executors shall out of the money arising out of my estate give to William Mcneely of Montgomery County in the state of Virginia the sum of sixty dollars[,] thirty Dollars of which to his daughter Polly Mcneety [*sic*] it being for their kind services and love which I do ~~have for~~ [written above "have for"] ~~bare~~ them. I do will that my executors Shall as soon as my two negro girls silva and leah is [*sic*] capable of Learning to spin flax hemp wool etc. & that they shall then Learnt to knit sew and after they acquired the Knowledge of the above businesses they shall Hired [be] out & to be Keept [*sic*] at those Businesses and I do in the next place Will that my executors shall sell all the residue of my estate real mixed and personal at such time in such manner and upon such terms whether private or public sales as to them may seem best & most proper and to convey transfer & do Whatever is right to be done relative thereto and I do hereby Will bequeath and devise all the proceeds therefrom & also my said negroes and hirage And every thing whatever exept [*sic*] the legasees [*sic*] above mentioned to my little child recognized & acknowledged by me as my child called & named Green Barnett now in the care aand [*sic*] of Susanah Gibbs except my dark Chestnut sorrel Mare called Spedel which I will to Joseph Hall and my will and desire is that my little child Green Barnett shall be well educated and Morally brough [*sic*] up untill [*sic*] twenty one years of age unless he shall die before and my will & desire is should he die before he arrives to the age of twenty one years that thereupon all which I have willed unto him herein and which he should hereby claim and have shall be equally divided share and share alike among the children of Joseph hall and my sister Ann Hall his wife together begotten and the children of my brothers James Barnett begotten by his present wife & my will and desire is that my executors hereafter named shall act as guardian for my said son and child Green untill he arrives to the age of twenty one and I do hereby constitute & appoint Joseph Hall and John Welsh Executors of this my last Will & testament in Witness Whereof I have hereunto subscribed my name and afixed my seal this fifteenth day of March in the year of our Lord one thousand eight hundred & five but I do further declare it is my will and Desire that my little child Green Barnett Shall be well cloathed [*sic*] at all times agreeable to the season and all moneys that may and shall be received by my Executors that shall arise from the proceed of of [*sic*] my estate shall be kept out on Interest for his benefit Ecept [*sic*] such part as I have otherwise otherways [*sic*] devised in such hands With security as will good

Executed in the presence of

Witnesses   John Barnett [seal]
Richard Gaines
Ja^s Welsh
Gab^l Lackey
Andrew Hall
State of Kentucky Lincoln county ___ [looks like "s F."]

At a county [*sic*] held for Lincoln county the 8th of Aprile [*sic*] 1805 this instrument of Writing was exhibitted [*sic*] in court as the last will and testament of John Barnett Dec^d and proved by the Oath of Richard Gaines Gabriel Lacky Andrew Hall and admitted to Record Witness Thomas Montgomery clerk of Lincoln county court of Lincoln.

Thomas Montgomery

John does indeed refer to Polly, wife of Elisha Moore, as his half-sister. What's especially interesting is how he refers to his son, Green, as his "little child recognized and acknowledged by me." Was this child born out of wedlock? Why else would he say that this child is "recognized and acknowledged by me"? Sharon searched for a marriage record for John prior to his death, but none could be found.

Look at all of the interesting details and information from these original records that you would miss if you confined your search to the Internet. Although Sharon exhausted just about all of the records in Lincoln County, Kentucky, and discovered a great deal about the John Barnett family, she still hasn't found any evidence of the names of John's wives, nor how many he actually had. But the search will continue, and I think the point is well made:

- start your search on the Internet, and gather as much information and as many clues as you can,

Important

- be alert to discrepancies and inconsistencies (and don't let them frustrate you too much),
- then seek out the original records.

If you can't make a trip to the Family History Library, the same results can be achieved by ordering the microfilms at a Family History Center, by writing to the county courthouse, or hiring someone to get them for you.

WHAT'S NEXT?
Sharing your research finds with the world.

TEN

Sharing Your Research

Idea Generator

A few years ago I received an e-mail that began, "Let me introduce myself. I'm Sheryl, your Aunt Alice's daughter." Sheryl, it turns out, had read an article I'd written and was sending her congratulations. The last time we'd seen or heard from one another was 1960. Sheryl's note began the slow reunification of our far-flung family. Our electronic "family reunions" have given us—and our aunts, uncles, and cousins—a chance to catch up on life, climb the family tree and share our memories. Two of my aunts, whose ages I am forbidden to reveal, bought computers and enthusiastically joined the ancestral hunt. One of them routinely e-mails me the Web sites that mention our family.

Sending an e-mail to family is just one avenue of sharing your research. **Why not post it to the Web and share it with the world?** After all, if it weren't for the hundreds of thousands of genealogy Web sites—most created by amateurs—there wouldn't be much to find on the Net. How can you share?

- post to forums and mailing lists
- create a research group
- build your own family Web site
- share old photos
- start an electronic family newsletter
- introduce other family members to genealogy

POST TO FORUMS

Remember back in chapter three when I mentioned the file sent to me by Mike Gregory? To refresh your memory, I had visited the Gregory Family Forum at GenForum.com and made a connection with Mike, who generously shared his findings. Wouldn't it be great if everyone were like him? Well, you can be by visiting the forums and message boards you found in chapter five and letting people know about your research findings and what you are willing to share.

Briefly, I'd like to mention a somewhat touchy subject: handing over your research to other people. It's a touchy subject because some people have abused the kindness of others. Here's how it can play out. Researcher A shares his information with Researcher B, then later finds his work on Researcher B's Web site, without proper credit given. It has happened. But should that keep you from helping others? No.

Facts, such as names and dates, cannot be protected by copyright. That means if you discover the birthdate of an ancestor named Paxton Jones and then share the information with other researchers, they can freely post that date. What is protected by copyright is the "body" of your work. That means someone cannot take your "creative expression" of those facts and post them without your permission.

Reminder

So please share your findings with others—but be sure to add a note saying that your material cannot be used without your permission. In fact, if you look carefully at most Web sites—even personal ones—there is a copyright notice somewhere on the page. For example, go to <www.rootsweb.com/~txlimest/faulkenberry.txt>, and you'll find a survey of a Limestone County, Texas, cemetery, transcribed by a volunteer. At the top of the page, the copyright notice is clearly displayed. This may all seem like a bother, but hopefully it will not deter you from becoming a generous participant in the online genealogy community.

So return to those forums and message boards, such as the USGenWeb, GenForum, and RootsWeb, and start posting. You don't have to leave a lengthy note detailing all of your research, just something like this:

> I have information on the family of Josiah Graves, b. about 1757, in Worcester Co., Massachusetts. Contact me to exchange or share research.

MAILING LISTS

Remember those mailing lists you joined back in chapter six? Perhaps you've already networked with a few Internet cousins via mailing lists. Now it's time to go back onto the appropriate lists to share your information.

What you'll post to the list depends on any rules specified by the list owner. She may prefer that you not leave lengthy posts about all your findings, but rather a brief note summarizing the family you're researching and what information you have to share.

Now that you've let people know what information you have to share, get prepared. That means either creating a GEDCOM that only pertains to the family line you're ready to share, or putting together a text file of your data. Here's how:

SPLITTING GEDCOMs

Do you keep every branch of your family tree in one huge GEDCOM file? Many people do. However, you don't want to e-mail your entire genealogy

Notes

to someone who is only interested in a tiny portion. There are a couple of easy ways to handle this situation. **One is to create separate files for each line; the other is to export a GEDCOM that only contains a specific portion of your file.**

For our purposes, let's assume you have one big file and you want to create a GEDCOM for the Graves branch. How you do this is dependent on your software program. In Legacy Family Tree, for example, you merely set a "focus group." The focus group may be a single family, an individual and ancestors, an individual and descendants, or an individual and an entire family line. Next, you select the individual (or family) then decide whether to include siblings and spouses. After all the options have been chosen, the software creates the appropriate GEDCOM.

Splitting a Family Tree Maker file involves the use of custom reports. Because the procedure varies depending on what version you are using, go to <www.genealogy.com/help/index.html>, click Knowledge Base, then type "splitting gedcom" in the search box. A list of pertinent articles will then be displayed.

Consult the Help files of your genealogy software for specific information on splitting a file.

CREATING TEXT FILES

Have you ever received a file that you couldn't read? That's because people use different software programs for note keeping or word processing, and their program saves it in a unique file format. Note: A format is the way a program stores information. You can tell which format is used by the file extension (the three letters after the file name). For example, the extension on a Microsoft Word file is .doc; a type of graphic file is .jpg.

If you have a Microsoft Word file, for example, it can be read by anyone else who uses Word. If someone is using a different word processing program, however, they won't be able to read the Word format. Word does allow you to save your file in other formats (including WordPerfect) by choosing Save As in the File menu, and then choosing WordPerfect in the pull-down "type" menu.

Another easy solution is to save your file as a text file. That means it won't retain any fancy formatting, but it can be read by just about any program, including EditPad, WordPad, Notepad and all word processing programs. Files can be saved as text files by using the Save As command, and then choosing text as the file type.

CREATE A RESEARCH GROUP

You know that old saying about two heads being better than one? Well, why not ten heads or twenty? As you know, genealogy can be a time-consuming hobby. In fact, it entails so much research most people concentrate on only a few of their lines. Who has time to tackle twenty or thirty? That's where research groups come in.

Once you start meeting other family researchers online, why not form a family research group? For instance, let's say you meet five people who are all descended from the same third-great-grandfather. (To help calculate finding your common ancestors see relationship chart on page 190.) How might you split research tasks? Maybe you'd split up the different family lines. Or, perhaps you'd divide by type of tasks, e.g., one person tackles the census, another marriage records, and another county histories. You could even divide tasks by locale, with each person doing research in a specific county.

Once the research group is formed, you could share findings via e-mail, or a Web site. If you decide on the e-mail route, be sure to adjust your e-mail filters so you can keep all related e-mail messages in a single folder. If you decide to build a family Web site, you can upload research findings, family photos, or scanned images of family mementos.

BUILD A FAMILY WEB SITE

If you haven't created a family Web site, you're missing the chance to collaborate on a global scale. In the past, long-distance families didn't have the luxury of sharing old photos around the dining room table. But today, the Internet has made that possible and more. Creating a family Web site allows distant cousins to divide research tasks, share findings, upload documents, and post old and new family photos.

When amateur genealogist Kevin Macomber grew frustrated with the duplicated research he found on the Internet, he created an organization to pool family data. His Macomber Project <www.macomberproject.com>, which began as an e-mail collaboration, evolved into a Web site that has grown to 160-plus active researchers. The site boasts online databases of military records, photos, and close to two thousand family burial sites. As new researchers come on board, Macomber identifies which branch of the family they belong to, then connects them with their own mini-research group.

If you'd like to build a collaborative site, here's a behind-the-scenes peek at what's involved and what you can include.

RESEARCH TASKS

Every family has scores of branches to research. Using a family Web site makes it easy to break down research tasks, avoid duplication of efforts, and share findings. Almost three hundred Wickware/Wickwire families use their Web site <www.wickware.com> and newsletter to share stories, photos, and genealogy research. Site guru Rick Wickwire says that when one person sends information, it inspires other members to participate and send their data.

The basis of the Wickware/Wickwire project is a book published about the family in 1909. Current members have attempted to update it by finding missing ancestors and bringing all of the lines forward to present day. Thanks to collaborative research, enough information has been added to expand the original 283-page book to between five and seven volumes.

Research tasks can include pooling census data, listings from city directo-

	1	2	3	4	5	6	7	8	9
	COMMON ANCESTOR	SON/DAU.	GRAND-SON	GREAT GRAND-SON	G-G GRAND-SON	G-G-G GRAND-SON	4G GRAND-SON	5G GRAND-SON	6G GRAND-SON	7G GRAND-SON
1	SON/DAU.	BRO/SIS.	NEPHEW/NIECE	GRAND NEPHEW	GREAT GRAND-NEPHEW	G-G GRAND-NEPHEW	G-G-G GRAND-NEPHEW	4G GRAND-NEPHEW	5G GRAND-NEPHEW	6G GRAND-NEPHEW
2	GRAND-SON	NEPHEW/NIECE	1ST COUSIN	1 COU 1 R	1 COU 2 R	1 COU 3 R	1 COU 4 R	1 COU 5 R	1 COU 6 R	1 COU 7 R
3	GREAT GRAND-SON	GRAND NEPHEW	1 COU 1 R	2ND COUSIN	2 COU 1 R	2 COU 2 R	2 COU 3 R	2 COU 4 R	2 COU 5 R	2 COU 6 R
4	G-G GRAND-SON	GREAT GRAND-NEPHEW	1 COU 2 R	2 COU 1 R	3RD COUSIN	3 COU 1 R	3 COU 2 R	3 COU 3 R	3 COU 4 R	3 COU 5 R
5	G-G-G GRAND-SON	G-G GRAND-NEPHEW	1 COU 3 R	2 COU 2 R	3 COU 1 R	4TH COUSIN	4 COU 1 R	4 COU 2 R	4 COU 3 R	4 COU 4 R
6	4G GRAND-SON	3G GRAND-NEPHEW	1 COU 4 R	2 COU 3 R	3 COU 2 R	4 COU 1 R	5TH COUSIN	5 COU 1 R	5 COU 2 R	5 COU 3 R
7	5G GRAND-SON	4G GRAND-NEPHEW	1 COU 5 R	2 COU 4 R	3 COU 3 R	4 COU 2 R	5 COU 1 R	6TH COUSIN	6 COU 1 R	6 COU 2 R
8	6G GRAND-SON	5G GRAND-NEPHEW	1 COU 6 R	2 COU 5 R	3 COU 4 R	4 COU 3 R	5 COU 2 R	6 COU 1 R	7TH COUSIN	7 COU 1 R
9	7G GRAND-SON	6G GRAND-NEPHEW	1 COU 7 R	2 COU 6 R	3 COU 5 R	4 COU 4 R	5 COU 3 R	6 COU 2 R	7 COU 1 R	8TH COUSIN

RELATIONSHIP CHART ABBREVIATIONS

The chart may be extended in either direction for identifying more distant relationships.

BRO = brother
SIS = sister
DAU = daughter
COU = cousin
R = removed (generations removed)

G-G = great-great
GRANDSON = grandson or granddaughter
SON = son or daughter
NEPHEW = nephew or niece

ries, marriages, land records, and wills. In the case of brick walls, sometimes the biggest leaps can be made by family members sitting around the cyber-table and "what-iffing." These brainstorming sessions can spark a long-forgotten name or story.

Images

Although hundreds of people may be descended from a common ancestor, sometimes only one branch ends up with old photos. Posting pictures to a family site is the easiest way to share valuable treasures and ensure that they don't get lost or further damaged over time. In addition, many old photos are unlabeled, and uploading them to a well-visited family site can help identify both people and places. **But use caution in posting images of living people, especially children.** You can't be too cautious, even with a password-protected site.

Warning

On the Wickware/Wickwire site, the Photo Album pages contain pictures of ancestors and current family members. Also included are photos from the family's English town of origin, Wickwar. On another family site called The Unwritten <http://library.thinkquest.org/C001313/index.html>, three teenage cousins, Karisa, Mandy, and Charanna, bring their family to life with "photo stories." These are family photos with an accompanying narrative, like a newspaper article or handed-down story. For example, the photo-story of their great-grandmother contains a picture of her as a young girl and tells how the family fought illness during the 1918 influenza epidemic.

Although family members can take digital photos of old pictures, the easiest way to convert a vintage photo to digital is by scanning. Scanned images can then be sent to the site's Webmaster for uploading. Scanners are now available for under one hundred dollars, and come with software, most of which includes Web imaging options (see page 193 for more on scanning).

Documents

Online images aren't always family photos. Your family site can contain entries from a journal or diary, a Civil War regimental history, wills, deeds, a dance card, Valentine, V-mail, calling card, or handkerchief. Anything that can be scanned or photographed can be included on your site.

The Wickwire's Museum page includes photos of an ad for the family business, a stock certificate, books written by family members, a business invoice, and promotional matchbook. They even included a photo of K2—one of the mountains climbed by Jim Wickwire. Each photo in the museum is pictured as a "thumbnail" (small image), which can be clicked on to see a larger picture.

The Webmaster

Although collaborative Web sites depend on the work of each member, the task of coordinating the efforts and keeping the site current usually falls on one or two members. In the case of the Macomber Project, Kevin's "cousin" Tim McCumber volunteered for the job of Webmaster, although he had no

Figure 10-2

Create an online museum of family memorabilia. *Charles F. Wickwire*

Web design experience. Tim bought a copy of Microsoft Front Page and learned it on the fly. As data comes in, Kevin organizes it and then passes it along to Tim to post online. Rick Wickwire and his son Trey use much the same method. Rick keeps everyone in the family informed about research, photos, and the Web site via an electronic newsletter; then, as information is returned to him, he sends it to Trey, the Webmaster. The father and son devote several hours each week to the family's site.

If you are just starting your family site, you may wear the hat of project coordinator, data organizer, and Webmaster. As coordinator, it is your job to organize the data that is already collected, then set up research groups with specific tasks, such as census transcriptions or the research of a specific line. As data is returned, you'll need to put it in an organized fashion to send along to the site's Webmaster.

Although Webmasters can get free Web hosting at a wide variety of sites, you may want to register a domain name (about fifteen to thirty-five dollars a year) and pay for a site host (eight dollars a month and up). See below for more on choosing a host.

Depending on how computer-savvy your family is, Webmasters may need to explain scanning techniques, photo formats, and e-mail attachments. Creating a Frequently Asked Question (FAQ) file for new members can be a time-saver. Although families are more geographically scattered than ever before, a family Web site can pool energy and resources unlike any time in the past. Isn't it time to get started?

Using a Pre-Built Site

If all this Webmaster talk makes your head spin, check out the free family Web sites offered by My Family.com <www.myfamily.com>. Layouts are pre-

Money Saver

designed, so you can't move columns, delete categories, or pick your favorite colors. Still, the sites are attractive, easy-to-use, password-protected, and are an easy way for families to connect—no matter how far apart they may live.

Password protected sites offer about 5MB of storage, and include features like a photo album, real-time chat, a bulletin board, and calendar. Creating these sites takes about five minutes. Each person you ask to join will automatically receive a password (you don't have to do anything), and no one can access the site without one. These sites are great for families who want to share genealogy data or just everyday life. You can post photos, plan a reunion, announce milestone events, and share family tree research. Everyone can use the site easily, without any knowledge of Web design, coding, or graphics.

Because the site is password-protected, you can exchange addresses and phone numbers without worrying about strangers gaining access to your personal information. And if someone moves or changes his phone number, he can easily update the information on the site.

Important

SCANNING MADE SIMPLE

These sites are filled with information on using scanners to get Web-perfect images and information on editing programs:

Adobe Photoshop
<www.adobe.com>

How to Scan Photos for Web Pages
<http://aspin.asu.edu/~pctp/photscan.htm>

MGI PhotoSuite
<www.photosuite.com>

Photo Impact Imaging Software
<www.ulead.com/pi/runme.htm>

Prep Your Photos for the Web
<www.graphicssoft.about.com/compute/graphicssoft/library/weekly/aa000516a.htm>

Restoration of Genealogical Photos
<www.scantips.com/restore.html>

Scanning 101, The Basics
<www.scantips.com>

Sizing Your Digital Photos for the Web
<www.attbusiness.net/channels/features/ft_digitalphotospart1.html>

Tips and Techniques of Image Scanning
<www.infomedia.net/scan>

SHARING OLD PHOTOS

Are you the lucky one who owns the old family photos? Sharing them online is easy if you have a scanner or digital camera. A scanner will convert "paper photos" to a graphic format, which you can then upload to a Web page or send via e-mail. Scanners usually come bundled with some kind of graphic-editing software, so you'll be able to crop unwanted portions of the photo and adjust color and brightness.

Digital Cameras in Genealogy

You can also use a digital camera to photograph old photos as well as capture current family images. If you don't already have one, the time is right to make that purchase. With camera prices down and features up, you'll wonder how you ever lived without it.

Idea Generator

Although digital cameras won't turn you into a photo pro or capture scenes any better than your favorite Kodak, they do have a leg up on conventional cameras. That's because they produce a digital file instead of a print, which means you can instantly share images with any computer-wired family in the world. For genealogists, that means no more hassle of getting prints made from negatives or mailing them across the country. Although that might not seem like much of a reason to switch from film, **the more you use digital, the more uses you'll find.** For example, you can

- convert old slides to digital files.
- upload family reunion photos to the Web.
- record family headstones.
- import pictures of official documents into family tree software.
- digitally preserve oddly-shaped mementos that are difficult to scan, e.g., an old teacup.
- shoot old letters or journals, then e-mail images of them to the family.

Figure 10-3
Use your digital camera to capture family treasures, then share them with others.

And just for fun, share a typical day with faraway family. Shoot your breakfast, where you work, the flowers that are in bloom, annoying construction in your neighborhood, a birthday party, dinner out, your new car, a retirement party, or the grandkids' new dog. Get the picture?

WRITE AN ELECTRONIC FAMILY NEWSLETTER

The Internet has made keeping in touch a breeze—why not take it a step further and create your own e-mail family newsletter? In fact, many publishers of traditional hard-copy newsletters are gradually making the change to e-mail or Web-based electronic versions. Like me, they've learned that e-mail and instant messaging means families that once corresponded with a yearly Christmas card now write daily. Laura Tasset Koehn, publisher of *Tasset Tree Trunks*, said, "I know that our newsletter has brought our family closer together. The newsletter has helped everyone exchange e-mail addresses and also to meet some new cousins. I also feel that it promotes love and pride of family." Rick Wickwire, editor of *The Family History Newsletter of the Wickware and Wickwire Families* <www.wickware.com/newsletters/newsletters.htm>, began his newsletter when he realized how much history he had lost of his own family. "At the time I didn't realize there were thousands of Wickwires in the world and that they were all related, but I was trying to get all the information on my immediate family that I could. Then I started a mail list and Web site, and then a newsletter. It was really just a realization of how much history was being forgotten that led me to start the newsletter."

If you are interested in preserving your family's history, sharing your heritage, or just keeping in touch, you can now start your own electronic family newsletter. **Not only can you easily reach family the world over, you can do it without the cost of paper, printing, and postage.** Here's how.

Planning Your Newsletter

Once you've decided to venture into the publishing game, you'll probably want to jump in with both feet. A little up-front planning will make it easier for you to have a first-rate publication—and maintain your enthusiasm down the line. Ask yourself

- How often do I want to publish?
- How long will the newsletter be?
- Will I be the sole writer or will I ask for contributions from other family members?
- Will my newsletter have a specific focus?
- How much time and effort am I willing to invest?
- Will I include ongoing columns on specific topics?
- What format will I use for the newsletter?
- What will I name my newsletter?

Most family newsletters are sent quarterly. If you're the sole writer, editor, publisher, and chief bottle washer, and uncertain of the time commitment, you may want to publish sporadically. Like Rick Wickwire, you may be lucky enough to have a family so actively involved in the project that you can publish weekly.

When first starting your newsletter, it's tempting to write about everything you know in the first issue. If you have a publication calendar—a rough outline of what topics you want to cover in each newsletter during

Money Saver

your first year—it will help make each issue shine with fascinating tidbits, legendary family stories, and current news. Advance planning also makes it easy for you to balance each issue with an interesting variety of topics.

If you don't want to be the sole contributor, e-mail your family members and let them know that you're publishing a family newsletter and would like their help. If a person has never seen a family newsletter, she may not know what type of information you want, so make it easy for them by listing the articles you want and a ballpark deadline of when you need material. Most of us lead busy lives and deadlines can be forgotten, so send follow-up e-mail reminders to those who have promised articles. Perhaps you will have a family of genealogy researchers, family historians, great cooks, poets, artists, photographers, and just plain old storytellers—all who want to help.

Naming your newsletter will probably be your easiest decision—many use the family surname, like *Hendrickson Newsletter*, others may be more creative, like *The Hendrickson Haven*. It's your newsletter, so have fun naming it.

Newsletter Topics

Once you've decided on a publishing schedule, it's time to write the first issue. Your choice of topics are almost endless—here are a few ideas to get you started:

- **Vital statistics.** Include the birth, marriage, and death dates of a few ancestors in each issue. This data gives family members an opportunity to check their own records and correspond about any discrepancies.
- **Cultural/religious heritage.** Does your family have a interesting cultural or religious heritage, like Acadian, Palatine, or Huguenots? If you've researched this background, share what you've learned in the newsletter. Your family members will be thrilled when given the chance to learn about their cultural heritage. I recently discovered one of my family lines was Quaker, and I'd love to read more about that faith.
- **Family recipes.** In an issue of *Tassett Tree Trunks*, Laura Tasset Koehn included her mother's recipe for zucchini nut bread, with the advice to make a double batch! Every family has a favorite recipe. In mine, it's Grandma's apple dumplings and Mom's potato salad.
- **I Remember Grandma (or Grandpa).** Ask family members to share their memories of one specific ancestor. You'll be surprised how each person's memories differ. In my family, cousin Sheryl remembers Grandma's homemade grape juice and lemonade. My sister Vicki remembers the hollyhocks in her backyard. Aunt Alice remembers Grandma's snoring, but I remember her most for teaching me to play checkers.
- **Single-topic issues.** Consider dedicating an entire issue to a single topic, like Our Indiana Ancestors or Our Civil War Ancestors. These "mini-biographies" are priceless additions to family histories, and help us see

our ancestors as real people.

- **Old documents.** For whatever reason, my family didn't save letters, military papers, diaries, or much else on paper. So of course, I'm in envy of all the families who still have these treasured mementos. If you own old documents, include excerpts in your newsletter.

- **Family events.** In every family, something is always going on. Marriages, new babies, graduations, deaths, promotions, engagements, and new homes all have a place in your newsletter. These current events are a wonderful way to keep the family in touch.

- **Preservation advice.** Carol Norris Vincent, a former museum administrator and editor of the *Norris Family Newsletter*, includes advice on preserving fabric, photographs, and other family treasures. If you have a background in preservation or access to a preservation class or book, let your relatives know how to keep their family treasures safe for future generations. Get ideas from Katherine Sturdevant's *Organizing and Preserving Your Heirloom Documents* (Cincinnati: Betterway Books, 2002).

- **Genealogy research projects.** If your newsletter goes to a group that's active in genealogy research, you can use the newsletter to share research discoveries, or even to split research tasks which can save duplicating efforts. Kevin Macomber's *The Macomber Project* announces which family members are searching for which ancestors. His family has had great success in matching information.

- **Where Our Family Lived.** Did your family come from a small village in France or a bustling German town? If someone in the family has visited the family homestead, his article accompanied by photos will get your readers interested in the family's heritage, and even inspire some to travel there themselves.

- **In Uniform.** Billie Jean Reese has three grandchildren, a nephew and great-nephew in the military, and other family members who are retired from the service. Adding an In Uniform section to her newsletter gives her a way to give special recognition to those who served.

Publishing Your Newsletter

You've notified all the relatives, you've made an editorial calendar, and your first newsletter is written. Congratulations! Now you can share all your work with the family. Using the Internet, you can publish your newsletter in one of four formats:

- text-only e-mail
- fully formatted document sent as an e-mail attachment
- Web-based newsletter
- HTML e-mail
- mailing-list newsletter

Text-Only E-mail Newsletters

The text-only newsletter requires the least work in terms of design and formatting. Because it is sent as an e-mail message, you are limited to text-only, with no photos, no color, and no formatting. Due to the limitations of some e-mail software, lines should be no longer than sixty-five characters. **Regardless of its design limitations, the text-only format is the one that can be most easily read by the largest number of people.** Although some e-mail programs allow HTML—e-mails which allow some formatting and color—not everyone's software is capable of reading them.

Using a text-only e-mail newsletter doesn't mean you have to sacrifice sharing family photos. Kevin Macomber's newsletter includes several links to Web sites that contain photos.

Fully Formatted Newsletters Sent as File Attachments

A fully formatted newsletter—the kind that looks beautiful when printed out—is the product of your word processor. Design the newsletter in your word processor, adding borders, shades, color, photos and fancy type, then send it to your family members as an e-mail attachment.

If you decide to go this route, poll your readers to make sure everyone can read the format you're going to send, and that their e-mail software is set up to accept attachments. Larry Quinto's *Belhumeur Newsletter,* which covers his Metis background, is sent as a WordPerfect document and contains borders and columns along with a table of contents. His WordPerfect file can be converted and read by Microsoft Word.

If you own Adobe Acrobat, you can convert any document, regardless of format, so that it can be read by Adobe Acrobat Reader. Refer to the program's help file for conversion instructions. Reader is a free program, which can be downloaded from the Web <www.adobe.com>.

Web-Based Newsletters

Bill Norin, editor and publisher of the *Mac Donald Newsletter* <www.geocit ies.com/Heartland/Pointe/9632>, has published his newsletter in hardcopy for thirteen years. Now issues can be accessed from his Web site. Bill's Web-based newsletter has the advantage of photos, handsome Web design, and music (he's currently playing "Mull of Kintyre"). The *Mac Donald Newsletter* is filled with articles taken from a book on family history that Bill wrote several years ago, along with new material like "We Met on the Net," a piece about the new cousins Bill has met online. Each issue of the *Mac Donald Newsletter* begins with the Gaelic *A Chairdean Ionmhuinn Mo Chinnidh* ("greetings to members of my clan").

If you have a personal Web page, or belong to one of the free family "gathering places" like Ancestry, you can upload the newsletter to the Web. **If you publish it on a Web page, you'll gain a wider reading audience, but because the people who may be reading it aren't known to you, you may want to delete any personal information,** such as phone numbers, addresses, or any intimate family stories you don't want made public.

HTML E-Mail

If you want to combine the good looks of a Web-based newsletter with the convenience (for your readers) of a text-only e-mail, consider producing an

HTML e-mail newsletter. You can create the newsletter just as you would a Web page, then attach it to an e-mail message that you send to newsletter subscribers. In the past few years, many more e-mail providers have become HTML e-mail-friendly, allowing users to open and view Web pages within their e-mail messages. For those subscribers that aren't able to view the HTML in an e-mail message, you could offer a text-only version or simply a link to the newsletter online.

Mailing-List Newsletter

A mailing-list newsletter is the same as a text-only e-mail newsletter, but instead of sending it via your personal e-mail, it is sent to all your subscribers by a mailing-list provider. There are several companies on the Internet that provide free mailing lists in exchange for tucking in a small ad at the bottom of your newsletter (see margin sidebar for a list of companies).

Although policies vary from company to company, in most you have the option of creating three types of mailing lists: announcement-only, moderated, and open. A newsletter is generally set up as an announcement-only list. This means that you are the only person who can post to the list, and the only messages people on the list receive will be from you. Some people who are new to the Internet are wary about being on any kind of list, so if you choose a mailing list newsletter, you may want to reassure them that they won't receive unsolicited e-mails (spam) as a result of receiving your newsletter.

Some families use mailing lists as a place for members to discuss events or share stories. These lists are set up as moderated or open. If the list is moderated, you, as the list owner, need to okay every message before it is e-mailed to the entire list. If open, every message posted is e-mailed directly to everyone on the list. Don Esslemont, who lives in New Zealand, set up an Esslemont mailing list so he and a Canadian cousin, Bob, and other relatives scattered across the world, can easily share their genealogical research.

Remember, not everyone likes to write. In fact some people hate it. To get your family actively involved in your newsletter, assure them that you aren't expecting them to write a Pulitzer Prize-winning novel. **Let them know that you're more interested in their stories than their writing style.**

Several providers of free mailing lists also offer the opportunity to be listed in their directory. If you're listed, anyone searching the directory will find your list. This may bring you family members you didn't know existed. To protect family members from having their messages read by someone not on the list, you may also have the option of having message archives available only to list members.

Once you've sent your first issue, regardless of the format you choose, you will probably be getting e-mails from your non-computer savvy cousins, asking how to open attachments, how to change their e-mail address, or how to set up their e-mail software to filter your newsletter into a special file. Welcome to electronic publishing.

You'll also receive e-mails from your cousins, aunts and uncles, thanking

Internet Source

FREE MAILING-LIST SERVICES

YahooGroups
  <www.yahoogroups.com>
Coollist
  <www.coollist.com>
Topica
  <www.topica.com>

Tip

you for your hard work, and asking how they can e-mail their own article for inclusion in the next issue. And, with each e-mail you receive, you'll feel a sense of pride, knowing that you're using the newest technology to bring the oldest of family stories to life. Congratulations!

TEN MORE NEWSLETTER IDEAS

Idea Generator

It also helps to give family members ideas on what to write about. (Chances are, you'll need a few ideas yourself when the creative juices are running low.) I'd be surprised if you couldn't squeeze plenty of articles out of these ten newsletter ideas. Keep them in mind as you plan your newsletter's content.

1. **Family Reunions.** Do you remember any family reunions from your childhood? I can recall long tables loaded with pies and covered dishes, and someone appointed to shoo away the flies. Writing about a long-ago family reunion will probably inspire someone in your family to start planning a future one.

2. **Interviews.** I love asking my aunts about their parents and grandparents, and every time I get off the phone I jot down my notes in my genealogy software. My aunts remember events that happened long before my birth, and I cherish their memories. Aunt Lu's story of her grandmother making ambrosia salad and leaving it on the screened-in back porch in winter leaves me with fond remembrances of a woman I never knew. Interviews, whether on the phone or in person, can add a special touch to your issue.

3. **Our Blacksheep Ancestors.** We all have one—the horse thief, army deserter, or no-account scoundrel. Instead of hiding them away, why not write a profile about them and all the facts and rumors you've ever heard? (Be aware, though, that some family members may not enjoy seeing ancestral skeletons brought out into the light.)

4. **When We Were Kids.** Ask your oldest living relatives to write about their childhoods; their remembrances will give your children a look at a society that they probably can't even imagine.

5. **Poetry Nook.** Save space in your newsletter for your budding poets and writers. It doesn't matter if the poem or essay isn't about genealogy or the family—it's a way to honor their talents. Imagine how wonderful it will be twenty or thirty years from now to go back and read their words.

6. **World War II Memories.** Whenever my mom visits my brother Mark, he asks her to tell him stories about World War II—what it was like on an everyday basis, what it was like for Dad to leave his family and go to war, or how ration books worked. We baby boomers want to know more about life during World War II, so start interviewing those who know.

7. **Guess Who?** If your newsletter is formatted to include photos, add several baby pictures and have a contest to see who can correctly identify all the photos.

8. **Slice of Life.** My dad loved butter and radish sandwiches. It's something that I'll always remember about him. I wish I knew tidbits like that about all my relatives. Your older relatives may know little slice-of-life tidbits about your ancestors; write them up and make them a part of your family's written history.

9. **Newly Found Cousins.** Your electronic newsletter is the place to note the names and e-mails of those cousins you meet on the Internet. It's amazing how many distant family members are online—and even more amazing that we are meeting so many of them.

10. **Family Web Pages.** If several of your family members have Web pages, highlight one in each issue. Describe what their page contains, e.g., photos, a family tree, family histories, or Civil War regimental information. Perhaps this will encourage other family members to publish their own Web pages.

GET THE FAMILY INVOLVED

It seems that every family has one person who is the designated family historian. If you're reading this book, you're probably the one! Wouldn't it be fun to get everyone else involved? Creating a family Web site, editing a newsletter, or even buying everyone a copy of this book as birthday gifts are wonderful ways to get the family climbing the tree. Sometimes it takes showing them how much fun they can have with all this family tree stuff.

Idea Generator

One of my favorite approaches is showing off my genealogy-related tech toys: a digital camera and personal digital assistant (PDA). As you can see from above, genealogy and digital cameras are a perfect match. But what about the PDA? Well, the last time I went to a family celebration, I took along dozens of vintage photos—all displayed on a PDA not much bigger than a deck of cards. It was fun to hear everyone "oooh" and "ahhh" as they watched the digital slide show I'd created earlier in the day using my Handspring Prism.

"That's a picture of my dad!" said my 85-year-old aunt, as she poked at the tiny screen. "How'd you do that?" Simple. All it took was installing a photo album on my PDA, transferring digital copies of old family photos, and selecting a five-second delay option for the slide show. Nothin' to it.

Turning your PDA into a photo album is a great way to share family mementos of all kinds, not just photos. Whatever you can photograph or scan can be transferred to your PDA album. In fact, my own slide show included my dad's grade school diploma and Grandma's dance card.

Albums range in cost from free to about thirty dollars and come with a "try before you buy" policy. Download as many as you want, try them all, and then pay only for the one you keep. Some trial versions will only let you transfer two photos to your PDA; others will disable themselves after a thirty-day trial period. Although installation instructions vary per program, the process is similar for most: During installation, a program is installed on both your desktop and the PDA, which usually must be connected to the desktop or laptop computer. The desktop part of the software is where a photo is converted to PDA format. The PDA part of the software is where the photo is viewed.

The desktop converter usually comes with a few basic photo-imaging functions, such as zooming, cropping, brightness, and contrast control. Options also include whether the image is displayed in 4-bit (16 grays), 8-bit (256 colors) or 16-bit (65,536 colors). A 4-bit display will take up about 15K of your memory, a 16-bit about 50K. Images you want on your PDA are selected through the desktop software.

After you select the image and choose the options, the image is transferred to your PDA via a hot sync. Once on your PDA, it can be viewed as a thumbnail, a full-size image, or as part of a slide show. You can label each photo, as well as add a description. If you really want to impress the family, set up multiple albums, such as one for your latest vacation, another for ancestor photos, and maybe one for ancestral headstones.

Aside from the cool factor, carrying family photos on a PDA is a practical use of handheld technology. The photos are displayed with a surprising degree of clarity and sharpness, and you can show off old photos that you may not want everyone handling. Got a family birthday or reunion coming up? Download your photo album and hot sync all those old pictures. Then when your elderly relative asks "how'd you do that?", you can say, "nothin' to it, why don't you give it a try?"

Figure 10-4
Carry all your genealogy data on a personal digital assistant (PDA).

PDA SOFTWARE

Handango
<www.handango.com>

PalmGear
<www.palmgear.com>

ZDNet
<www.zdnet.com/downloads/ce>
<www.zdnet.com/downloads/pilotsoftware>

For machines running the Palm Operating System
Address Album
<www.evolutionary.net/aalb-info.htm>

Album To Go
<www.clubphoto.com/tools/atg.php>

Fire Viewer Suite
<www.firepad.com>

Pocket Photo
<www.dreamhs.com>

Splash Photo
<www.splashdata.com/splashphoto>

For Pocket PCs
CoolViz
<www.realviz.com/products/coolviz>

Photo Explorer
<www.aidem.com.tw/English.htm>

Picture Perfect
<www.applian.com/pocketpc/pictureperfect/index.htm>

Picture Viewer
<www.resco-net.com/resco/en/solution_picview_p.asp>

Pocket Album
<www.conduits.com/products/album>

PEDIGREES IN THE PALM OF YOUR HAND

Pictures aren't the only way you can introduce everyone to the family history with your PDA. You can carry around your entire GEDCOM file and fun genealogy utilities on it, as well. For example, Ron Chenier never travels alone. Wherever he goes, tucked inside his shirt pocket are 22,500 of his ancestors, all stored on a handheld computer the size of a 3- by 5-inch index card. Whether researching in the Ottawa, Canada, archives or walking local cemeteries, his genealogy records are all in the palm of his hand.

Ron's Palm and its rivals (Sony Clie®, Handspring Visor®) are pint-sized Palm OS powerhouses that weigh about six ounces and come with 2 to 8MB of memory. Their 2.5 by 2.5-inch screens display text or graphics in sixteen shades of gray, with the Palm Tungsten boasting a 65,000-color screen. Although you can add a keyboard, most data entry is done with a stylus or by tapping an on-screen keyboard. Pocket PC systems are often much more robust, with 64MB of memory and programmed with Microsoft Word, Excel, etc.

Notes

Handhelds come packaged with calendar, calculator, and address book software, as well as a program that allows communication with a desktop computer. Additional software is downloaded into a unit by placing it in a cradle that is connected to the desktop via a USB or serial port, and then "hot-synched" to exchange data. Handheld prices range from just around one hundred dollars to close to six hundred dollars.

Since many genealogists already own a laptop or take notebooks to the library, is there a need for yet another electronic gizmo? I loaded my Visor with a half-dozen programs to find out.

PEDIGREE SOFTWARE

GedStar
<www.ghcssoftware.com/gedstar.htm>

GedStar (v.4.3) is an $11.95 program which runs on the Palm Operating System 2.0 or later and requires Win 95/98/ME/NT/XP/2000. It comes with a GEDCOM converter, and an easy-to-follow manual. There is no limit to the number of people you can have in your database; in addition you can set up multiple databases. During the conversion process, you can choose whether you want any of your notes imported, and if so, whether you want them to be of unlimited length (up to 32K in characters) or limited to 1,024 characters. If free memory is a consideration, don't import your notes.

GedStar is a "genealogy viewer" that alphabetically lists every individual in your database. Tap on any name to go to the Family View where you can quickly navigate to any notes, or details about the individual's parents, spouse, or children. Once on an individual's Detail View, a single tap creates a two-generation ancestor tree or a two-generation descendant tree. From the tree, navigating generations is simple, as a single tap on any name creates a new tree with the specified person the new "root."

Although you can't add new notes directly into the program, you can add them from your desktop software via a new hot synch. In addition, notes can be exported to your handheld's built-in memo software. GedStar is a compact program, using only 45K of your unit's memory. Although the conversion process minimizes the size of your data, memory requirements are about 100 bytes per individual, depending on the length of your notes. The program comes with a free forty-five-day trial.

My Roots

<www.tapperware.com/MyRoots>

My Roots (version 2.01), a $19.95 program, is a full-fledged, Palm OS genealogy program for Windows and Macintosh. Unlike other "file viewer" PDA genealogy programs, My Roots lets you enter data directly into the program, then transfer it back to your desktop software. The program's import routine is limited to a database with no more than ten thousand people.

Using My Roots you can create multiple databases and do a one-tap navigation from an individual to her children, spouse, or parents. A Find Person dialogue box allows for quick jumping to a new person. A convenient feature is the ability to set filters to show all of the people in your database, or only living individuals. My Roots also allows you to filter by birth or death location, surname, given name, birth or death year, or any combination. For an overview of a particular family line, you can easily create an ancestor or descendant tree for any individual, with new generations indicated by indents. Event types include common (birth, death), religious, LDS, legal, other (burial, immigration, residence), and user-defined. Adding event types or editing data is simple and intuitive. You can download a trial version from the Web site.

GedWise

<www.gedvisor.com>

Formerly known as GedVisor, GedWise allows you to transfer data from your desktop to PDA via a GEDCOM transfer. The program consists of two components: the GEDCOM conversion software that resides on your desktop, and the file viewer which is installed on your PDA.

GedWise allows up to a hundred databases, and will display information in a variety of views, including individual, ancestry, descendancy, and family. A built-in Soundex code converter tool comes in handy when you're at the library and doing a Soundex-based search. The program also supports multiple entries for an event. For example, if you have more than one birthdate for an individual, GedWise will list them all. This Windows-based program costs $17.99; a free trial download is available from the Web site.

Pocket Genealogist

<www.northernhillssoftware.com/pgenie.htm>

Pocket Genealogist is designed to work with Windows CE devices running CE 2.0 or higher. This includes PocketPCs, Palm-size PCs, Handheld Pro, and Handheld PCs. The Casio BE-300 (Pocket Manager) is not supported. Pocket Genealogist works with Windows 95, 98, NT, ME, 2000, and XP systems.

It has been tested with GEDCOM files from Legacy Family Tree, Family Tree Maker, The Master Genealogist, Generations, PAF, and other genealogy software. Pocket Genealogist is available in Basic and Advanced versions. The Basic version ($20) of 2.x for Pocket Genealogist will support limited data entry. The Advanced version ($35) will eventually support full data entry and two-way synchronization.

Databases

When Steve Johnson of The Cemetery Column <www.interment.net> decided he wanted to use his Palm III to record cemetery inscriptions, he installed a database application, JFile 3.2, and created his own database. He designed the database for a nearby cemetery where he wanted to record the section, row and marker numbers, and input the surname, given name, birth date, death date, and inscription. After designing the database, which he says took about ten minutes, he entered data by writing with a stylus in the Palm's text area.

Once the data was entered, JFile converted it to a comma-delimited text file which could be imported into several applications including Access, Excel, or Word. Using JFile <www.land-j.com> ($24.95), or similar programs such as HanDBase <www.handbase.com> ($24.99), you can use your handheld to create an endless number of genealogy-specific databases. You may want a cemetery one like Steve's, or one for census or land records.

Donald Keiffer wrote two genealogy databases, GenRes and Gen2Do, for use with HanDBase. GenRes keeps track of any new resource you've found, with fields for name, event, date, person, location, and source. Gen2Do is a genealogy to-do list that displays research items for your next trip to the library. Fields include the person or event you want to research, the location, and whether you want to search microfilm, fiche, or books. There's also a results field and a place to keep notes. Both databases are free. If you search the free databases for keyword "genealogy," you'll also find a free database for keeping track of microfilms ordered at the Family History Center <http://handbase.com/gallery.html>.

Don't want to purchase HanDBase but want GenRes and Gen2Do? They're available as stand-alones for six dollars each at PalmGear <www.palmgear.com>.

Soundex Utilities

Soundex is an indexing system that convert surnames into a four-character code consisting of one letter and three numbers. The most familiar usage of Soundex was by the U.S. Census Bureau, which used Soundex to group names by phonetics (sounds) rather than spelling. The 1920 census has a Soundex index for every state. These two utilities make converting your surnames a snap.

- **pSoundex** (v1.01) is a freeware program written by Jim Knopf that converts surnames to their Soundex value. This little utility takes up only 10K of memory. Just write your surname in the Input Dialogue box and it's instantly converted.
- **Soundex Calculator** is a $4.95 shareware program that converts surnames to Soundex.

Both programs are available at PalmGear <www.palmgear.com> (keyword search: Soundex).

Who of your relatives could resist getting involved in such a fun hobby?

WHAT'S NEXT?

If you started this book with the question: "Can I find ancestors online?" I hope you can now answer with a resounding "Yes!" You've learned the techniques for poking into every corner of the Web—and developed a talent for asking the right questions, formulating the most effective search strategies, and following every clue until you strike gold or strike out. And if you strike out, I'm confident it's because that piece of information simply wasn't online.

I know some of your own searches might seem too complex or overwhelming to attack. But if you divide them into the four search strategies I know you'll succeed. Don't forget how to eat the elephant.

Final Thoughts

fter you've finished this book, you may ask yourself, "What next? And how do I sort out all the discrepancies I found online?" Good questions. The answers depend on your goals.

If you want to keep finding ancestors online, just keep practicing the same search strategies you've learned. In particular, hone your search engine skills—they will serve you well. Additionally, learn to go at a research problem like a dog with a bone. Chew it from one end, then the other, then grab it in the middle. The more "doggedly" you approach a search, the better your results.

If this book has helped you realize a particular area of interest, pursue it. For example, my own searches have uncovered a passion for reading period journals and for locating photographs of the places my ancestors lived. Yours may be delving in women's history or the history of period firearms. Now that you've become a search engine wizard, those topics are ripe for your picking.

For those of you who have discovered a yen to know more about genealogy and how to find those original documents I've been recommending you get, **check out these classics:**

For More Info

The Handy Book for Genealogists, edited by George Everton (Logan, Utah: Everton Publishers, latest edition)

The Researcher's Guide to American Genealogy, by Val D.Greenwood (Baltimore: Genealogical Publishing Company, 2000)

The Source: A Guidebook of American Genealogy, edited by Loretto Dennis Szucs and Sandra Hargreaves Luebking (Salt Lake City: Ancestry, 1997)

Map Guide to the U.S. Federal Censuses, 1790–1920, by William Thorndale and William Dollarhide. (Baltimore: Genealogical Publishing Co., 1987)

Unpuzzling Your Past, by Emily Anne Croom, 4th edition (Cincinnati: Betterway Books, 2001)

Printed Source

In addition, **visit the *Family Tree Magazine* bookstore** <http://familytreemagazine.com/store> and browse through the wonderful selections there. You'll find great books on searching for your ethnic ancestors (Italian, English, Irish, etc.), helpful guides for writing a family newsletter, and books to give you a solid research footing.

Lastly, if this book has helped you discover an interest in preserving and sharing the information you've found online, think about starting your own Web site, creating a digital photo album, or even getting your "electronic family" together for a real-life reunion.

Whatever course you take, the key to your success is staying focused.

And as we all know, the Internet makes that quite a challenge. But it's not impossible. The next time you find yourself surfing all over the Web, use these ten quick tips to get you back on course. You may even want to copy the tips and post them around your computer.

TEN QUICK TIPS FOR ONLINE GENEALOGISTS

1. Before logging online, write down your goal, e.g.
   - Find and join the Jackson surname mailing list.
   - Locate a Revolutionary War-era map of Connecticut.
   - Get the mailing address for ordering a death record.

2. Depending on the goal, use the appropriate search strategy (or a combination of all four). If you are unsuccessful with one strategy, try another, then another.

3. Attack your search problem from every conceivable angle. Follow your hunches.

4. Keep an electronic or paper file of every site you visit in your search. Date the search and note whether you need to research this site at a later time. You may even want to create a file that contains the URLs of Web sites which need revisiting.

5. Note the pertinent information on each query you leave, e.g., the date, the URL, the name of the site, and the subject ancestor.

6. If you find a site brimming with possible goodies, but it doesn't pertain to your current search, finish the current search first, then return to the goodies. This is a tough one, and I speak from experience!

7. Keep an electronic or paper file on your genealogy-related e-mails, and be sure to date when they're sent. This will keep you from sending the same question to someone you've already contacted.

8. Know when it's time to say "uncle." If you follow the search strategies in this book, and attack the problem every way you can think of, and you still can't find what you're looking for, it's possible it's just not online. Save the search and run it again in six months. Or see if the record you need is on microfilm at a Family History Center.

9. Weave back and forth between online and offline research. As much as we all love the ease of online research, you will need to contact local agencies for vital records, as well as ordering land, probate, and other records. Check to see if your local library has genealogy records, or if it participates in an interlibrary loan program. Become friends with your local librarian! Visit a local Family History Center to see what records are on microfilm. Go to the FamilySearch site to find a center near you.

10. Ask for help. When a research goal becomes tough, ask other researchers on your mailing lists—or your local genealogy society— for suggestions. They may think of an approach that never occurred to you.

Online Resources/Blank Forms

O nline ancestor hunting can leave you feeling like you're lost in a vast Internet maze. You've found countless dead ends among the millions of genealogy sites out there, but the proverbial pieces of cheese—those digital clues to your family history—keep eluding you. Your path may produce the prize, but it's often fraught with frustration.

That's why the editors and experts at *Family Tree Magazine* are endlessly navigating that labyrinth of online roots resources. They weed out the junk and point you to the best sites for your search—in each issue of the magazine and the Sites of the Day <www.familytreemagazine.com/categories.asp>, featured on our home page.

Once a year, they whittle down all those worthy Web sites to the ones that rise above the rest: 101 destinations that will make your online searches easier, faster, and more productive. Some are "classics" you'll recognize from past years' picks, others have arrived on the genealogy scene only recently. All appeal to a wide audience, are easy to use and have a clean design. You'll find free databases, tools and references, maps, original documents, and millions upon millions of searchable records. For the current 101 Best Web sites for genealogists, check out <www.familytreemagazine/101sites>.

When you're done with the current list, check out the archives for previous years at <www.familytreemagazine.com/101newsites> and <www.familytreemagazine.com/101 sites>.

And while you're finding your roots online, be sure to utilize the forms provided on the following pages or download these forms and others free of charge at <www.familytreemagazine.com/forms/download.html>.

Family Group Sheet of the _____ Family

Source #   Source #

Full name of husband	Birth date
His father	Birth place
	Death date
	Death place
His mother with maiden name	Burial place

Full maiden name of wife	Birth date
Her father	Birth place
	Death date
	Death place
Her mother with maiden name	Burial place

Other Spouses

Marriage date, place, etc.

Source #s   Source #s

Children of this marriage	Birth date & place	Death date, place, & burial place	Marriage date, place & spouse
Source #s			
Source #s			
Source #s			
Source #s			
Source #s			
Source #s			

Reprinted from Unpuzzling Your Past Workbook

Source #   Sources (Documentation)

Reprinted from Unpuzzling Your Past Workbook

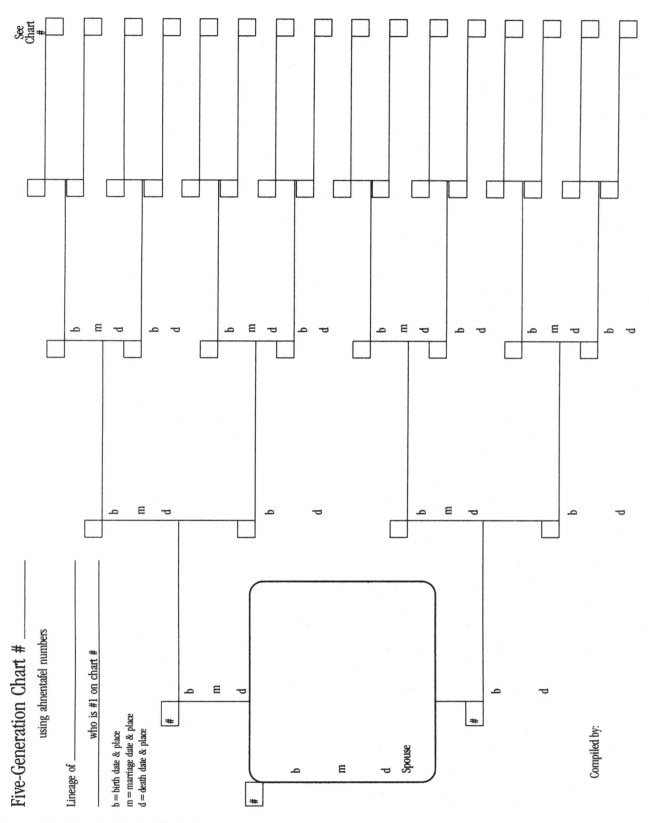

Five-Generation Chart # _____

using ahnentafel numbers

Lineage of _____

who is #1 on chart # _____

b = birth date & place
m = marriage date & place
d = death date & place

Spouse

See Chart #

b
m
d

Compiled by:

Reprinted from Unpuzzling Your Past Workbook

Military Records Checklist for _____

Ancestor Name & Life Dates	Colonial Wars (state records)	American Revolution 1775–1783 (check state & federal records)	1784-1811	War of 1812 (1812–1815)	Indian Wars 1815–1858	Patriot War 1838	Mexican War 1846–1848	Civil War 1861–1865 (for Confederates, check state & federal records)	Service 1866 forward	Spanish-American War 1898–1899	Philippine Insurrection 1899–1902	World War I 1917–1918	World War II 1941–1945

Reprinted from Unpuzzling Your Past Workbook

Glossary

Abstract—Summary of a record or document; usually contains only the most important information from the original document.

Ahnentafel numbers—A numbering system used to identify each individual in a family tree. The formula states that an individual's father is twice that individual's number, and that an individual's mother is twice that individual's number plus one. For example, if your Ahnentafel number is 1, your father's is 2, and your mother's is 3.

Aliquot parts—A notation used on U.S. Bureau of Land Management General Land Office records, representing the exact subdivision of a *section* of land. Aliquot parts are described as a half or quarter of the largest subdivision of the section, except fractional lots, which cannot be described by aliquot parts.

Batch number—A number used in FamilySearch's International Genealogical Index and Scottish Church Records to find the original source of information in an entry.

Bookmark—A Web site address that's been saved in your browser for future reference (also known as a "favorite").

Boolean search—A computer search technique that uses various operators to find specific files or Web pages. The "and" operator between two words or other values (for example, "pear *and* apple") will find documents containing both of the words or values, not just one of them. An "or" operator between two words or other values (for example, "pear *or* apple") will find documents containing either of the words.

Bounty land—Land promised as a reward for military service.

Bulletin board—A Web page that allows users to share or exchange information.

Browser—An application that provides a way to look at and interact with all the information on the World Wide Web.

Clipboard—In word-processing programs, this is where information that you cut or copy is temporarily stored for pasting elsewhere.

Common ancestor—An ancestor shared by two or more people.

Deed—A transfer of ownership of property.

Digest mode—A type of mailing list subscription that sends you messages in batches, rather than one at a time.

DOS—Disk Operating System; first widely-installed operating system for personal computers.

E-mail—Electronic mail; exchange of computer-stored messages by telecommunication.

Emigrant—A person who leaves one country for another.

Enumerator—A census taker.

FAQ—Frequently Asked Questions; many Web sites offer a FAQ page to address its users' common questions.

FHC—Family History Center; a local branch of the Family History Library in Salt Lake City, Utah.

FHL—Family History Library, the world's largest genealogical repository. It is run by the Church of Jesus Christ of Latter-day Saints in Salt Lake City, Utah.

Firewall—A set of related programs, located at a network gateway server, that protects the resources of a private server from users from other networks.

Gazetteer—Book that alphabetically lists and describes the places in a specific area.

GEDCOM—A standard file format for exchanging information between genealogy programs. The acronym GEDCOM stands for GEnealogical Data COMmunications. The Family History Department of the Church of Jesus Christ of Latter-day Saints (LDS Church) developed the GEDCOM standard.

GPS—Global Positioning System; satellite-based system that uses specific coordinates to mark or pinpoint locations anywhere on the globe.

Hack—To break into a computer system.

Home page—The first Web page that is displayed when a user starts a Web browser; also the first page presented when a user selects a site or presence on the World Wide Web.

Hot sync—To synchronize information stored on a personal digital assistant with information stored on a desktop or laptop computer.

HTML—Hypertext Markup Language; the set of markup symbols or codes inserted in a file intended for display on a World Wide Web page.

Icon—An image that represents an application, a capability, or some other concept or specific entity with meaning for the user.

ICQ—"I Seek You"; a program you can download that will let you know when friends and contacts are also online on the Internet.

IGI—International Genealogical Index; a computer file that lists several hundred million names of deceased persons from throughout the world. It also lists some vital information, such as a birth or marriage date and place. Many names in the index come from vital records from the early 1500s to 1885. Others have been submitted by members of the Church of Jesus Christ of Latter-day Saints. The International Genealogical Index, which was created by the Church of Jesus Christ of Latter-day Saints, is available on the Internet, on compact disc, and on microfiche.

Instant messaging—The ability to easily see whether a chosen friend or co-worker is connected to the Internet and, if so, to exchange messages with them.

ISP—Internet Service Provider.

Lineage-linked database—Files linked together by common ancestor.

Link—Using hypertext, a link is a selectable connection from one word, picture, or information object to another.

Mail mode—A type of mailing list subscription that sends you messages one at a time, rather than in batches.

Mailing list—A list of people who subscribe to a periodic e-mail distribution on a particular topic.

Malware—Malicious software; programming or files that are developed for the purpose of doing harm.

Meridian—An imaginary north-south line (used on land patents).

Meta-search—A search engine that searches multiple search engines at once.

Metes-and-bounds—A land survey method that uses compass directions, natural landmarks, and distances from one point to another.

Modem—Modulates outgoing digital signals from a computer or other digital device to analog signals for a conventional copper twisted pair telephone line and demodulates the incoming analog signal and converts it to a digital signal for the digital device.

NARA—National Archives and Records Administration; the United States' repository of important federal documents and records.

PDA—Personal digital assistant; a term for any small mobile hand-held device that provides computing and information storage and retrieval capabilities for personal or business use; also called "*handheld*."

Public domain land—Land owned and administered by the United States government. Public land states: Alabama, Alaska, Arizona, Arkansas, California, Colorado, Florida, Idaho, Illinois, Indiana, Iowa, Kansas, Louisiana, Michigan, Minnesota, Mississippi, Missouri, Montana, Nebraska, Nevada, New Mexico, North Dakota, Ohio, Oklahoma, Oregon, South Dakota, Utah, Washington, Wisconsin, and Wyoming.

Query—A request for information, such as information about a particular ancestor.

Range—A row or tier of *townships* lying east or west of the principal *meridian* and numbered successively to the east and to the west from the principal meridian.

Rectangular survey system—A way of surveying land that uses imaginary "nets" of big rectangles superimposed on the land. The center of a net is anchored at a known geographic position. Two base lines cross at the center, one north-south and the other east-west. The big rectangles of the net, each generally twenty-four miles by twenty-four miles, are described according to their position in relation to the base lines. Each big rectangle is then subdivided into smaller rectangles, and the smaller rectangles into even smaller rectangles, and so on.

Sanborn fire insurance map—Maps created by the Sanborn Map Company between 1867 and 1967 containing data used in estimating the potential risk for urban structures; includes such information as their construction material, height, and function as well as the location of lot lines.

Search engine—A coordinated set of programs that includes a *spider* (also called a "crawler" or a "bot") that goes to every page or representative pages on every Web site that wants to be searchable and reads it, using hypertext links on each page to discover and read a site's other pages; a program that creates a huge index (sometimes called a "catalog") from the pages that have been read; a program that receives your search request, compares it to the entries in the index, and returns results to you.

Section—In a U.S. land patent, a section is a regular tract of land, one-mile square, containing 640 acres, within a *township*. It is approximately 1/36 of a township.

Signature file—A short text file you create for use as a standard appendage at the end of your e-mail messages.

Soundex—An indexing system of grouping words together with similar sounds but different spellings, e.g., Lee, Leigh.

Snail mail—Slang for sending mail by post, as opposed to sending e-mail messages.

Spam—Unsolicited e-mail on the Internet.

SSDI—Social Security Death Index; a computer file that contains records of deaths reported to the United States Social Security Administration. Most records start in 1962, but the file does contain a few records of deaths that happened before that date.

Thumbnail—Small image that represents a larger version of that image, usually intended to make it easier and faster to look at and manage a large group of images.

Township—Division of public land. Contains thirty-six sections, with each section being one square mile.

Transcript—A typed or handwritten copy of data from an original record.

Trojan horse—A computer program in which malicious or harmful code is contained inside apparently harmless programming or data in such a way that it can get control and do damage to your computer.

Uniform Resource Locator (URL)—A Web site address, <www.familytreem agazine.com>, for example.

Virus—A piece of programming code usually disguised as something else that causes some unexpected and usually undesirable event.

Vital records—Records of birth, death, marriage, and divorce.

Webmaster—The individual who maintains and controls a Web site.

Wildcard—A wildcard character is a special *character* that represents one or more other characters. The most commonly used wildcard characters are the asterisk (*), which typically represents zero or more characters in a string of characters, and the question mark (?), which typically represents any one character.

Windows—A personal computer operating system from Microsoft that, together with some commonly used business applications such as Microsoft Word and Excel, has become a de facto "standard" for individual users.

Index

Look for These Other Great Genealogy Titles From Betterway Books!

Your Guide to Cemetery Research—Cemeteries can help fill the holes in your precious family history! With this book, you'll learn how to determine when and where a person died, locate the exact cemetery in which a family or individual is interred, analyze headstones and markers, interpret funerary art and tombstone iconography, and more!
ISBN 1-55870-589-9, paperback, 272 pages, #70527-K

The Family Tree Guide Book—This invaluable resource—from the editors at *Family Tree Magazine*—combines genealogy basics, online directories and region-specific travel information in one book. Divided into seven regions of the United States, plus a chapter covering Canada, each section introduces you to a specific region and provides guidelines for finding and using its records.
ISBN 1-55870-647-X, paperback, 352 pages, #70595-K

Genealogist's Computer Companion—Master the basics of online research and turn your computer into an efficient, versatile research tool. Respected genealogist Rhonda McClure shows you how, providing guidelines and advice that enable you to find new information, verify existing research, and save valuable time. She also provides an invaluable glossary of genealogical and technical terms.
ISBN 1-55870-591-0, paperback, 192 pages, #70529-K

Your Guide to the Federal Census—This one-of-a-kind book examines the "nuts and bolts" of census records. You'll find out where to view the census and how to use it to find ancestors quickly and easily. Easy-to-follow instructions and case studies detail nearly every scenario for tracing family histories through census records. You'll also find invaluable appendices, and a glossary of census terms.
ISBN 1-55870-588-0, paperback, 288 pages, #70525-K

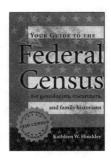

More Great Books to Help Find and Preserve Your Family History!

Your Guide to the Family History Library—The Family History Library in Salt Lake City is the largest collection of genealogy and family history materials in the world. No other repository compares for both quantity and quality of research materials. Written for beginning and intermediate genealogists, *Your Guide to the Family History Library* will help you use the library's resources effectively, both on site and online.
ISBN 1-55870-578-3, paperback, 272 pages, #70513-K

The Weekend Genealogist—Maximize your family research efficiency! With this guide, you can focus your efforts in searching for family documents while still gaining the best results. Organization and research techniques are presented in a clear, easy-to-follow format perfect for advanced researchers and beginners. You'll learn how to work more efficiently using family history facilities, the Internet, and even the postal service!
ISBN 1-55870-546-5, paperback, 144 pages, #70496-K

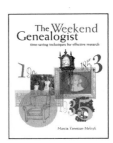

Long-Distance Genealogy—Gathering information from sources that can't be visited is a challenge for all genealogists. This book will teach you the basics of long-distance research. You'll learn what types of records and publications can be accessed from a distance, problems associated with the process, how to network, how to use computer resources and special "last resort" options.
ISBN 1-55870-535-X, paperback, 272 pages, #70495-K

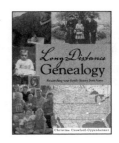

Preserving Your Family Photographs—Learn how to care for your family photograph collection by applying the concepts used by conservators and photocurators every day. Maureen Taylor shows you how to organize your photographs for both family history research and display, create a scrapbook using archive quality guidelines, select a restoration expert to restore damaged photos, use photo identification techniques and more.
ISBN 1-55870-579-1, paperback, 246 pages, #70514-K

These books and other fine Betterway titles are available from your local bookstore, online supplier or by calling

1-800-448-0915.